Reparenting the Child Who Hurts

A Guide to Healing Developmental Trauma and Attachments

Caroline Archer and Christine Gordon
Foreword by Gregory C. Keck, Ph.D.

Jessica Kingsley *Publishers*
London and Philadelphia

First published in 2013
by Jessica Kingsley Publishers
116 Pentonville Road
London N1 9JB, UK
and
400 Market Street, Suite 400
Philadelphia, PA 19106, USA

www.jkp.com

Library of Congress Cataloging in Publication Data
Archer, Caroline, 1948-
  Reparenting the child who hurts : a guide to healing
developmental trauma and attachments / Caroline
Archer and Christine Gordon ; foreword by Gregory C. Keck, Ph.D.
    pages cm
  Includes bibliographical references and index.
  ISBN 978-1-84905-263-4 (alk. paper)
  1. Child psychology. 2. Child development. 3. Adoptive
parents--Handbooks, manuals, etc. 4.
Parenting--Handbooks, manuals, etc. I. Gordon, Christine Ann, 1949- II. Title.
  BF721.A6943 2012
  649'.1567--dc23
                                        2012033827

British Library Cataloguing in Publication Data
A CIP catalogue record for this book is available from the British Library

ISBN 978 1 84905 263 4
eISBN 978 0 85700 568 7

Printed and bound in Great Britain

We would both like to dedicate this book to our grandchildren. The challenges of the next generation continue to allow us to practise and hone our developmental reparenting principles. Thanks to them all, and our children, for the opportunities they have given, and are giving us, to have fun whilst continuing to learn.

Contents

Foreword

As I read the book that you are about to begin, I felt excited that so much recent information is included. Caroline Archer and Christine Gordon have clearly researched the most recent literature in neuroscience, trauma, human development and developmental parenting.

As a professional, I felt that the material contained in this book offers those people working with hurt children and their families insight and information which will better inform their practices and enhance their efforts to help traumatised children move forward in their development. As an adoptive parent, I felt the strong encouragement that is offered on almost every page. As I read through the manuscript a couple of times, I was glad to see theoretically sound and well-researched information presented in a manner that will be palatable to frustrated and challenged parents.

When a child who has been traumatised enters a family either for foster care or for adoption, they bring a lot with them. Much of what he/she brings may not be expected by the family, and even more importantly, it is almost certain that the family – parents and children – will not expect the child's trauma experiences, emotions and behaviours to have a negative or even traumatic impact on the family. When professionals see prospective adoptive families, they appear to be healthy, excited, optimistic, forward looking and hopeful that they will be able to raise a hurt child; they often feel that their love and acceptance will erase the hurt or, at least, mitigate it enough so that the child will have a bright and productive future.

Hurt children bring their hurt – their many hurts – with them, and often both parents and other children in the family feel as if they are now living in an environment that is both traumatic and hurtful. I feel that Caroline Archer and Christine Gordon offer hope for families who may be struggling and flailing about trying to find their feet, so to speak. While the book is not a step-by-step guide, which I don't even believe could be written, *Reparenting the Child Who Hurts* offers readers a conceptual framework for understanding the complex dynamics of living with a child who, indeed, has developmental trauma disorder. It also provides explicit details of how parents may respond to difficult situations – complete with examples of verbal responses that may be helpful in ameliorating extremely intense situations.

New developments in neuroscience offer us so much insight, and this book integrates this new knowledge with the long-understood dynamics of child and human development. I believe that when parents are able to maintain a focus on developmental issues as they make their way through the maze of emotions, behaviours, challenges and difficulties, they are able to keep their heads high enough above the water to allow them to make reasoned decisions about what they want to address and what they may want to do. When parents can make a shift in how they see the problems the hurt child has and in how they respond to the child, the child will have fertile ground for developmental re-activation and progress.

I think that readers of *Reparenting the Child Who Hurts* will find, as I did, that this book will help them understand the dynamics they either work with or live with and, more importantly, it will help them make the kinds of shifts that will facilitate their efforts to parent and help hurt children.

Gregory C. Keck, Ph.D., Founder/Director of the Attachment and Bonding Center of Ohio; co-author of Adopting the Hurt Child *and* Parenting the Hurt Child; *and author of* Parenting Adopted Adolescents

Part 1

Stepping Forward

Exploring the Foundations

Introduction

When we first met in the late 1980s and began work with colleagues at Adoption UK (then Parent to Parent Information on Adoption Services (PPIAS)) to explore how parenting 'hurt' children (Keck and Kupecky 2002) differed from parenting securely attached children, little did we know that, two decades on, we would still be working together exploring the needs of traumatised children and discussing how best to parent them. Little, too, did we know the extent to which new developments in neurobiology would increase our understanding of the continuing day-to-day struggles that affect the lives of many traumatised children even when they have been removed from their traumatic circumstances and offered the security of loving families.

When we first started writing together in the late 1980s a climate change in the way adoptive family life was perceived was beginning. John Bowlby's research on attachment (1969, 1973, 1988) was increasingly recognised as pertinent to our understanding of how our earliest relationships, particularly those with our mothers, crucially determine how we relate to the world and our relationships within it. This eventually led to greater awareness amongst the 'adoption community' that early trauma continues to have an adverse impact long after children are placed in loving families. This began a movement away from blaming adoptive parents for the ongoing difficulties their children presented to an understanding that on its own love does not conquer all.

This climate of change had its drawbacks. With the label of 'Reactive Attachment Disorder' (RAD) that many traumatised children were then given came the implication that the behavioural and relationship difficulties central to this diagnosis were virtually impossible to alter, in effect consigning children to a lifetime of difficulties and failed relationships. Also implicit was the belief that traumatised children's behaviour was, to a significant degree, under their personal control and that, if parents wished to make family life more tolerable, they needed to wrest control from their children and take it into their own hands. Although it was accepted this should be done in loving and empathetic ways, the message that children 'wouldn't do' rather than 'couldn't do' predominated. This thinking influenced early attempts to create alternative parenting approaches for 'hurt children'.

Our first output therefore concentrated on control issues and on strategies for confronting and containing specific behavioural issues. Little attention was paid to the underlying feelings that drove 'hurt' children's behaviour.

By the time Caroline wrote *First Steps in Parenting the Child Who Hurts: Tiddlers and Toddlers* and *Next Steps in Parenting the Child Who Hurts: Tykes and Teens* (1999a, 1999b) our awareness of the impact on children of early traumatic experiences had moved on considerably. Developments in neuroanatomy (structure) and neurophysiology (function) had increased our understanding that children 'can't do' rather than 'won't do' and that 'horse whispering' was preferable to 'horse breaking'. Hence we were able to recognise that control-based strategies alone would not substantially affect 'hurt' (traumatised) children's ways of understanding and relating to the world. *First Steps* and *Next Steps* emphasised a change in parental mind-set, with strategies reflecting the change of emphasis from containment to understanding and healing.

Whilst these two books continue to be very relevant today, particularly the developmental focus on babies and young children in *First Steps in Parenting the Child Who Hurts*, research and understanding in this exciting field have continued to grow apace, increasing our awareness of the impact of early trauma on every aspect of our children's being: their body, feelings and thoughts and their expression through their behavioural 'language'. The study of mirror neurons (MN) exemplifies how neurobiological findings can confirm what previously we could only surmise: that experiences and patterns of interaction learned in the womb and early months of life can profoundly influence our daily lives throughout childhood and adulthood. This book builds on our journey of exploration in *First Steps* and *Next Steps* to integrate recent scientific, psychological and social scientific developments and to provide parents, caregivers and professionals with the latest insights into the nature of early relational trauma and its impacts on children at the neurobiological as well as behavioural level.

MIRROR NEURONS

Towards the turn of the century, neuroscientists identified nerve cells in specific areas of monkeys' brains that were seen to fire, as if the animals were carrying out those actions themselves, when they simply observed other monkeys' actions (e.g. Rizzolatti, Fogassi and Gallese 1997).

This suggests that the firing of neural circuits in these premotor areas plays a vital role in the acquisition of new skills or, conversely, that imitation facilitates the development of mirror neuron (MN) systems (Nishitani and Hari 2000).

Using functional Magnetic Resonance Imagery (fMRI), Iacoboni and his colleagues (2005) observed that in humans neural firing occurred in areas of the right inferior frontal cortex in response to perceived intentional actions, specifically to encode 'the "why" of the action and respond differently to different intentions'. The sound associated with an action was also shown to evoke firing in these premotor areas (Kohler *et al.* 2002). These findings shed important light on the development of communication and social interaction in animals that form close social communities, including humans.

Since gesture and facial imitation are observable in two-day-old human infants (Meltzoy and Moore 1989) this area of functioning must have high survival value. A popular evolutionary view is that hand gestures provided an important means of communication between members of a social group (Roth 2012). For example, during hunting activities, gesture facilitates communication, allowing co-ordination of activities and improving survival chances. With time, specific vocalisations in primates enhanced this process; in humans the gradual development of language, in these same neo-cortical areas, conferred greater survival value.

In Chapter 7, 'Seeing Eye to Eye', we consider the hugely important part eye-to-eye contact and 'mirroring' play in young children's development. Baron-Cohen (1999) identifies 'shared attention', the capacity to draw other people's attention to an object and to 'know that they know I am looking at this' as significant to social communication. This in turn plays a vital part in the communication of intention at close quarters. Similarly, eyes are often used to establish the 'pecking order' in a social group, with weaker individuals lowering their eyes as part of a submissive posture. This has species survival value, where intentionality, such as in 'battles for dominance', can occur 'symbolically' through eye-to-eye communication, rather than through 'fight to the death'. Thus the firing and wiring of MN circuits allow us to 'read' others' minds, enhancing the security, trust, flexibility, adaptability and stability that lie at the core of wellbeing.

Children who experienced early maltreatment tend to 'misread' situations (d'Andrea et al. 2012). Since in their early lives they experienced others' actions, such as being looked at, addressed or approached, as frightening or as having painful consequences, their MN circuits are 'hot-wired' to 'fight, flight or freeze' responses. Their 'survival MN wiring' means they frequently display inappropriate responses, often perceiving actions as threatening in 'neutral' situations, or when others' intentions are, in fact, well meaning.

The understanding offered by neurobiology also presents us with exciting opportunities to help children repair from early trauma.

Allan Schore (1994, 2001a, b) and colleagues worldwide refer to the 'plasticity' of the brain, implying that children can alter the ways they respond both neurobiologically and behaviourally if provided with consistent experiences of an alternative, healing environment. In our subsequent book, entitled *New Families, Old Scripts: A Guide to the Language of Trauma and Attachment in Adoptive Families* (2006) we explored this phenomenon, offering parents focused discussions of how, as the 'prime agents for change' for their children, they could create a family environment where change became a real possibility.

In this new book, we look towards integrating the body and the emotionally based nature of traumatic experiences, from the 'bottom storey' brainstem and limbic 'middle storey', to the neo-cortical (top storey) cognitive functions of our thinking brains. This enables us to formulate important basic principles for developmental reparenting from which parents can tailor-make their approach to their children's real needs. We start where parents and professionals need to start: at the beginning of children's physical, emotional, social, behavioural and cognitive development. This is the 'bottom up' thinking that informs this volume: starting with ways of sensing, moving on through ways of feeling and doing, and ending with ways of thinking and being. We demonstrate how these are integrally connected and how they make up who and what we become.

In doing so we continue to develop the ideas and suggestions featured in *New Families, Old Scripts*, and explore the basic principles of caregiving that create an environment where real change becomes a reality for some of our most vulnerable children. The terms 'therapeutic', or 'developmental reparenting' imply that adopters and foster carers offer the best 'therapeutic medium' within which maltreated children can feel sufficiently safe and 'held' to set out on the road to healing. Using this awareness we can make the changes in parenting mind-set that our children require so that they, too, can change: in their bodies, their feelings and their thoughts and behaviours. Change then becomes not so much a challenge as a gift: to ourselves, our children and our communities.

Traumatic early experiences are not confined to those children who are, or were, overtly maltreated or spent long periods in the 'looked after system'. Children born into families where there is persistent parental discord experience uncertainty and fear that 'prime' their perceptions and responses. It is often difficult for birth parents to be fully 'there' for their children when facing the fear of domestic violence, or to acknowledge that their children see, hear, feel and store these events in their bodies, brains and minds. If these experiences occurred in their earliest months of life when neurobiological development is at its most rapid, children develop trauma-based responses that profoundly shape their lives over the long term. Other children face even more 'invisible' adverse early experiences pre- or post-natally. Infants who spend periods in special care baby units experience traumatic early separations that mirror those of fostered and adopted youngsters. Young children who undergo painful hospital procedures experience hurts as inexplicable to them as the pain of abuse, often accompanied by distressing periods of separation they cannot comprehend. Maternal distress and depression create the same feelings of abandonment and unpredictability in young children as neglect. Even if these youngsters are lucky enough to remain with caring birth families they remain prone to trauma-based stress responses that affect their attachment security, relationships and development.

Our book is therefore designed to help all parents of children presenting behavioural and relationship difficulties derived from sub-optimal early life experiences. One of the bedrocks of our approach is the belief that healthy attachments are fundamental to healthy development. All of us are impacted by the way we were parented and almost everyone experiences some degree of attachment-stress (trauma) during their journey to adulthood. Securely attached adults will, as a rule, raise securely attached children, who in their turn will raise securely attached offspring. Theoretically they are well placed to help traumatised children develop healthier attachments. However, securely attached parents may well have differing expectations of the parent–child relationship from those of their traumatised children. Such 'mismatches' need to be acknowledged so that caregivers can make sense of their children's responses and best meet their needs. Other caregivers may have had difficult childhood experiences that affect their parenting style. Whilst it is more challenging to parent children in healthy ways when our own attachment experiences have been sub-optimal, such adversity can allow us a clearer 'window' into our children's inner world than is available to our more securely attached counterparts.

Whatever our parenting style, it is essential to be able to reflect on our own attachment experiences and those of our children and to have faith that, given the plasticity of the brain, change is always possible. Therefore to become therapeutic parents we need to consider our attachment style and how well this 'fits' our children's trauma and attachment histories. Understanding the neurobiological influences on ourselves and our parenting, alongside those of our children, is vital if we are to adapt to meet our children's needs effectively. We believe this book provides the foundations that will make change and 'rebuilding' more possible in our families and make our journey through life more comfortable and rewarding.

Chapter 1

Knitting Your Kid!
Patterns of Knitting and Nurturing Attachments

Although making an analogy between raising children and knitting woollies might seem fanciful it can be a useful tool in developing our understanding of the impact of trauma on children's attachment, resilience and global development. So let's begin at the beginning and see where we go!

Raw wool from the fleece comprises matted strands of dirty, oily fibre. To produce the balls of wool to create complete garments we need to strip, wash, tease out, card and spin the disconnected, tangled threads into longer, more even, inter-linked strands. This represents, metaphorically, the sequence of frenetic division, determining of potential function, and building of vital connections between the myriad cells that define the individual, taking form within the womb. The process of wool creation must be undertaken with great care and follow the correct production sequence. Then, irrespective of colour, texture or minor individual variation, we have the makings of a fine garment: as long as we have enough material, time and skill to follow the appropriate pattern, using suitable knitting needles. The same principle holds for the creation of human beings.

At birth babies possess more than a lifetime's worth of brain cells, neurons that must become specialised and inter-connected to create a mature, feeling and thinking human being. Normally at birth the 'raw wool' (fertilised embryo) has been spun into an identifiable 'fluffy ball' (new-born baby) with the potential to influence, for example, colour, size and strength. These characteristics, drawn from the gene templates of both parents, are tempered by experiences in the womb, creating the unique pattern for development of each human being. Within this early environment (metaphorically represented by the washing, carding, spinning and refining process) many unseen, poorly understood and underplayed influences can have a defining impact.

Provided there are reasonably adequate environmental opportunities, with safe space to grow, good enough maternal nutrition, a sufficient developmental period, limited stresses, and absence of toxic or traumatic experiences, the fertilised egg moves gradually towards becoming a healthy, 'neurotypical', individual. However, adverse experiences during this time, such as poor maternal diet, use of tobacco or other drugs, or chronic emotional or socio-economic stress within the family, may significantly affect the weight, development and future physical and mental health of the baby.

Many of the 'invisible' factors that adversely affect babies' development before birth have a common link: the destructive effect of maternal stress hormones, such as cortisol, passing directly from the mother to the ball of cells forming the infant in the womb (Schore 2001b). Although early foetuses may be unable to identify sensations and feelings such as pain, depression or anxiety, they certainly experience the neurobiological distress with which such emotions are intrinsically linked (Fisk 2000; Jennings 2011) and their neurophysiological systems adjust to achieve 'best fit' to ensure survival in adversity. Just as the secretion of hormones like adrenalin allow us to prepare for 'fight, flight or freeze' under stress to promote survival and perpetuation of the species, similar patterns of 'emergency response' occur in distressed and helpless infants pre-birth.

Where the perceived threat is ongoing, or repeated post-birth, these neurobiological adaptations become relatively fixed patterns (Schore 2001b). For developing infants this means continually raised stress hormone levels, making them tense, fractious, demanding, 'jumpy' and hard to settle, or, conversely, overly sleepy, 'poor feeders' and unresponsive. These factors, in turn, make it harder for caregivers to 'get to know' their infants and to feel confident in their parenting. In such circumstances babies' capacities to self-regulate are significantly affected, since the 'setting' of regulatory 'thermostats' begins before birth, with basic brainstem functions, and continues after birth via co-regulatory interactions with parental figures.

If things do not go well in the womb, the primal 'ball of wool baby' comes into the world in less than peak condition, though external appearances may seem normal. Beneath the surface there may be tiny 'breaks', 'kinks', 'knots', 'threads of fluctuating thickness and strength', variations in the 'twisting together' and connecting of individual 'fibre strands' and other potential 'flaws'. If the 'raw fleece' has been exposed to contamination, or 'quality control' during the cleansing process is poor, potentially toxic elements may persist. These factors, alone or together, can adversely affect growth, flexibility, durability and resilience and hence babies' subsequent 'knitting up' potential. Subsequent handling by 'workers' who are inadequately trained, in ill health or working in challenging conditions can further perpetuate poor outcomes.

From this point, 'standard patterns' may be insufficient to offset poor early 'manufacturing processes'. There may be 'poorness of fit' between the healthy 'knitting patterns' of securely attached or experienced 'knitters up' and the 'distressed yarn'. Such differences can accentuate developmental 'flaws', failing to repair early 'manufacturing' deficits. The 'manufacturing ergonomics' can become altered, through complex system feedback loops, affecting future production and organisation of 'output' of the 'garment' that is our growing child. The situation may be more problematic for a baby who remains with a 'knitter' who has not learned how to 'knit' well, 'knits without a pattern', 'drops stitches', uses different 'tensions' or 'tugs at the wool' to try and release the 'knots', rather than gently 'teasing' them out.

Unfortunately there is little we can currently do to influence children's pre-birth experiences directly, although it is to be hoped that, through raising public awareness of pre-natal influences, and systemic and individual pre-natal and birthing practices, this will change for the better over time. However, it is now possible, using therapeutic reparenting techniques derived from our growing understanding of children's attachment and developmental pathways, and the impact of early distressing experiences, to effect improvements in outcomes for traumatised youngsters in our care. These are discussed in greater depth throughout Part 2.

The brainstem forms the 'bottom storey' of the 'triune (three-layered) brain' – the layers of which are frequently described as 'reptilian', 'mammalian' and 'human' according to their level of evolutionary development. It is responsible for the establishment of life-promoting functions such as respiration, heart rate, blood pressure, body temperature, ingestion and excretion (Gerhardt 2004) and informs the autonomic nervous system (ANS), which itself controls automatic reactions to the environment. The brainstem provides the foundation upon which the internal and external sensory, motor, perceptual and socio-emotional functions can build, within the 'middle storey' limbic areas of the mammalian brain (Siegel 2010). Complex biofeedback loops that evolve between 'bottom storey' and 'middle storey' areas in infants' early months establish the neurobiological templates for physical regulatory systems throughout the lifetime.

In turn, these response patterns form the basis for the development of the 'top storey' neural networks of the cerebral cortex: the 'grey matter' of the human 'thinking' brain that allows mature reflection and organised, considered responses (Schore 1994). The limbic area and the cerebral cortex of each brain hemisphere (imagine a three-storey semi-detached house here) must follow specific neurodevelopmental sequences that begin after birth. Thus it is essential that good enough, basic regulatory patterns are set in place within the 'bottom storey' of the foetal brainstem to allow optimal organisation, regulation and integration of children's bodily, neurological and mental systems throughout the lifespan.

Exposure to toxic stressors in the womb can seriously compromise global developmental progress, 'pre-setting' unborn infants' regulatory brainstem functions in 'emergency mode': affecting breathing, sleeping and eating patterns, alongside other basic bodily functions, like heart rate, blood pressure and body temperature. These 'bottom storey' adaptations, once established, tend to persist even where living conditions improve considerably. Individuals will have higher reactivity to perceived stress, less flexibility of response, and a reduced sense of wellbeing and resilience.

WELLBEING

We might visualise wellbeing as a well from which a supply of pure, free-flowing water can be drawn, providing a dependable life-giving resource; whatever the demands placed on it, a consistent stream remains readily available. Wellbeing develops through positive attachment experiences, particularly during the first thousand days of life. It enables children to regulate their neurobiological stress responses, return to their 'comfort zone' and feel good in body and mind. The 'inner well' of securely attached children develops to meet their basic needs, providing them with a powerful source of clear, 'inner flow' and a healthy sense of confidence, consciousness, connectedness and creativity. They are ready to face almost everything the world throws at them with equanimity.

On the other hand, children's 'inner flow' is compromised by serious early adversity. The 'water-table' may be unreliable, with periods of 'flood' or 'drought'; the supply may appear 'tainted'. There will be continued lack of trust over 'supplies' that limits youngsters' expectations, exploration and free expression. Such children cannot 'go with the flow': their very being is constrained by fear of unfathomable, potentially life-threatening, events that threaten to 'drown' them. They remain on unrelieved 'flood-alert', at odds with themselves and the world; their life-chances and long-term health are likely to be compromised.

RESILIENCE

Wellbeing and resilience are integrally linked: both are created in the interactive 'dialogue' of attachment. Children are not born resilient; the lucky ones inherit a genetic coding that enhances their capacity to deal with life's challenges with equanimity. Such coding is promoted by positive, nurturing experiences within 'good enough' attachment relationships, conferring important advantages in terms of neurobiological responses to stress. This enhances children's ability to feel good in their bodies and minds, allowing them, both physically and emotionally, to 'bounce' or 'spring back' under stress: to find their 'comfort zone' and 'resume normal service as soon as possible'. We can consider the conjunction of wellbeing and resilience as the 'wellspring' of healthy, fulfilled life.

Conversely, trauma and poor early attachment experiences inhibit the development of well-regulated, organised, 'joined up' neurobiological systems. The lack of basic organisation and balance compromises inner flexibility (Cicchetti 2010); response patterns become rigid or chaotic, or may swing between these two extremes. These characteristic attachment patterns, the antithesis of resilience and wellbeing, are associated with significant, longer-term physical and mental ill health (van der Kolk 2005).

Research has shown that foetal exposure to high levels of cortisol can alter or destroy neurons in 'middle storey' limbic areas of the brain such as the hypothalamus (Gerhardt 2004). Within this essential component of the regulatory hypothalamic-pituitary-adrenal (HPA) feedback system, cortisol can further dysregulate vital neurophysiological systems. These include the dysregulation of cortisol production itself (Schore 1994, 2001b), the volatility of the emotionally based memory system and learned emotionally loaded responses co-ordinated by the twin amygdalae, and the under-development of 'feel-good factor' neurochemicals such as dopamine, endorphins and oxytocin (Cozolino 2002). This neurobiological 'cascade' provides a clear example of a complex biofeedback response, altering internal control systems in response to direct experience. Long-term poor management of stress appears unavoidable, leading to difficulties in areas such as self-awareness, self-control, thinking and reasoning, and in the functioning of the immune system.

Moreover, cortisol is known to affect the development of the neurons of the limbic hippocampi during the pre- and peri-natal period (Eliot 2000; Schore 2001b), although, functionally, they do not come 'on line' until the third year of life and recall of memories of events below five years of age is usually limited. The hippocampal structures are intrinsically involved in the creation of explicit, long-term, verbally based memories and the formation of the 'coherent narrative', or real life-story, which underpins children's awareness and understanding of themselves as beings. The hippocampus of each cerebral hemisphere logs the who, what, when and where of youngsters' experiences, although each functions in distinct ways: the left lays down the bare facts and the right records personal, 'episodic' events.

Siegel (2010) describes the paired hippocampi as masters of 'puzzle piece' (jigsaw) assembly; together they communicate with other 'higher' limbic areas, such as the orbito-prefrontal cortex (OFC), and connect to the top-storey 'thinking brain'. This integrative function is vital, enabling us to make sense of, learn from and adapt to individual circumstances appropriately. The hippocampi can continue to grow throughout the lifetime, facilitating the creation and storage of new memories and their integration into our awareness. It is likely that stress-related over-production of cortisol will continue to inhibit neural growth in the long term and hence to interfere with explicit memory formation and conscious recall. Without the facility of conscious, focused 'remembering', our flexibility of response to circumstance is compromised; choices will be 'closed'; and 'knee-jerk' emotionally driven reactions, rather than 'open' and considered responses, will predominate.

Both a fundamentally dysregulated neurobiological 'alarm' system and a weakly developed sense of self, accessible memories and 'personal narrative' affect our potential for self-awareness and our capacity to understand, relate to and infer the intentions of other people meaningfully. This complex, developmentally acquired, process of self-knowledge includes both 'emotional literacy' (of self) and 'mindreading' (of others) (Fonagy and Target 1997); both involve the 'wiring up' of mirror neuron (MN) circuits. Thus the relative lack of intrapersonal and interpersonal 'literacy' we may see in later childhood and adulthood is underpinned by the dis-stressing and dis-organising relational experiences of the earliest years, highlighting the importance of beginning the repair process as soon as possible and helping our children develop the 'coherent narratives' that help them make sense of their past, present and future.

MINDFULNESS ('MINDSIGHT', 'MINDREADING', 'THINKING ABOUT THINKING')

 The capacity for logical, reasoned thought becomes possible when children acquire sufficient sensory and emotional literacy, language and memory of objects and events to make sense of, and express, themselves, plus the wherewithal to become mindful of others' thoughts and feelings ('think about thinking'). The origins of mindfulness lie in the attunement of caregivers in healthy attachment relationships (Siegel 2010) that allows children to transform 'concrete' thoughts, centred around themselves in the moment, into more abstract concepts that can be categorised, considered and stored 'symbolically', in language-based form, and readily available for recall.

Parents must continue to help their children extend their range of experience and vocabulary and provide more detailed explanations and insights into their inner and outer world.

By helping youngsters become more socially and emotionally aware, mirroring, modelling and putting feelings, actions and thoughts into words, parents provide meaning for their children and make vital cognitive connections for them, so that they can extend their capacity for reasoned thought, mature social interactions and intellectual growth. MN circuits play a major role in the development of mindfulness (Siegel 2007), making the world more coherent, predictable and hence safer, for children to function well, form meaningful relationships and thrive.

Having insufficient experience of being 'mirrored', of 'sharing attention' and 'sharing minds', or of being 'held in mind' within consistent, nurturing attachment relationships, neglected and abused children are unable to be mindful of other people: they struggle to identify their feelings, reflect on their actions and thoughts, or predict their intentions. Consequently they are frequently 'out of synch' in social situations and struggle with close relationships, including with peers. This, in turn, increases their sense of alienation and inherent 'badness'. Lack of mindreading abilities is also likely to interfere with children's ability to plan and organise, and hence executive functioning.

Events at and following birth can also have adverse effects on infants: where the 'choice of knitting needle size', 'selection of pattern', the mode of 'casting on' and 'choice and number of stitches' form the next vital developmental stage. These processes, passed down through generations, bring expectations that 'texture', 'thickness of wool', 'diameter of needles', number and form of 'stitches', and 'wool handling' characteristics will follow established protocols. Any minor variations due to individual characteristics and cultural practices remain within well-defined parameters. In families where knitting patterns and handling methods diverge more markedly, the potential for – further 'breaks', 'holes', 'tangles', variations in 'texture', 'fibre structure' and 'tensile strength', the establishment of incomplete or distorted 'stitch loops', and altered 'tension' – to adversely affect outcomes increases significantly. Moreover the earlier the interruption to the overall developmental process the greater is the potential for continuing 'flaws':

causing further 'cascades' of 'pattern' distortions that affect individual potential and making repair more difficult.

Sensitive and timely structural and functional 'quality checks' are therefore essential, with a clear focus on identifying subtle but significant factors that can disrupt the 'manufacturing' process and affect longer-term outcomes. Putting these safeguards in place is clearly cost-effective and should be given the highest priority: it is much easier to pick up a 'dropped stitch in row four' than if it remains undiscovered until 'row 50'.

As an example, 'standard' forceps deliveries are known to raise cortisol levels significantly (Gitau *et al.* 2001). Premature or ill babies placed in special care (SCIBU), though owing their survival to highly skilled clinical interventions, are significantly distressed by untimely separation from their mothers, with whom they have become intimately connected in the womb. New-borns are able to identify their mothers' smell (MacFarlane 1975) and voice (DeCasper and Fifer 1980) within hours or days of birth: these essential sensory adaptations, promoting bonding and survival, are recognisable throughout the mammalian kingdom. For new-born infants, even brief periods of separation are experienced as a 'lifetime' and can seriously raise stress, and hence cortisol, levels (Schore 1994, 2001b). Thus the traumatic separations and frequent changes in handling and sensory input intrinsic to many clinical situations can compromise early bonding in sick and pre-term infants, exaggerate their experiences of distress, and affect the basic 'stress response settings' that vitally underpin their future developmental pathways.

Absent, too, will be the essential two-way 'mirroring experiences' and intimate contact, both tangible and visual, which soothe and regulate infants' brainstem functions such as breathing and heart rate (Reebye and Stalker 2008; Trevarthen 2001). The subsequent reduction in serotonin receptor formation and the 'neurophysiological cascade' of unhealthy stress responses (Schore 1994) increases basic arousal levels, further alters biofeedback processes and compromises long-term wellbeing and resilience. Under normal circumstances, 'good enough' parents have continual opportunities to recognise their babies' responses and the capacity to reflect these in their own interactions: beginning a 'mirroring' process that promotes the growth of 'mirror neurons' (Iacoboni *et al.* 2005).

These, in turn, facilitate ongoing understanding and learning. Simultaneously, the spontaneous pleasure and wonder infants evoke in their caregivers is reflected back and encourages further pleasurable sensations in babies, stimulating the secretion of neurotransmitters, such as serotonin, and the formation of numerous neural receptors: 'messengers of wellbeing'. Benefits include physical good health, through the intrinsically linked immune system (Schore 1994, 2001a), as well as the positive effects of these chemical messengers on children's emotional health (Siegel 1999).

Infants and young children who remain with, or swiftly return to, stable birth families are likely to fare much better than those subjected to further breaks in caregiving, whether through changes in parents' relationships, multiple caregivers or entry into the care system. Sadly, in the latter the burgeoning 'garment' that is the young child is exposed to unpredictable changes of 'knitting needle' properties, such as 'gauge, length, material and colour' and 'stitch choice'. These factors, alongside unavoidable alterations in 'handling patterns', greatly increase the potential for individual variation. Inevitably there will be continuing changes in 'tension': just as no two persons knit with precisely the same 'tightness or looseness' so, too, each caregiver parents in unique ways, to which children must try to adapt and of which they must try to make sense. The potential for further 'dropped', 'twisted', 'picked up' or 'out of sequence stitches' abounds.

Let us now consider the circumstances for changes in 'tension and style' inherent when any 'knitter' takes over from another temporarily and then returns the garment to the original 'handler'. It is important to recognise that this will be the case during even brief periods of contact or respite, both formal and informal, or when infants attend nursery, arrangements that are common for looked after children and in the histories of adopted children. Furthermore, experienced professional carers, including nursery staff and respite and longer-term foster carers, can become set in their caregiving patterns and less sensitive and flexible to the individual needs of their charges: less ready to 'switch needles', 'alter tension' or 'change stitch' from ways they have previously found effective.

Foster and nursery care providers may, over time, develop seemingly functional patterns of dealing with 'troubled children', based on perceiving them as 'controlling', 'manipulative', 'aggressive' or 'attention-seeking'. Consequently they may unwittingly adopt parenting patterns that reinforce children's own 'stuck' perceptions of themselves as 'difficult' or 'unlovable', consolidating their difficulties. Friends and family members may contribute to these negative self-images, for example giving parenting advice, based on their own experiences of having raised 'neurotypical children' (Cartwright and Morgan 2008), that is unsuitable for troubled ones. Siblings may play on the 'bad reputation' of youngsters to displace blame for their own actions; older distressed children may take advantage of younger or more vulnerable youngsters, perhaps re-enacting the abuse they witnessed or experienced in their families of origin.

Bear in mind, too, that not all knitting is done with 'one pair of needles', representing a parenting couple. There are many 'single-needle knitters' (lone parents and carers), represented by the 'circular needle' and 'four needle knitters', families where caregiving may be shared by several generations. Looked after, or adopted, children often move through several households in their formative years and experience several of these variations: posing further challenges to their sense of stability, security and predictability. Consequently they can become increasingly set and inflexible in their social, emotional, cognitive and behavioural responses, feeling ever more helpless in the hands of changing caregivers and an unpredictable world.

Unfortunately, inadequate, ineffective and destructive 'knitters' bring an additional dimension of stress to the 'knitting process'. Unpredictable 'knitters' can exacerbate existing 'irregularities', with additional tendencies to 'unravel' or 'slip stitches' that further compromise growth and development. Abusive 'knitting' contributes powerfully to 'tangles, knots and dropped or picked-up stitches', alongside further changes in 'stitch pattern'. Moreover, inattentive, neglectful 'knitters' frequently 'drop stitches', creating serious 'holes' and 'lack of connection' in the growth of the 'delicate garment': hence neglectful parenting is likely to create the greatest degree of damage to the developing and 'finished product'.

This emphasises the need to make decisions about children's welfare as soon as possible, offering support to birth parents likely to struggle and establishing clear expectations for standards of caregiving. Assessing opportunities for change within realistic time-limits and determining whether parental 'knitting' is 'good enough' can mitigate the damaging impact on children of repeated, failed rehabilitation attempts.

Throughout the developmental phase from birth to three years of age, there are exponential changes in the nature and form of the neural networks that link mind and body, alongside the establishment of increasingly specific areas and structures of the brain itself. When young children experience consistent, sensitive and attuned feedback from their caregivers (during the moment-by-moment 'dance of attachment') their physiological and neurological development and the formation and specialisation of brain structures, such as areas of the prefrontal cortex, will go well (Trevarthen 2001). These, in turn, form the basis for the integration and healthy development of the 'top storey', thinking brain and establishing essential wellbeing and resilience over the lifetime (Siegel 1999). We now explore some of these processes in greater detail.

During their first three years, well-cared-for youngsters' growing sense of safety, comfort and belonging allows the 'thermostats' of their ANS to become well modulated and further, healthy neurological connections to be created and strengthened through the myelinisation of the nerve fibres with a 'protective outer coat' (Siegel 1999). The secretion of essential neurotransmitters such as serotonin and dopamine also permit the smooth flow of information from external receptors (such as skin, ears, eyes, nose) and internal receptors (e.g. muscles, joints and internal organs) (Reebye and Stalker 2008) to increasingly defined 'receiving' areas of the brain: allowing swift and appropriate physical and emotional responses. During this period, youngsters develop an increasingly intimate awareness and mastery of their physical selves, begin to identify and make sense of their bodily and emotional feelings, and develop confidence in the predictability of their world and of themselves. These form the 'internal working models' (IWMs) described by Bowlby (1973), an essential 'representational memory' function of the orbito-prefrontal cortex (OFC) (Schore 1994).

Initially activated by 'natural' feedback from caregivers' eye contact, gestures and 'baby talk' (Gerhardt 2004), the 'dance of attachment' between parent and infant that encourages positive IWMs to develop also provides the optimal environment for the establishment of the mirror neuron system (MNS), allowing youngsters to anticipate and infer others' actions and intentions (Siegel 2010). It is also believed to facilitate the recognition and 'decoding' of emotions in others: in turn enhancing children's 'emotional literacy' and the development of empathy (Carr *et al.* 2003). This capacity to 'read' the feelings of both self and others is understood to be mediated through the caregiver's unconscious mirroring of the neurobiological state of the observed infant and the neurobiological linking of these physical feelings to the emotions they represent (Siegel, 2010). This can be described as 'the feeling of feelings', an essential function that comes 'on stream' gradually within the reciprocal 'dance of attachment'. Areas most closely identified with the MNS lie in the middle prefrontal cortex and insula (Siegel 2007), contributing to the building of a 'staircase' of connections between the lower, middle and top 'storeys' of the brain.

Simultaneously, the consistent, attuned responses of primary caregivers during the early months encourage the development of object permanence (OP) (Goldman-Rakic *et al.* 1983). This provides the basis for youngsters' increasing recognition that they themselves exist, even when alone: reducing feelings of abandonment and powerlessness that could otherwise be overwhelming. This can be understood as acquiring the sense of 'feeling felt' (Siegel 1999) and understood: of increasingly being 'held in mind' by attachment figures (the figurative 'secure base' (Bowlby 1969) from which children feel safe to move out into the world). Damasio (2006) suggests that this challenges Descartes' well-known statement 'I think therefore I am', proposing that a more accurate statement might be 'I am therefore I think'.

OBJECT PERMANENCE

 Object permanence (OP) plays a major part in the establishment of a secure base. Continuity, consistency and responsiveness of caregivers are all essential for children to acquire OP (Bomber 2007). At birth, babies have no concept of themselves or of the world: it is only through repeated experience that they learn that objects and people continue to exist when they cannot be felt, seen or heard. From this youngsters become aware that they, too, continue to 'be' whether or not their caregivers are in close proximity (Williams 2004): that they do not disappear or cease to exist but remain 'held in mind' over time (object self-permanence, OSP)(van Gulden 2010).

The acquisition of OP is directly related to the development of our memory systems. Our earliest memories are sensory-based, and are processed and stored according to their emotional value by the mid-storey amygdala, particularly in the right hemisphere. These non-verbal memories, also known as implicit, procedural or body memories, begin to be consolidated from around eight months; they are not readily brought to mind through conscious recall. It is only in the third year that explicit, verbal, narrative memories begin to be stored in the mid-storey hippocampal areas, particularly in the left hemisphere. Here memories of objects, people and experiences are symbolically represented through language and are 'hooked' to specific events, locations and perceived causality; they can be intentionally accessed and recounted. Both memory systems are significantly involved in the establishment of OP and object constancy (OC).

Interrupted early attachment experiences interfere with the development of OP (Bomber 2007), leaving children, young people and even adults with a sense of abandonment and isolation. They have a persisting sense of helplessness and hopelessness, feeling they have little or no control over their chaotic world. They believe there is no-one predictably 'there' for them whom they can trust to keep them safe and lack affirmation that they themselves continue to exist (OSP). To infants these felt like potentially life-threatening situations; even brief separations in the present can trigger overwhelming feelings that profoundly affect their behaviour. Since all memory is experience-based, neglected and abused children's memory systems reflect their early sensori-motor and emotional distress and continue to affect their perceptions and responses through their MN systems.

SECURE BASE

Parents need to establish a secure base (Bowlby 1988) for their children to allow them to feel safe, cared for, worthy of love, able to be healthily dependent, and to trust that their needs will be met appropriately. Parents should be attuned to their children's needs, responsive and readily available for them both physically and emotionally, throughout their childhood. By providing a predictable, dependable, nurturing environment, caregivers create a solid foundation upon which young children can build a sense of trust, acceptance and belonging. They can then move into the world with growing confidence in their self-worth and competence, able to form meaningful relationships and to develop resilience and wellbeing.

Failure to provide a consistent secure base means that infants and young children experience the world as confusing, unpredictable and hostile (Solomon and George 1999). They remain on physiological 'high alert', unable to trust that caregivers will take care of, protect and guide them. Their sub-optimal neurobiological response patterns will continue to adversely affect their sense of security and trust, their emotional and behavioural responses, and their capacity to form meaningful relationships throughout their lives.

Subsequent to the development of OP, object constancy (OC) can be established. Here any given 'object', animal, vegetable or mineral, can be perceived as remaining the same, despite variations in appearance or behaviour. For example, the cherry tree in the garden is recognised as the same tree, whether leafless in winter, bearing buds and blossom, or in full leaf. Similarly, 'Mummy' is recognisable as 'Mummy', whether wearing a hat, in her nightdress, watching TV, smiling or scowling. In particular 'Mummy' remains 'Mummy' through all her moods and actions, 'good' and 'bad'. Youngsters can also see themselves as 'all round' individuals, rather than one-dimensional beings represented by one dominant feeling or behavioural state.

OBJECT CONSTANCY

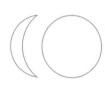

Opportunities for exploration of self, other people and the world around them allows children to make greater sense of their body sensations, feelings, responses and thoughts across a wider range of experiences. Gradually, as their experience, awareness, memory and understanding expand, children come to know that things such as 'my teddy' stay the same whether they are clean or dirty, wearing their jacket or hat, or have both eyes or have lost one along the way. Similarly other people can be recognised as the same over time, place, action or mood. Eventually children 'get it' that they, too, are the same individual whether at home or outside, in the morning or the afternoon, dressed up or wearing no clothes, sleeping or awake, or happily playing or on their own and feeling upset.

As for every step along the developmental path, parents need to provide a wide infinite range of experiences and opportunities for their children to acquire object constancy (OC) at the 'right time'. Ongoing nurture and structure (see p.52) must be complemented by a new and gradually changing balance between consistency and predictability, novelty and variety of sensations and feelings. Often this is the time when caregivers take their children to 'parent and toddler' groups, playgrounds and soft ball areas, broadening children's horizons whilst remaining readily available in the background.

In addition, healthy attachment figures tune into their youngsters' feeling states, reflecting and modulating them accordingly (Schore 2004; Siegel 1999). In this way they help their children practise moving smoothly from one feeling and behavioural state of being to another. They accept all aspects of their children, 'good' or 'bad', whilst helping them return to comfortable 'baseline' states and practise pro-social behaviour. In doing so they help children to identify, accept and integrate every part of themselves: consolidating their sense of object self-constancy (OSC).

Without access to attuned and consistently nurturing caregivers, young children cannot come to know themselves as 'whole', assured that they are loved and valued for all of themselves, however they are feeling and behaving. They will have insufficient opportunities to practise managing controlled state transitions and take responsibility for all of their actions, or acquire the OSC vital for self-awareness, self-control, self-confidence and self-esteem.

The acquisition of OC protects youngsters against the challenges of external inconsistency, encouraging the expectation of overall predictability and stability whilst fostering flexibility and adaptability. Young children also learn to integrate their own shifts in feelings and behaviours: to know and accept that 'all of this is me'. An overwhelming emotional state can be recognised as transient, not 'forever', shielding children from the potential distress created by internal feeling state changes. For Dan Siegel (2010) the ability to be flexible, adaptable, consistent, energised and stable (FACES) forms the core of resilience, defined as 'the maintenance of high levels of positive affect and wellbeing in the face of adversity' (Davidson 2000). Thus OP and OC contribute to youngsters' capacity to 'bounce back' when faced with difficulties and to avoid being overwhelmed by them, or developing rigid behaviours to circumvent them.

A key area of the prefrontal cortex linking all three storeys of the brain is the orbito-prefrontal cortex (OFC). It has been shown (e.g. Schore 2001a, 2001b) that a consistently 'good enough' 'dance of attachment' with primary caregivers fosters the development of those bilateral areas of the limbic brain that forge pivotal 'staircases' to the cortex and its maturing capacity for reasoning, negotiating and impulse control. With its direct and powerful connections to the emotionally driven amygdalae of the limbic 'middle storey', particularly in the right hemisphere, and its capacity to integrate powerful feelings within the hippocampal memory storage system, more highly developed on the left side of our 'semi-detached' brain, the healthily functioning OFC encourages balance, coherence and flexibility of response. Sadly, in youngsters with histories of early maltreatment, especially of neglect, development of the OFC tends to be inhibited: their sense of security will be compromised, leading to more rigid (depressed, 'shut off', avoidant), or chaotic (over-reactive, impulsive, 'switched on'), responses than would ordinarily be expected in toddlers.

THE SEMI-DETACHED BRAIN

 The human brain can be visualised as a house divided horizontally into three storeys and vertically into two semi-detached dwellings. The brainstem, limbic areas and neo-cortex ('grey matter') are represented by the horizontal layers. The vertical division represents the two brain hemispheres, each half having similar room layouts. There are connecting 'walkways' that link the two halves (the corpus callosum, or 'white matter'). All areas of the building share plumbing and electrical systems running both vertically and horizontally (the neurobiological systems). From here neurobiological connections run throughout the body, linking external and internal sensory and motor systems to relevant parts of the semi-detached brain.

Just as the owners of each semi-detached house 'customise' their home, perhaps turning a 'bedroom' into a 'library' or 'playroom', we find differentiation and specialisation of function of brain areas between the hemispheres. For example, the OFC develops more, and matures earlier, on the right-hand side than on the left. From an evolutionary perspective, differentiation of function confers greater survival value, allowing increased brain functioning from the same basic number of brain cells. There is a concomitant need for enhanced communication systems throughout the semi-detached brain in order for disparate brain areas to function as an integrated whole.

Adverse early attachment experiences interfere not only with the growth and specialisation of specific brain areas but also with the connections between them. Some plumbing and electrical (neurobiological) circuits may not become established, whilst others form 'closed circuits'. So, for example, children may exhibit sensory integration difficulties (SIDs), difficulties with emotional and behavioural regulation and literacy; 'higher' cognitive skills, such as executive function (EF) (see p.41) and mindfulness, are likely to be impaired.

Moreover, children's capacity to over-ride 'bottom storey' brainstem systems also remains limited: meaning basal physiological responses such as heart or respiration rates will be more frequent, powerful and dysregulated. Since these somatic sensations are transmitted, via the energising of powerful vagal nerve responses (the 'fight, flight or freeze' reactions), to internal sensory and emotional receptors (Porges *et al.* 1996), they evoke potentially overwhelming feelings of loss of control in children. Over time this pattern of volatility becomes relatively fixed and forms the basis for children's perceptions (IWMs) of themselves: 'what I do' and consequently 'who I am'. This perpetuates 'out of control' behaviours and influences others' perceptions and responses, leading to a destructive, self-reinforcing cycle involving distorted OC formation. Once established it can prove highly resistant to change. Letting go of 'this is me and how I do things', however unhelpful, may be too terrifying for children to contemplate: a challenge that may, in turn, test the most securely attached of caregivers.

In summary, youngsters raised by maltreating caregivers experience serious attachment-trauma which seriously impacts their global development. This is evident in markedly different configurations of perceptions, beliefs and behavioural responses that appear fixed and resistant to change. Research shows that the majority of these children display disorganised attachment patterns (Shemmings and Shemmings 2011): the most serious and dysfunctional of insecure attachment patterns. Often recognised in early aggressive or compliant behaviour and employed unconsciously by youngsters to provide an illusory sense of control in their otherwise inexplicable world, such patterns are said (Spangler and Grossmann 1999) to be underpinned by patent dysregulation and disorganisation of children's emerging neurobiological systems.

At this point a timely reminder that neuroplasticity continues to offer hope for change throughout the lifetime is reassuring. The good news is that understanding neurotypical development and awareness of children's early developmental history allows us to create effective therapeutic reparenting programmes individually tailored to their needs. Although it is vital to begin the 'reshaping' and 'repairing' process as early as possible, when body–mind mechanisms are at their most malleable and less 'collateral damage' has occurred in terms of self-concepts, social interactions and expectations and the brain–body mechanisms that underpin these, it is never too late to 'take youngsters back', 'reset their thermostats', reprogramme their response patterns and offer them opportunities for lasting, healthy change.

NEUROPLASTICITY

 No matter what individuals' early experiences, their degree of dysfunction or their age, the capacity for repair persists (Siegel 2010). For example, current research suggests that people with Parkinson's disease, an as yet incurable degenerative condition, can be helped to 'reprogramme' their neurological systems to maintain residual control of their movements. There is considerable over-production of neurons during foetal development, so, despite periods of rapid 'pruning' in the early years, during adolescence and during the natural process of aging (reducing the total neuron count), it remains possible to 'turn on' 'redundant' brain cells throughout the lifespan.

This adaptability, or neuroplasticity, allows the formation of new neurological circuits capable of at least partially repairing 'faults' in the neurobiological system. Clearly the earlier opportunities become available for neural 'rewiring' the better the outcome is likely to be. Not only will there be a larger available neuron 'pool', there will also have been less time for the 'firing and wiring' of unhealthy circuits and thus for distorted perceptions, responses and cognitions to become 'hot-wired' and habitual.

Moreover, opportunities for developmental reparenting strategies are greater in the early years, when the social acceptability and expectations of close physical contact and supervision are higher; this also holds true for many children with physical and learning disabilities. Sadly older children may become pseudo-independent, resisting parental help, insisting on 'personal freedom' or developing 'manipulative' patterns which can work against them getting what they need. We must help all our hurt children find opportunities for developmental repair. Hence an understanding of attachment and development must underpin any therapeutic reparenting programme (Archer and Gordon 2004).

From our experience, equally fundamental to repair and healing is the understanding that 'there is always a way'. Having confidence in our capacity to bring about healthy change using a developmental attachment template is at least half the battle. We must also learn to take good care of ourselves in order to be at our best to take good care of our children.

Continuing our knitting metaphor, we might think of children in the 'middle years', beyond early years schooling, as representing the main 'body' of our garment. They have taken on their basic shape but have several more years of continued growth before reaching the extended reshaping periods of puberty and adolescence. It is during this 'middle years' stage that consolidation and continuation of 'good enough' patterns already acquired occurs in the steady hands of 'good enough knitters'. Some natural variation within expected norms is to be expected, as the individuality of each garment becomes apparent and contributes to its maturing style and character.

This period should continue to be one of vigilance for 'quality controllers' at home and school, where more atypical 'pattern settings' and wider variations in the strength and nature of 'knitting materials' and 'styles', due to early 'mishandling', can become more evident alongside increasing expectations of 'age and stage' conformity. The potential disparity between home and outside-the-home 'handlers' (e.g. teaching staff) may also become increasingly apparent to 'handlers' themselves or their 'co-workers' (partners), to fellow 'garments-in-formation' (peers) and frequently to the 'proto-garments' (children) themselves. This last element is readily overlooked yet fits with the distorted OC formation of maltreated youngsters.

Expressed in the now familiar phrase 'neurons that fire together wire together', nerve cells, located throughout the body's nervous system and concentrated in the brain, have the greatest opportunity or incentive to interact in their formative stage, allowing them to establish and maintain the strongest connections over the lifetime. Thus the 'smart brain' that can anticipate and predict events is created, enhancing individual life-chances, health and wellbeing.

In our 'knitting' we might think of adjacent 'stitches', horizontally and vertically, forming solid connections that continue to run through and influence the functionality of the 'garment' – at least until the inevitable wear and tear of age takes its toll. By then, hopefully, it will have been much loved and valued, able to offer comfort to its owners, and inform design patterns for future 'models'! Contrariwise, the 'stitches' of poorly cast-on or mishandled 'pieces of knitting' have weaker, often 'tangled', connections, inappropriate 'links' and 'loops', 'knots' or 'gaping holes'.

The dysfunctional patterns becoming established adversely influence outcomes: these 'garments' may lack basic 'shape' or 'strength', readily 'unravel', be less likely to lead to pleasing 'finished products', fail to meet 'normal standards', or be subject to negative perceptions and even rejection within mainstream circles. Such 'garments' are also more likely to be 'left on sale' or 'returned as unsatisfactory'. Of some concern is the potential for 'self-destruction', or attempts by inexperienced 'handlers' to 'make good'. The latter may employ ineffective 'cover up' strategies that aim to compensate for fundamental 'snags' or apply more radical and potentially damaging strategies such as wholesale 'pulling back of the yarn' or untimely 'unpicking of the joins'. The 'garment' may, quite literally, be 'torn apart at the seams', rather than receiving the gentle 'handling and reshaping' it requires.

Returning to our human adult-in-formation, the body–brain–mind mechanisms of primary school children must continue to connect and consolidate. At this developmental stage, neurotypical youngsters show a maturing capacity for self-regulation (e.g. physical and emotional self-soothing, self-calming, self-awareness and impulse control) and for increasingly rational and reasoned thought (Siegel 1999). The billions of neurons that 'fire together' and 'wire together' form increasingly complex 'information networks' facilitating perception, categorisation and memory formation. Thus key cognitive processes of interpretation and anticipation of future events and capacities for self-reflection and 'mindreading' come 'on line'. MN circuits play a critical role in these maturing functions.

Throughout the 'middle years', children require countless opportunities to consolidate and refine their neural connections according to individual needs, influenced both by environmental factors and innate genetic potential. During this highly complex interactive process, the structure and mechanisms of children's brains demonstrate further differentiation according to function and further refinement and speed of response (Schore 1994). Developmental focus is increasingly on cognitive 'top storey' processes. Executive function, the capacity to conceive of, plan, instigate and carry out more complex thinking, now becomes a key feature (Dawson and Guare 2004). Over and above differences due to 'nature and nurture', personal, social and intellectual development will be affected by children's expectations and belief systems, alongside the pressure of peers, caregivers and educators.

EXECUTIVE FUNCTION

 A major step in children's development is the acquisition of the capacity to evaluate situations and to plan, organise and respond appropriately at home, at school and in the community. This demands a high level of self-regulation, large 'well-programmed' knowledge and memory banks, both non-verbal and verbal, the capacity to draw on this information, and to apply it efficiently. It involves mature integration of sensory and motor systems, facilitating physical co-ordination and allowing youngsters to organise their bodies in order to carry out actions conceived in their 'thinking' brains.

An ability to sustain attention, alter focus appropriately, inhibit impulsivity and anticipate outcomes is also essential. Sufficient 'bottom up' brainstem and limbic developmental connections must be established to allow a growing degree of 'top down' regulation, monitoring, reasoned thought, self-awareness and self-control. Areas of the PFC are particularly associated with executive function (EF).

Inconsistent, neglectful and abusive early caregiving means that young children have inadequate opportunities for the 'firing and wiring' of well-connected, well-organised neural networks, including MN circuits. Areas of the brain, such as the OFC, may not have been 'turned on' and fail to 'light up' when needed.

Since this area has been identified (Schore 1994) as the 'hierarchical' link between the brain's middle and top storeys, executive functioning tends to be significantly impaired.

Moreover, neurobiological 'short circuits' keep children in 'high arousal' ready to respond through 'fight, flight or freeze' responses. This further precludes the 'switching on' of vital 'thinking' areas of the neo-cortex, leaving children prone to emotional reactivity, impulsivity, poor attention control, limited access to linguistically based memory banks and impaired cognitive abilities. Relationship difficulties are also likely due to limited impulse control and behavioural inhibition, and reduced capacity to identify and predict others' intentions appropriately. Impairment of EF is associated with specific learning difficulties, attention deficit hyperactivity disorder (ADHD), obsessive-compulsive disorder, autistic spectrum disorders, Tourette's syndrome, depression and schizophrenia (Encyclopedia of Mental Disorders 2012).

The gradual extension from the 'inner circle', or secure base, of primary caregivers and close family that becomes consolidated in toddlerhood 'takes off' during this period. Schools, clubs and organised group activities play increasingly important roles in the lives of primary school-aged youngsters, as the influence of non-family adults and peers gains ground. This represents a continuation of the 'exploration' phase of toddlerhood that allows safe, limited practice of brief separations followed swiftly by reunion with primary caregivers. In toddlerhood, youngsters experiencing a 'secure base' begin to 'internalise' the security with which 'good enough' caregivers have surrounded them, as the closely linked concepts of trust, predictability, OP and OC become increasingly embedded.

EXPLORATION

 Young children need to learn more about their bodies, sensations, emotions and awareness of the wider world through exploration and expanding experience. As their secure base extends, and their sense of OP becomes more firmly established, toddlers literally begin to 'find their feet': starting to move out of the intimate, 'closed' space they shared with their parents and using their growing control over their bodies and minds to expand their world.

It is from this extended secure base, with continuing 'external' reassurance and safe guidance, that young children take on board parents' behavioural expectations and ideals and begin to monitor their own behaviour using these internalised guidelines. Young children learn they can 'keep in touch' with their caregivers metaphorically when away from them, knowing they are still being thought about, 'held in mind' and cared for by them. Typically, toddlers glance back regularly for confirmation of their parents' continued presence and approval of their intended actions.

'Good enough' caregivers continue to enlarge and consolidate this secure base, whilst simultaneously encouraging their youngsters to try out new experiences and test themselves in different situations. They remain 'there' for their children, responding when they need to be protected and shown safe boundaries, or when they need to 'check in', for reassurance, and 'check out' parental reactions to their growing exploits, while encouraging them to take their first steps towards independence.

As a consequence of inconsistent, unpredictable and hurtful care, neglected and abused children are unable to 'internalise' the security and boundaries they need. The resulting inhibition of exploration, or lack of awareness of safe limits, in this 'practising' stage of development means that children remain fearful of separation and change or, conversely, seem oblivious to danger (rigid or chaotic behaviours typically associated with lack of wellbeing).

Feeling 'held in mind' (Siegel 1999), neurotypical pre-school children engage in increasing exploration of their world, pushing the boundaries yet feeling 'held' by the clear, safe limits provided by their caregivers. In evolutionary terms, this facilitates the gradual acquisition of independence that is vital in adulthood. The 'primary years' provide exponentially greater opportunities for practising and honing these essential 'survival' skills, within graduated and 'boundaried' conditions, encouraging an increased sense of self-awareness, individuality and self-efficacy. These developmental processes are accompanied by the strengthening of self-control and self-confidence, increasingly mature thinking, reflection and decision-making skills.

The early attachment experiences of poorly nurtured or overtly maltreated youngsters provide them with neither the basic security and OP and OC, nor the maturing self-awareness and cognitive capacities they require to face the challenges of this period (Schore 1994). A significant number bring with them poorly integrated sensori-motor systems, meaning, for example, they are over-sensitive to touch or sound, or remain poorly co-ordinated (Reebye and Stalker 2008). Yet simultaneously circumstances demand that they deal with the same age-and-stage interactions, and are subject to the same behavioural and educational pressures and expectations, as their peers. It is not surprising that they struggle to conform and appear demanding and 'attention-seeking' or unco-operative and withdrawn.

Many youngsters attempt to disguise their difficulties through over-active behaviour, 'showing off', 'playing the clown' and 'challenging' behaviour, or by over-compliance or 'giving up'. They are often misunderstood, described as having 'emotional and behavioural difficulties' rather than educational difficulties in the classroom, making the accurate recognition of, and provision for, their special needs challenging (Bomber 2007). Essential learning support systems may not be put in place and children may slide further away from peer norms: generating animosity in adults and peers, confirming their negative self-images and perpetuating the behaviours they so desperately need help to modify.

Typically, 'polar opposite' behavioural patterns emerge at this time. On the one hand, youngsters present as quiet and inhibited: 'daydreamers' experienced as 'no trouble'. They passively yet firmly resist change, are wary of unfamiliar people and reluctant to undertake new challenges or make simple choices. 'Compliant' children try hard to be likeable and to fit in: sometimes appearing 'desperate' to make and keep friends at all costs. They can appear over-dependent on adults, yet attract little negative or focused attention, since overall they strive to conform; consequently their special neurodevelopmental, social and educational needs can pass unrecognised.

Other traumatised youngsters can appear precociously independent, often unable to ask for, or accept, help from others. They may be described as 'bright', yet are easily distracted and struggle to sit still and focus their attention, leading to disturbance of peers and educators. These youngsters frequently lack basic social skills and find peer relations problematic. Difficulties with following instructions and co-operating with rules and requests can lead to maladaptive behavioural strategies, further compromising their learning potential. Children in this cohort tend to be 'in your face' as they struggle to 'feel felt and held in mind': yet this frequently results in their being left out of shared peer-group activities and can lead to more formal exclusions by the adults in charge. Increasingly, parents, group leaders and school staff find it difficult to understand or deal with the challenges such children pose, particularly in the context of a classroom, playground or communal activity.

Lacking age-appropriate neurobiological organisation, many previously maltreated youngsters find it harder in general to exert impulse control, pay attention, follow instructions, stay on task and organise themselves, their time, their thoughts and their belongings. All these are vital prerequisites for effective learning and executive functioning. Specific learning difficulties such as dyslexia, dyspraxia, dyscalculia and receptive and expressive language problems are common and can be understood in terms of poor integration of sensory and motor systems alongside the relative developmental immaturity of 'top down' cognitive regulation of 'bottom' and 'middle storey' systems (Reebye and Stalker 2008).

The compensatory strategies struggling youngsters adopt to deal with these difficulties contribute further to a negative cycle of development. Since these behavioural adaptations use up vital energy, such children (even the ones described as 'on the go 24/7') are more readily exhausted. This in turn weakens their already poor impulse control and capacity for reasoned thought and they rapidly begin to decompensate. Whilst 'good enough' caregivers readily attribute toddlers' angry or 'naughty' outbursts to tiredness and make allowances accordingly, it is more difficult to bear this in mind when dealing with a 'stroppy' nine-year-old. Yet in neurodevelopmental terms that nine-year-old may at that moment be functioning as a toddler. Negative feedback continues the downward spiral as youngsters recognise that they are perceived by others as 'out of control' and 'bad'. Since this confirms their negative self-image it consolidates their shame-based, one-dimensional view of themselves: 'this is who I am' with the concomitant 'this is what I do'.

SHAME

Maltreated children frequently experience extreme, inconsistent and abusive socialisation interactions, without attachment repair: leading to chronic, toxic shame. They are unable to recognise or practise pro-social behaviours and their behavioural repertoire can be both inappropriate and limited. Moreover their attachments will be compromised, leaving them feeling abandoned, helpless and hopeless. So children enter our families with continuing, unmanaged levels of dis-stress and dysregulated neurobiological systems. Furthermore the overwhelming shame experiences to which they were exposed significantly affect their self-image; they come to believe that it is not their actions that are unacceptable but that they themselves are unacceptable and inherently 'bad'.

Rather than 'I made a mistake' our children internalise the message 'I am a mistake'. As a result shame-based children are highly sensitive to criticism, feeling that making mistakes is potentially life-threatening, similar to the feelings engendered when they were maltreated in infancy. Some develop coping strategies based around an endless struggle to be 'good enough', interspersed with 'meltdowns' when, inevitably, they 'get it wrong'. In turn, this confirms their worthlessness and saps their reserves of energy, heavily compromising their wellbeing and resilience.

Others become adept at 'inverting' their feelings and responses: denying any sense of wrong-doing and blaming everyone else for the situations in which they find themselves. They frequently fail to learn from their mistakes, leading to a persisting pattern of anti-social behaviour. They feel alienated and frequently respond with 'shame-rage': becoming verbally or physically abusive or destructive. Their sense of self and their resilience and wellbeing are also adversely affected.

There is a marked change in pattern of a 'knitted garment' once the 'main body' reaches the appropriate 'size'. In our metaphorical raglan-style jumper, there is a gradual reduction in the 'stitch count' as the outline narrows to form the 'neck'. Shaping must proceed at the right time, at a well-defined rate according to pre-determined patterns, to ensure that the 'sleeves' and 'neck' fit 'seamlessly' alongside other parts of the 'garment' as they too take shape and contribute to the finished article. An orderly sequence of 'decreasing' and 'casting off stitches' is also required to facilitate a good enough fit, ensuring the overall design criteria are met and articles are 'fit for purpose'.

Significant individual, or system, faults and issues in connection or completion at this stage can affect final outcomes, albeit in fundamentally different ways to the stages of 'casting on' and 'early increasing stitch' patterning. Now, instead of streamlining the finished 'product', 'manufacturing glitches' make it more difficult for the essential 'joining up' of parts and adversely affect its functionality. However, there remains a 'wider window', within which temporary 'meltdown', 'downing of tools' or 'go slow' interruptions to the 'manufacturing' process are less likely to seriously alter final outcomes. Greater variation in input here, within limits, is not only likely to have fewer adverse effects but it can, conversely, contribute to the unique qualities of the 'garment'. Major 'faults' are more likely to be the result of poor 'care and repair' at the earliest stages of 'manufacture' than from 'glitches' at this stage. Putting right any noticeable 'faults' will also be simpler, since they will be more localised and less well established.

So it is with young people as they approach the challenges of puberty and adolescence. During this major developmental 'double' transition there is significant 'neural pruning' (Schore 1994), contrasting markedly with the 'neural network' building that is a major feature of earlier developmental stages. Now the number of functional brain cells is proportionately reduced, preparing young people for further brain–mind–body integration, developmental 'joining up' and maturing executive function (Dawson and Guare 2004) and enabling them to meet the complex demands of independent adulthood. This paves the way for teens to become unique, separate individuals, able to connect in quite different ways with their birth and adoptive families and to establish lasting relationships and families of their own. These 'cutting back' and 'joining up' processes must operate in sequence and in concert to facilitate the transition to adulthood.

However, despite the concurrent widening of the neurobiological developmental 'window', adolescents are vulnerable to the expanding opportunities and social challenges they face in their daily lives. Ironically, as the maturation of their bodies and brains occurs at differing rates and, simultaneously, important hormonal changes are taking place, teenagers often act in immature and risky ways. As if that were not enough, the social pressures of peer groups begin to replace those of the family as the major influence in the thinking and behaviour of even the most stable individuals. Loyalties become increasingly allied with peers, and previously acquired relationships, social mores and responsibilities may be set aside temporarily in the quest for new 'grown-up' identities, outside existing family circles and influences.

We might compare this to the 'exploratory phase' of toddlerhood, when young children first practise separation from caregivers and broaden their horizons. The teen years bring with them many similar challenges, alongside the same outbursts and control battles toddlers engage in, although with significant changes in the power dynamics. Many adolescents are as large as, or larger than adults and are rightly encouraged to stand up for themselves and be treated as equals in society. Unfortunately their maturity of thinking and understanding of the responsibilities of adulthood may not keep pace. The current gradual expansion of the period of formal education and paucity of employment opportunities may further contribute to the 'gap' between the ideal of increasing independence and the reality of continuing dependence, as well as between 'teen norms' and the 'norms' of adult society in general.

In many mammalian species, adolescents separate themselves from their families, often with active encouragement from their parents, to form 'roaming peer packs'. In time the 'pecking order' of individuals becomes established, new alliances and relationships built. Frequently males strive to prove themselves physically to gain a foothold in the adult hierarchy whilst females often seek less confrontational ways towards this goal. However, sexual activity and procreation play a major role for both sexes; the concepts of 'survival of the species' and 'the selfish gene' help us make sense of these behaviours. These age-and-stage related trends have their counterparts in humans, although they tend to be modified by social expectations of altruism, mutual responsibilities and 'the common good'.

Clearly the quality of early caregiving and subsequent developmental attachments strongly influence the extent to which this turbulent human adolescent 'rite of passage' becomes a temporary 'blip' or heralds an adulthood of social and emotional turmoil, anti-social behaviour and challenging or offending behaviour. The evolutionary-based 'testing' or 'proving' behaviours of temporary peer-group formation, aggressive interactions, risk-taking and brief sexual encounters will, in the former case, be transformed into species-determined adult norms or, in the latter, become embedded in individuals' behaviour, leading to continuing personal and social difficulties. In human society, continuing socio-emotional connections to caregivers, family and community often remain strong and can 'hold' adolescents whilst they make the transition to maturity. Sadly, such psychological connections and supports are not readily available to young people with poor attachment patterns.

Take, for example, the occasional teenage 'experimentation' with illegal substances. This is much more likely to lead to serious misuse and addictions in young people with compromised attachments than in securely attached individuals, where acceptable social norms are more deeply embedded, neurobiological systems are relatively well balanced and the 'top storey' thinking brain is well established and functional. Unfortunately the disorganisation of physiological systems and neural networks and poor executive function in young people with poor attachment histories makes them particularly vulnerable to risk-taking behaviours and continuing drug use, as they attempt to 'self-medicate' and create more order and balance throughout their dis-stressed bodies and minds. The combination of lack of neurobiological homoeostasis (systems balance) and poor cognitive function, leading to weak 'top down' controls, can be a lethal mix.

Maltreated individuals are often driven to behave beyond social norms and expectations, since they possess poorly organised brainstem and limbic circuits and have had fewer opportunities to build mature cortical systems through which to apply reasoned thought and impose top-down impulse controls where needed. Since these young people also lack somatic self-awareness, any real sense of self or positive identity, the adolescent stage of 'proving' themselves and establishing their adult identities will necessarily be problematic. There is also a tendency for troubled young people to group together and take their lead from the most powerful and 'wildest' of the 'gang', meaning there are less opportunities for positive peer role models to influence them for the better.

Furthermore, young people with compromised developmental attachments find this stage of separation and individuation particularly challenging, since they have limited healthy experiences of positive attachments to stand them in good stead. Not having been able to practise healthy separation as youngsters they struggle to manage healthy separation as they approach adulthood. Instead the unresolved fear of abandonment, loss and isolation felt in the past is mirrored in chaotic or rigid responses in the present. Typically as young adults they avoid intimacy, make fleeting yet often intense and dependent relationships, or allow themselves to be victimised by more dominating friends or partners in their struggle to avoid further abandonment and create some sense of belonging.

Sadly, a significant number of adopted and fostered young people attempt to separate sooner rather than later, often by their mid-teens – despite their underlying need to remain and feel 'held'. Here the 'push me, pull you' dynamic between fear of rejection and fear of closeness creates unbearable opposing 'tensions' that may overwhelm the whole family. Preventing 'casting off' from turning into 'casting out' can require almost blind faith that one day our hurting young people will realise where they truly belong and return 'home'. Almost inevitably, as parents, we will struggle to balance being ready to 'pick up' our young people again and ensuring they do not slip back into old, distorted patterns of relating within the family. Some teens and young adults may 'drop more stitches' or seem to 'unravel wildly' on the way, yet by holding out ongoing opportunities to 'pick up where we left off' we provide the vital, powerful message that 'we can work it out' – together.

In essence, adopting the maxims 'slower is faster' and 'less is more' is invaluable in encouraging independence in previously traumatised children. Since they had serious interruptions to their attachment ('casting on') process we must anticipate, and help them manage, corresponding difficulties with 'casting off' (separation, moving out and moving on) in adolescence and early adulthood. Almost inevitably they will require a longer period of 'casting off' in order to *'fill in the gaps'* and complete the developmental attachment process. Inevitably, when it comes to the final *'joining up'* of the *'garment'*, there will be some *'pieces'* that are less well finished than others, making the *'sewing together'* potentially problematic. While some young people may appear *'ready to roll'*, their true state of *'readiness'* should be judged in light of their early history, all-round *'joined-upness'* and *'good fit'*. Whilst the *'survival pieces'* of the young person may be well developed, the *'trust'*, *'relationship'*, *'thinking'* and *'self-awareness'* pieces may be much less mature, requiring additional opportunities to develop fully.

Families, friends and professionals involved at this stage need to recognise the true dynamics of the challenges faced by adoptive families. Encouraging adopters to 'reclaim' their young people and identifying effective ways of providing the 'nurture and structure' intrinsic to attachment, often well into adulthood, is vital to young people's wellbeing. Simultaneously, an awareness of functional, rather than chronological, age can obviate potentially damaging 'casting out' scenarios, where parent–young adult dynamics become increasingly untenable and 'explosive'. Enabling families to 'hang in there' and 'hang together' by providing therapeutic mentoring is more effective than facilitating premature separations and independence. Where personal or family safety is threatened, meaning physical separation is advisable, continuing familial connections should still be encouraged, so that attachment 'strands' are not irretrievably broken.

NURTURE AND STRUCTURE

A balance of nurture and structure is vital to the formation of early developmental attachments. Whilst nurture plays the dominant role in the establishment of a secure base, the regular patterns of daily life provide a consistent, predictable framework within our earliest attachment relationships. In the exploratory phase, beginning in toddlerhood, the focus changes, as the provision of a clear structure becomes increasingly important to young children's security.

Nurture represents all the caring, loving, giving, playing and sharing activities that 'good enough' parents provide intuitively for their children. In general, irrespective of children's age, we recognise these in moment-by-moment, sensory, motor and socio-emotional parent–child interactions. They 'speak' directly to the bottom and middle levels of the brain, laying the foundations for the structural connections and functional development of children's body–brain–mind systems.

Babies' neurobiological systems are immature, lacking the integration and organisation they need to live meaningful, independent lives. It is through the **structure** of consistent, predictable, stable caregiving that the essential 'firing and wiring' takes place. Rhythms, routines, co-regulation and simple house rules provide the order, and hence the essential structure, for children to feel safe, protected and 'held' within firm, loving boundaries. Both nurture and structure are vital to the development of secure attachment patterns.

As toddlers become more mobile and begin to 'move out' into the world and face new challenges, they need greater parental structure and guidance in order to stay safe. Through 'shame socialisation' (see Schore 1994) good enough caregivers begin to create 'temporary emotional breaks' in attunement that generate just enough anxiety (guilt) in their youngsters for them to recognise unacceptable behaviour. Then almost immediately, they reconnect with their children to 'repair' these attachment breaks: providing children with messages that whilst they disapprove of their actions they still love and cherish them. Together, parents and children are able to identify and practise pro-social behaviours that, in evolutionary terms, ensure children's acceptance within their families and communities.

Due consideration must also be given to the effects on subsequent generations of interrupted developmental attachments. Parents with unresolved attachment issues, who have poor self-awareness, impulse controls and social and organisational skills, find it difficult to attune to, make sense of and care for their children appropriately. Parents' compromised capacity for self-regulation means they experience high levels of stress, remain on neurobiological 'red alert' and may 'unravel' rapidly. Their relationships are often 'tangled' and turbulent, their lives chaotic. Seeking early independence, many of these young adults appear driven to make intense, often inappropriate, relationships and reach parenthood prematurely.

If adopters and foster carers have kept 'the windows and doors open' and 'kept hold of the strands firmly', they are better placed to provide a degree of stability for these young families. Whilst the importance of grandparents as a 'third-party secure base' for their grandchildren cannot be under-estimated, the role is often fraught with difficulties. Conflicts between the needs of children and grandchildren can be challenging; grandparents may feel helpless to intervene or become the major caregivers for the next generation. Currently there is little recognition of these issues, yet it is an area that demands attention and the development of both formal and informal support networks.

Chapter 2

Fitting the Pieces Together

In Chapter 1 we identified specific issues that are pivotal in influencing children's physical, emotional, social, behavioural, educational and cognitive development at each developmental stage. We emphasised the impact that youngsters' environment (nurture) has on the extent to which they reach their genetic potential (nature) from the moment of their conception to way beyond the conception of the next generation. We explored why the quality of physical and psychological caregiving has the most significant influence on youngsters' health and wellbeing during the earliest developmental periods. We identified specific factors that are implicated in the way children grow and develop and began to examine how early identification of vulnerability at each stage, alongside age-appropriate, developmentally based attachment interventions, could enhance children's lives and, indeed, those of every member of their family and community. In all, we hope we have been able to clarify some *knotty* issues and *tangled* concepts that are sometimes beset by *woolly* thinking and practice at the systemic level.

DEVELOPMENTALLY BASED ATTACHMENT INTERVENTIONS

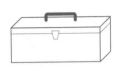

Children who experience insufficient nurture and structure develop insecure attachment patterns; good foundations of vital 'bottom up' developmental sequences fail to be laid down; poor internal wiring occurs; and mature 'top down' controls are compromised. Since neurobiological systems remain 'plastic', by providing a healthier caregiving environment we can encourage the firing of new neuron patterns and begin to 'rewire faulty systems'. The more developmentally informed adopters and foster carers can be, the earlier they can begin the therapeutic process of reparenting, and the more opportunities they can provide for their children to receive the 'good enough' nurturing and structured caregiving they lacked, the greater are the therapeutic benefits. Parents are in a unique position to undertake this life-enhancing work, since they are, and can create and control, the '24/7' healing environment their children need.

Using our extended knitting metaphor we attempted to bring the complexities of neurobiological development within the grasp of a broader audience. In particular we tried to speak directly to caregivers, since they represent the 'hands on' resource that is most effective in untangling the strands, identifying the distorted patterns shaping our children's lives and working more confidently and accurately. Simultaneously we endeavoured to avoid turning clarity and simplicity into 'reductionism', implying a 'one size fits all' approach to setting things right. It is a 'no-brainer' to state that every one of us is unique and a clear 'yes-brainer' to take account of developmental body–brain–mind patterns that can guide us in devising templates for individual intervention and caregiving.

The 'tailor-making' of a developmental, or therapeutic, reparenting programme is invaluable (Archer and Gordon 2006) and is only possible with a clear, shared understanding of 'why children do what they do' and of why being creative in offering youngsters repeated opportunities to practise doing things differently is vital. Hence we encourage caregivers to create and practise 'fridge-mantras' such as:

- 'We need to know what was *done* to our child to make sense of what it *did* to our child.'

- 'It's not "*won't do*", it's "*can't do*".'

And, consequently:

- '*We* need more practice.'

These seemingly simple concepts not only bring more understanding to parents and other significant adults, they introduce the empathy and self-confidence that are fundamental to achieving healthy changes of balance in relationships, perceptions, thinking and behaviour. Printed and attached to the fridge door they provide apt reminders for caregivers when they most need them and are least likely to recall them: when they are under most stress.

Every 'knitter' holding the 'baby wool', at whatever stage, needs to be able to select not only the most appropriate 'needles' and 'stitch sequences' but also the most effective 'handling skills' and 'tension'. They then hold in their hands the means of engaging in that two-way, interactive process, or 'inter-subjectivity' (Trevarthen 1979, 2001), which is as fundamental to attachment and development as it is to knitting. From this position they will be able to establish the best balance between nurture (the loving, unconditional caregiving) and structure (the loving setting of firm but fair boundaries), to begin to establish a 'secure base' for even the most troubled children and young people. This approach, in turn, must be founded on carefully observed behavioural patterns of children within their current families, and interpreted in the light of their past family experiences, ideally with the support of an experienced parent mentor, or 'knitting coach'. In the absence of access to this information, the potential for further developmental damage is intensified and the task of making good children's distorted somato-sensori (bodily), social, emotional, behavioural and thinking patterns made more difficult.

As a physical example, where children are identified at placement as 'small for age' or 'underweight' due to neglect, new caregivers may 'play catch up' by substantially increasing their youngsters' intake, especially of carbohydrate- and fat-rich foods. However, recent research shows that rapid 'catch-up growth' is associated with an increased incidence of raised blood pressure, coronary heart disease and diabetes (Criscuolo *et al.* 2008). These findings are consistent with the proposition that serious childhood adversity increases the likelihood of subsequent development of heart disease, cancer, stroke, diabetes, skeletal fractures and liver disease (Felitti and Anda 2009). Moreover, this challenge to physical health compounds the long-term, traumatic-stress-related emotional, relational and learning difficulties that many maltreated children and young people exhibit.

Interestingly, Gluckman and Hanson (2005) propose a physiological 'default' pattern in consumption directly linked to parental exposure to raised stress hormone levels during pregnancy. The same pattern is evident, through persistently raised core regulation, in infants exposed to other environmental stressors such as from parents with serious mental health issues. These youngsters, too, become biologically prepared, or 'programmed', to survive adversity. The 'inherited survival setting' needs to be understood by subsequent caregivers so that they gain increased empathy for their youngsters' behaviour, be it craving for unhealthy foods, need for excitement or general volatility, and can explore ways to introduce, practise and 'reprogramme' new, healthier, patterns of behaviour. We might visualise this in terms of knitters, through the right balance of nurture and structure, slowly but steadily increasing the diameter of the needles to achieve optimal size, shape and quality, without creating undesirable tensions, holes or snags in stitch loops and inter-connections that will adversely affect final outcomes.

We hope it is now clear that awareness of youngsters' early history, and its potential impact, is fundamental to the interpretation and handling of their behaviour and that observation of children's overt behaviour can be highly misleading without this 'historical lexicon'. We need to recognise that behaviour is children's 'first language' (Archer and Gordon 2006) and, perhaps, the only language they know, as a result of their early adverse experiences. Since many of our children have missed valuable opportunities, during the appropriate developmental period, to acquire emotional literacy and language, they continue to rely on non-verbal behaviours to communicate vital information both about their past experiences and their current feelings and needs: their actions certainly speak louder than words. Experienced therapeutic parent mentors can often help caregivers make 'informed guesses' and 'fill in the knowledge gaps', in the absence of sufficient, essential information on children's early attachment experiences, and support caregivers to utilise their growing understanding of developmental trauma to 'hear' and understand what their children and young people are communicating.

We have found that establishing greater awareness, competence and self-confidence in parents leads to an increasingly shared 'parent–child language' which, in turn, evokes greater self-awareness, self-control, self-confidence and competence in children and young people (Archer and Gordon 2004). This two-way communication process replicates the inter-subjectivity of early infancy within healthy attachment relationships. Since there are only so many ways in which children act, a good deal of 'trauma-programmed behaviour' will often be 'heard' in terms of 'All children do that!' Consequently youngsters' vital communications may be overlooked. Conversely some behaviours provoke strong negative feelings and labels like 'attention-seeking', 'inattentive', 'manipulative', 'controlling' or 'anti-social', meaning that children's developmental special needs are overlooked. Less overtly pejorative, yet equally unhelpful, descriptions of traumatised children's unspoken behaviour might include: 'daydreamer', 'natural clown', 'quiet', 'compliant' or 'likes to stay close'.

These behavioural patterns, already touched on in Chapter 1, represent the twin predominant patterns of disorganised attachment behaviour identified by Lyons-Ruth, Bronfman and Atwood (1999) from observing school-age children. They should be understood as 'trauma-normal' behaviour, since they are persisting adaptive responses to early adversity, standing in strong contrast to the 'neurotypical' behaviour of children experiencing healthy, early attachment relationships. Early disorganised attachment patterns are predictive of subsequent emotional, social and mental health difficulties across the lifespan (Spangler and Grossmann 1999). However, by school age, children's behaviour can appear highly 'organised' and 'structured' (e.g. Lyons-Ruth *et al.* 1999), since they have evolved adaptive survival strategies that confer an illusory sense of control in an otherwise unpredictable and hostile environment. For example, children who act 'in your face' usually get what they need: reactions that help them feel 'held in mind' by caregivers, albeit in highly negative ways. These stereotypical behaviour patterns also demonstrate a reduced range of actions and interactions that adversely affect children's potential long-term wellbeing and resilience.

It is therefore essential that therapeutic parenting interventions begin as early as possible and are focused on the 'child behind the mask', holding in mind that the *meaning* behind the actions of children with developmental attachment difficulties is likely to differ markedly from the norm. This is evident in the high *frequency*, *duration* and *intensity* of their behaviours, in whether their actions are 'biologically driven' via experientially acquired expectations, rather than through conscious choice, and in the way they often make their closest caregivers feel. It can be a mark of the level of affinity 'knitters' feel for the 'garments' taking shape in their hands that caregivers experience levels of distress which actively mirror the neurobiological and socio-emotional distress of their children, via their MNS. Skilled parent mentors can help caregivers identify these somatic and visceral cues (physical responses and 'gut feelings'), alongside behavioural clues, to better manage their own reactions and adopt more effective reparenting strategies for their children. Caregivers can then avoid perpetuating unhealthy survival patterns and devise creative ways of repairing vital (and literally life-promoting) developmental attachment relationships.

For example, youngsters who have tantrums beyond 'the terrible twos' pose challenges often experienced as 'controlling': particularly as they can appear selective about their timing, audiences and 'performances'. Such outbursts may occur several times each day, last for hours and be voluble, violent and distressing. We know that paying scant attention to mistakes, big or small, in knitting tends to perpetuate, or exacerbate, faults throughout the garment. Part of the 'in-house training' of good enough 'knitters' is to detect such potential problems and intervene to correct minor difficulties in their infancy, before they become major problems likely to compromise the overall quality, reliability and durability of the finished product. Similarly, caregivers need preparation, specific training and support so they can recognise that the frustration, fear and lack of self-competence and control they feel reflect the frustrated, fearful, out-of-control and powerless feelings of their children and young people. Overlooking the 'cry for help' of full-on tantrums neither resolves children's distress nor puts things right. On the contrary, it reinforces the basic set-up of children's body–brain–mind systems, compromises developing parent–child relationships and sets in train increasingly unhealthy interaction patterns.

Thus, ignoring the negative frequently causes the negatives to increase, complicating unhealthy patterns and making putting things right more difficult. Ignored children feel increasingly unheard, out of touch, 'out of mind' and 'out of control': in much the same way that we might become frustrated and raise our voices when we feel we are not being heard. Conversely, children who feel listened to and 'held in mind', by caregivers able to accept and verbalise their deep-seated, unspoken fears, learn to identify and make sense of the chaos of their inner and outer lives.

Here the gradual 'unpicking' of their trauma-based responses under the guidance of their parents gives children and young people the chance to create, and build on, new and healthier life patterns. Since the natural parenting style of caregivers may differ from the structured parenting their youngsters need, effective preparation, training and support are essential to allow them to 'get in synch' with, and 'recalibrate', distressed youngsters' trauma-normal, base-level responses without being thrown 'out of kilter' themselves (secondary trauma – see p.247).

Again, direct observation of overt behaviour must be balanced by an awareness of trauma history in selecting the parenting style most appropriate to children's functional, or behavioural, age. If, for example, 'knitters' select their 'pattern' according to youngsters' chronological age or size, or their overtly independent behaviour, it is likely that experiential and learning 'gaps', sensory, emotional and cognitive 'tangles' and the acquired, altered or additional 'stitches' of survival-based adaptive behaviour will continue to affect their growth and development adversely. Children of, say, ten years old who have good enough early experiences can be expected to take a good deal of responsibility for self-care tasks, such as bathing, hair-washing, teeth-cleaning, bedroom-tidying and organising themselves for school. There is often greater, more disparate and more confusing variation in the abilities displayed by youngsters placed in adoptive or foster families.

Although maltreated children can demonstrate 'age and stage normal' self-care skills, many will, at least at times, refuse to do so, or appear unable to complete the task to 'reasonable' standards. At these times they may seem 'oppositional', 'lazy', 'attention-seeking' or 'babyish'. It is vital that we recognise that, at that moment, it is more likely 'can't do' rather than 'won't do'. Conversely some youngsters appear 'precociously' independent and resist offers of adult help or guidance, replicating inverted patterns of care that are common in families of origin. Whilst it is natural to wish to encourage the chronologically 'neurotypical' development of autonomy, we should turn perceptions on their head for children with traumatic histories and compromised attachments. It would be more 'trauma normal' for them to struggle with self-care skills, since early caregiving was absent, inconsistent or inadequate: therefore they will benefit from additional care, support and practice.

Frequently, youngsters' problems with self-care come from their lack of self-awareness, including of their own bodies, their poor or negatively defined self-regard, and from fear of relinquishing control to others, particularly parent-figures. In situations like these therapeutic parent mentors encourage caregivers to 'read' children's behaviours in terms of their unfulfilled developmental needs. Lacking the basic foundations of good care from others, these youngsters are letting us know at the bottom and middle storey (somatic and emotional) levels of functioning what their top storey, thinking brains cannot know: that they need to complete this 'shared care' stage before they can move on to healthy self-care. When parents reframe these situations as opportunities to be seized it allows them to give the early nurturing care they would love to have given and their children to have received. Where youngsters resist nurture, parents can empathise aloud that they had to grow up too quickly and take care of themselves and often younger siblings, pointing out that now, thankfully, they have parents to play this important role. In these situations we can offer a second chance for children to practise something vital they missed out on in their young lives. Although it may take a great deal of patience, time and creativity to alter these early-acquired patterns of behaviour, it is well worth the effort!

By reflecting on their youngsters' needs, and on the state and stage of the work so far, caregivers can gently and painstakingly identify and correct early 'manufacturing faults', however large, so that the 'finished article' carries as few 'flaws' as possible. Parents can be helped to identify the 'dropped stitches' and embrace the opportunities this gives them to 'go back' with their youngsters and make good: initially setting aside expectations of independence and encouraging much-needed, healthy dependence. Creative adopters might manage teeth-cleaning difficulties by encouraging 'teeth-cleaning races' (preferably snail's-pace), provide toothpastes with sparkly stars or use toothpaste drawings on the bathroom mirror to engage their children. Adding some much-needed fun and off-the-wall humour are powerful tools in defusing potentially distressing or confrontational situations. Additionally, and vitally, caregivers communicate to their children that they are 'there for them' and 'on hand': both providing nurture and reinforcing object permanence.

Whatever the situation, being confident that this is the best and healthiest thing to do to move children towards sounder independence is essential. Simultaneously, introducing an element of play allows some good experiences to 'slip past' children's well-practised defences, so that all involved can relish the process of filling in their 'experiential gaps'. Since, according to Panksepp (1998), we cannot feel fear and the joy of play simultaneously, this is a clear 'win-win' situation! Similarly, it is helpful to break down seemingly simple tasks into a number of smaller steps, asking children to take responsibility for just one part; a pictorial chart showing the whole process could serve as both visual prompt and reminder of the eventual goal. In this way parents set their children up to succeed, continue the essential nurturing process and, simultaneously, avoid shame-induced opposition: 'win-win' again!

These brief examples are intended as 'tasters': to start us thinking and make us eager to know more. We hope we have *teased out* some of the most important *strands* in the neurobiological sections, to provide an increased understanding and a firmer basis for action. Although Part 2 is written so that it can be read as a 'stand-alone' work, we hope readers will be tempted to peek into the 'science bit' at some points! We have learned a good deal in putting this volume together and have enjoyed ourselves along the way: we encourage others to join us and gain as much from it as we have. Finally, in addition to the explanatory sections given within the text (with some concepts, such as object permanence and object constancy, explored in greater detail in Part 2), a more inclusive glossary and relevant reference list can be found at the end of the book.

What Can We Do?

Introduction

Our focus in Part 2, 'What Can We Do?', is on enabling our traumatised children to begin the healing process. We attempt to integrate what is currently known of the neurobiological impact of early attachment-trauma with an awareness of our children's histories: to make sense of 'why they do what they do', and help them develop more coherent narratives of their lives.

This in turn helps us understand our children in the 'here and now' and identify the stepping stones on the 'road to repair' and the path towards healthier, happier lives. The task we will be embarking on can seem one of the most daunting, yet simultaneously one of the most important, projects that we will ever undertake. Quite literally we are setting out to change and develop our children's brain structures and connections, their body sensations and their emotional responses, to help them develop new neurobiological pathways and increase their resilience and wellbeing. In doing so we may face the challenge of making radical changes in the way we relate to our children; this can take a great deal of time and commitment and we are bound to make mistakes along the way. Indeed making mistakes is a prerequisite to change, as it sends two important messages to our children: that we do not have to be perfect and that, if mistakes occur, they are valuable learning opportunities, not the end of the world.

A major theme throughout our book is the need to display empathy for children's difficulties and, while not necessarily accepting their behaviour, to let them know we understand their struggles and accept them as special human beings. This recognises that many of their difficulties stem from their early traumatic experiences and are their primary way of communicating predominantly unconscious thoughts and feelings. Sadly, empathy can sometimes feel impossible when faced with the challenges our children present. Even the most patient parents 'lose it' at times, reacting with anger or rejection; a crucial element here is to repair the attachment breaks immediately. A simple hug, followed by '*Sorry! I'm having a bad hair day*', can be enough to convey a message of love and repair the temporary break in attachment connections.

Such messages are important for children who have learned that making mistakes can lead to abuse, rejection and feelings of shame ▢: where mistakes can have seemingly life-threatening consequences. By helping our children 'unlearn' these distorted beliefs we set in motion the process of neurological and somatic change. Simultaneously we can learn that the task we are undertaking is surmountable, that learning occurs in numerous ways and that we can help our children through making and owning our own mistakes: 'setting things right' and 'getting things right'. Remember that the most important learning pathway for children is via mundane interactions. It is the way we eat breakfast together, the games we play together, the smiles and laughter we share, the bedtime stories we read and the interest we show in their activities which make the crucial difference.

As adopters we wish we had known when our children were young what we know now. There were times when we were unhappy with the way things were at home, when we felt sadness, anger or despair, when we wished we could find ways to improve family life. We cannot pretend that reading this book will make such feelings disappear, or transform our children, overnight: however, we believe it can bring renewed confidence and hope, lessen stress levels within our families, and create real possibilities for change. We are also convinced that adopting our reparenting principles is much less energy-sapping, isolating and guilt-inducing than struggling to manage children's trauma-based behaviour using our old parenting patterns, however 'tried and tested'.

A main priority in bringing about changes in our families is to effect changes in ourselves. While parenthood clearly implies that we should prioritise our children's wellbeing, it is also essential that, at times, we take care of ourselves first. It is a universal flight requirement that we don our own oxygen masks before helping others. This injunction is equally relevant to our family journey: we need energy and enthusiasm to care for our children. We cannot do this well if exhausted and distressed. This can require a sizeable mind-set shift and plenty of practice: we therefore explore this issue in greater depth in Chapter 17, 'Taking Care of Ourselves'.

In Part 1 we emphasised that it is never too late to help traumatised children build healthier lives and that repair is easier the sooner the repair process begins 🏠. Reparenting traumatised one-year-olds, by going back to very early babyhood, is easier than beginning a similar 'bottom up' developmental process with needy eight-year-olds struggling, in addition, to cope with school and peer relationships. They may, chronologically, be expected to deal with these challenges yet are unlikely to be emotionally capable of doing so. Not only are the challenges greater but so too are the social expectations we and our children may face. So we must learn to trust that the 'bottom up' path is the right path for our families and become creative in providing opportunities for our children to 'go back' to babyhood and toddlerhood, albeit in ways appropriate to their actual age.

We focus here on the principles of developmental reparenting (Archer and Gordon 1999b) rather than taking a 'how to' approach, using examples of specific behavioural issues to highlight these principles. In doing so, we aim to develop a mind-set that can be adapted to a variety of challenging situations. In this way we hope to lay down foundations that lead to lifelong changes in relationships with our children. With these basic principles at our fingertips we can create an individual strategic approach, rather than referring back to 'the manual', just as experienced 'knitters' develop the confidence and 'know how' to create their own patterns as they go.

Developmental reparenting deals with all aspects of children's difficulties and all areas of home life: helping us create the optimal environment for change. Early trauma has a huge neurobiological impact on our children's bodies, brains and minds. It is often a case of 'can't do' rather than 'won't do', and we will need to take into account the developmental, trauma, attachment and executive functioning issues that affect our children's competence. Altering the emotional atmosphere of our homes is crucial to changing our children's view of themselves, of us and of the world we share. We know that babies and children learn best during periods of 'quiet alertness', that were often very limited in their early lives, and we must strive to create such opportunities now. Turning our families' 'emotional thermostat' down if it is 'over-heating', or up if there is a 'chill in the air', can be a learning curve for us and an even greater learning curve for our children.

Similarly, altering the physical environment, for example by reducing levels of stimulation, enables children to respond more readily to our attempts at co-regulation, since we will lower the overpowering sensory input that threatens their immature systems at brainstem and limbic levels. Consequently they will be less 'out of balance' and more readily helped to practise 'resetting' their neurobiological 'default' positions. Since our children's monitoring and modulating 'neurotechnology' is poorly calibrated we might visualise them as being akin to fire alarms that go off at the least puff of smoke, or conversely fail to react to billowing fumes. Moderating 'total sensory input' in our homes allows children, with our help, to learn to monitor and modulate sensory information more effectively and consequently develop healthy self-regulation.

While the principles of our approach are relevant to traumatised children of all ages, the way we approach the developmental reparenting task must reflect our children's current age-and-stage of development. The key tasks of babyhood are ones of attachment, feeling securely 'held'. Babies need nurture and structure in their lives: unable to make choices for themselves they need parents who can reflect their feelings and needs and co-regulate them. As they move into toddlerhood, children reach the stage of exploring their world and taking risks; they need practice in making decisions for themselves, albeit limited ones. They need increasingly overt structure, alongside nurture, to provide them with the safe environmental 'scaffolding' that allows them to explore the world safely. Thus the balance of nurture and structure that will be most beneficial to our children, and reflects their developmental needs, requires careful consideration. Frequently this will be an ever-changing mix of chronological age, developmental age and all the years between!

In practice

- Children will only change if parents can change first. Change is necessary not because we are 'getting it wrong' but to allow us to find better ways of 'getting it right', using developmental principles.

- As parents we need to be able to explore our own attachment histories, to help our children feel more comfortable in exploring their infancy, childhood and upbringing. We will inevitably find some attachment issues of our own along the way, from which we can gain essential insights into why we respond to our children as we do. These can prove invaluable in making sense of ourselves and our children and guiding them to greater understanding of their own 'inheritance'.

- Before children join our families, they will have developed disorganised patterns of feeling (physically and emotionally) and of relating. They will naturally act in ways that fit their historical 'mental map' (IWM) of how parents should be. We need to be able to 'download' healthy patterns of relating to enable our children to integrate new patterns of relating. This takes conscious effort, time and practice: remember we are teaching our children a new 'language' at the same time as trying to learn our children's 'language'.

- We should start by recognising the fears underlying children's behaviour and help create an environment where they can feel safe and secure.

- We cannot do this with words, as our children have not yet gained 'top down' understanding and self-control. Instead, working with youngsters at the physical level helps them recognise the body feelings and responses underpinning their emotional feelings and responses. Subsequently we can support them to reflect on their inner stress levels and practise ways of monitoring these more effectively.

- Where appropriate, we can explore ways of working through the 'bottom and middle storeys' of children's brains, by talking to them about their feelings and thoughts, creating essential links to their 'top storey' thinking brains and improving their ability to recognise and manage their feelings for themselves.

- Children learn about feelings predominantly through the cues, clues and messages given to them by caregivers. To help them recognise feelings of happiness, sadness, fear and anger, we must 'model' these feelings appropriately. For our children, as for babies and toddlers with good enough parents, this will initially be through facial expressions, gestures, body language and tone of voice via our inter-communicating MNS . As our children 'upload' these systems, verbal communications will eventually increase.

- A combination of relaxation and stimulation is vital to maintain a sense of wellbeing. Modulation is not uni-directional: good enough parents give their babies lots of opportunities to 'go up and down' through a wide range of physical and emotional states and then return to a comfortable 'baseline'. Our children need huge amounts of practice to acquire this essential capacity. It is *vital* we ensure we have the support to do this by creating both time to *be* and time to *do*.

- We must give boundless love and affection before our children can in turn learn to receive, or give, love and affection. We may have to endure months or years of lack of response or rejection before they learn to do this. In the meantime we need to go on loving and giving, consistently resisting the survival pattern of hurt and rejection they acquired in their birth families.

- Physical expressions of love and affection such as cuddles, eye contact and soothing voice tone are fundamental to building positive self-esteem and enabling children to feel loved and accepted. Again this may be a long-term project requiring all our understanding of, and commitment to, our children.

- We must model curiosity and learn to play with our children in developmentally appropriate ways to give them opportunities to try new things, take 'safe enough' risks and explore the world around them. It is through play that children, like all young mammals, learn about their physical sensations, how their bodies work, how to control them and how to interact with others.

- We now know that this involves learning about what other people do, how they 'work' and hence being able to predict their responses. Engaging our MN circuits contributes directly to our capacity to learn and integrate information at the social, emotional and cognitive levels, including learning within formal education. Recognising that our children may not yet have integrated a bodily sense of themselves, or any sense of themselves in space and time, let alone in relation to others, we should be prepared to continue to be playful well beyond the stage their chronological age might suggest. Not only are we helping our children, by having fun, we improve our own resilience and sense of wellbeing.

- Living with traumatised children can create splits within adult relationships. It is vital to take time to nurture our adult relationships for our own sake and for our children's sake.

- Be human! Acknowledging and expressing our own feelings of joy, grief, anger, despair and frustration is crucial. If we deny these natural feelings, we will lose the ability to have empathy for similar feelings in our children.

Although developmental reparenting is essentially a lifetime shift in the way we interact with our children, it begins with small steps that allow our children to 'feel felt' and experience the benefits of managing life in healthier ways. Concurrently it will also help us internalise the belief that we are good enough parents.

Our journey towards embracing developmental reparenting principles is likely to be a difficult one: long-established patterns are not easy to change. We must recognise that no parent is perfect and that our children have special needs which make parenting them particularly challenging. Inevitably we will sometimes act in ineffective or unhelpful ways. The despair and anger we feel at times may be in part a reflection of our children's inner world, in part a reflection of our own inner world. It will mirror the complex inter-relationship between our attachment histories and that of our children. Our mistakes will not harm our children if we recognise them and, following periods of misattunement, we work to 'repair' our relationship with our children as soon as we are able.

Finally, we should remind ourselves that we are the most valuable resource our children have in their journey to emotional health. Valuing ourselves means we will be more able to be 'there' for our children and help them to value themselves.

Chapter 3

Key Concepts

The concept of therapeutic, or developmental, reparenting

Dan Hughes (2000) proposes that therapeutic parents should parent their children in **P**layful, **L**oving, **A**ccepting, **C**urious and **E**mpathetic (PLACE) ways. We expanded this acronym to PARCEL in *New Families, Old Scripts* (2006) to include the reciprocal interactions, which are fundamental to 'good enough' parenting. Within this 'dance of attunement and attachment' we must be sensitive to our children's unique needs, seeing them as individuals and choosing the **P**layful, **A**ccepting, **R**eciprocal, **C**urious, **E**mpathic and **L**oving parenting patterns that 'fit' them best and enable them to achieve optimal physical, emotional, social, behavioural and cognitive growth and development.

Fundamental principles of developmental reparenting

Below we provide a point-by-point guide to our therapeutic parenting principles.

Looking backward, looking forward
CAREGIVERS NEED:

- Full access to children's histories.

- Awareness of 'what was done' to children and 'what it did'.

- An understanding of the underlying developmental neuro-biology.

- Support to plan for change.

- Opportunities to begin as early as possible to change.

- Faith that change is always possible.

Going back, going forward
CAREGIVERS NEED:

- An awareness of developmental 'gaps': physical, psycho-logical, behavioural.

- Understanding and time to fill in the developmental 'gaps'.

- Help identifying child's socio-emotional and functional age.

- To treat children at the age they seem at any given moment.

- Support to identify which 'brain storey' children are 'in': bottom, middle or top.

- To adopt a 'bottom up' approach for 'top down' self-awareness and controls.

- To remember that if in doubt, going lower and slower.

- And that 'boring is best'.

- To accept that progress may be 'three steps forwards, two steps back'.

- To Practise, Practise, Practise.

Nurture and structure
CAREGIVERS:

- Consistent, nurturing care encourages security.

- Providing a safe base allows children to explore themselves and their world.

- Emotional 'environmental regulation' enhances self-regulation.

- Creating a safe structure, 'firm and fair', allows children to feel safe.

- Clear guidelines help children develop internal rules.

- Nurtured children nurture relationships themselves.

- Parents need time to nurture themselves and be nurtured.

Regulation, regulation, regulation
CAREGIVERS SHOULD HOLD IN MIND THAT:

- Co-regulation from caregivers develops children's self-regulation.

- Co-regulation can be an arduous and lengthy process.

- Children can become dysregulated by 'invisible' triggers.

- Early identification and avoidance of triggers is essential.

- Re-regulation (see p.100) should occur immediately.

- Children met at the same level of emotional intensity (see p.96) are more readily re-regulated.

- Caregivers can become dysregulated by dysregulated children.

- Traumatised children can generate secondary trauma in caregivers.

- Parents need time and space to re-regulate.

Learning to play, playing to learn
CAREGIVERS SHOULD HOLD IN MIND THAT:

- Children learn through play.

- They need caregivers to play with them, helping them learn to play.

- Play is fun.

- Children and parents feel good when having fun.

- 'Controlled over-excitement' provides opportunities for practising co-regulation.

- Firing 'play circuits' reduces 'fear circuit' firing.

- More play, less fear increases self-regulation.

- Self-regulation underpins self-control and executive functioning.

Validation, consolidation, integration
CAREGIVERS SHOULD HOLD IN MIND THAT:

- Behaviour tells us how children feel.

- Insecurity and fear underpin children's behaviour.

- 'Hearing' behaviour increases understanding.

- Shared understanding increases children's self-awareness.

- Feelings met with equal intensity of (but controlled feeling) 'feel felt'.

- Validating feelings reduces children's need to 'show us'.

- They must help children practise finding their 'comfort zone'.

- Reducing 'out of control' feelings increase opportunities for 'practising'.

- 'Practising' rewires neural circuits.

- Rewiring enables integration: bottom, middle, top (upwards and downwards).

Talking, telling, timing
ESSENTIAL POINTS TO REMEMBER:

- Use statements not questions.

- Short, empathic responses 'go in'.

- Provide acceptance not reassurance.

- Say '*we need to*' rather than 'you need to'.

- Timing is everything.

- Calm moments allow optimal sharing.

- Slower is faster.

- Traumatised children were 'there' yet lack the words to 'remember'.

- Gentle exploration develops understanding.

- 'Speaking the unspeakable' reduces the power of past trauma.

For better, for worse
CAREGIVERS SHOULD HOLD IN MIND THAT:

- Every child has a silver lining.

- Accept children not the behaviour.

- Set children up to succeed not fail.

- Stay aware that separate states mean separate 'being', separate 'truths'.

- Model seeing and being all of ourselves.

- Use mistakes as vital learning opportunities.

- Moderate praise, moderate arousal: too much overwhelms.

- Good enough is good enough.

- Accept that change can take a lifetime.

The needs of traumatised children
TRAUMATISED CHILDREN NEED:

- Parents able to contain their own and their children's fear and anger in safe and nurturing ways.

- Acceptance and recognition that they are doing the best they can, understanding of their formative early histories and empathy for their struggles.

- Parental support to explore and practise making changes in their perceptions, belief systems and responses.

- Caregivers committed to 'the long haul', who can make sense of their struggles and show empathy rather than blaming and shaming.

- Parents who say 'together we can' rather than 'you should'.

- Parenting at their developmental age rather than their chronological age: recognising that 'functional age' can range from day to day and sometimes minute to minute.

- Gentle help to reflect on their confusing inner world, the way they feel about themselves, and the world around them, at any given moment.

These principles form both the central tenets of our book and the rationale for our approach. They recognise that children who have been hurt and traumatised by early abuse, neglect, rejection, separation and loss have socio-emotional 'gaps' that compromise their social functioning, affect their relationships and prevent them from developing into healthy, secure adults. Alongside these emotional 'gaps' go physical 'gaps', affecting bodily regulation, sensation and co-ordination, and cognitive 'gaps', like the poor reasoning and organisation that underpin executive function(ing). Children and young people with these 'gaps' struggle to be 'happy kids', 'healthy kids' and 'smart kids', which makes growing into happy, healthy, smart adults very difficult indeed.

Exemplifying this is the story of the 'three little piggies' where each piggy chose different foundations on which to build homes and subsequently experienced the 'big bad wolf' trying to blow their houses down. Each house looked solid, yet it was only the house built on stone that could provide a safe haven for its owner. Traumatised children can be likened to the little piggies whose houses were built on sand, which fall down at the first blow, or of sticks, that quickly blow apart. Therapeutic parents are the builders who carefully move the house from its sandy base and rebuild it brick upon brick, on foundations set on stone.

Thus we can see that a fundamental principle of developmental reparenting is that children need to 'go back to go forward'. It recognises that children who have lived through traumatic events in their earliest years have not laid down firm foundations from which to develop a sound awareness of their bodies, of where they 'fit' in the world, a sense of trust and self-worth, the ability to understand and relate to others in meaningful ways or the reasoning capacities needed to organise and manage their lives. A key aim of developmental reparenting is therefore to help our children repair their sensory, motor, social, emotional and intellectual 'gaps'. It implies treating our children at an age younger than their chronological age when their behaviour indicates this is needed: for example, by acting 'babyish' or not managing tasks they can usually accomplish, or that might be expected of similar-aged children.

Achieving the mind-set of 'congratulating' ourselves and our children for being dependent, rather than independent, runs counter to what is naturally perceived as 'progress'. However, this is one of the counter-intuitive concepts we need to embrace as therapeutic parents: instead of encouraging children to 'grow up' and 'act their (chronological) age', it is important to recognise their emotional (developmental) age and respond accordingly. In doing so we offer them vital opportunities to 'fill in the gaps', 'get what they need' and practise 'getting it right'. Encouraging children's dependence also validates that they are taking huge risks to embrace emotional closeness: an extremely scary prospect for children who have suffered abusive, neglectful or inconsistent parenting.

Instead of teaching our youngsters to tie their own shoe laces, we can encourage them to let us do this task for them. In doing so we may experience approbation from parents who vie with each other in boasting about their children's precocious exploits, such as: 'My wee Janey now gets into the car and fastens her own seat belt.' In contrast we can practise saying to ourselves, *'Fantastic news! My wee Janey let me carry her to the car today, instead of insisting on walking on her own. Isn't that amazing? I'm so pleased and proud of her.'* If we are confident enough to voice this aloud we might just set a counter-intuitive trend and slow down the 'rat race'!

It is also important to remember that change in our youngsters will not follow a steady progression. It can be highly frustrating to parent children who can dress themselves one day, only to be unable to do so the next. It is all too easy to feel they are being deliberately defiant or manipulative. Instead, we should recognise that our children may well be more capable one day than another, either because 'something on the inside' is affecting their body systems, and hence their ability to respond, or because circumstances in the external world are getting in the way. These two factors are inter-related and are crucial to our understanding and parenting approach. Often our children do not cope well in environments with high levels of stimulation, especially if they are tired, hungry, uncomfortable or hurting. It may help to reflect on how we, too, manage better when we are not stressed: as common phrases like 'I can't think straight' or 'I've lost it' indicate.

At such times youngsters' ability to 'compensate' for their poorly organised body–mind–brain systems can collapse and they 'regress' to earlier ways of functioning. Their fear-based early experiences mean they have highly aroused, 'bottom storey' brainstems within which the 'filtering' and 'regulating' mechanisms are (temporarily) compromised. It could also be that the current level of stimulation overwhelms their mid-storey limbic system, meaning their ability to access their top-storey 'thinking brain' to make sense of the environment and over-ride their 'knee-jerk' reactions is 'out of action'. Often it can be a combination of all of these factors. As therapeutic parents it is essential that we consider the sensory environment in our homes and 'turn it down' to levels that fit with our children's ability to manage at their most vulnerable times.

Traumatised children often feel responsible for the abuse and neglect they suffered. In many ways this is the 'safest' belief system for children living in unsafe environments as it provides a sense of control and supports the belief that their maltreating parents might treat them more favourably if they can find ways of changing themselves. Conversely, accepting the reality that abuse and neglect are always the responsibility of adults caring for them means children must accept they have no-one to protect them, are powerless and that things will never change. Recognising the dissonance between the internal feelings of responsibility for their maltreatment and the reality of parental responsibility, and feeling simultaneously in control and powerless, would mean the world makes no sense. To avoid the inner chaos, children 'choose' the lesser of two evils: blaming themselves, rather than blaming their birth families.

Recognising that these may well be the feelings children wake up with and carry with them minute by minute allows us to understand why it sometimes seems impossible for them to dress or organise themselves. Rather than experiencing frustration when children cannot do these things themselves on days when their inner world is overwhelming them, we can express delight that they have found ways to manage well on other days. Recognising that their level of ability is a barometer of their internal world will help us feel calmer and more able to provide additional help when needed.

Developmental reparenting means much more than encouraging our children to 'regress' and is often a complex and protracted process both for us and for them. Traumatised children are scared and hurt children. They may hide these feelings from us, and even from themselves, or act them out in behaviours that are hard to understand and manage: including aggression and rejection towards us and their siblings. Conversely they may be compliant and 'good', fearing that any misdemeanour will incur further abuse, neglect or abandonment. However they signal their needs and inner distress, traumatised children need us to recognise the underlying reasons for it and empathise with their struggles. They need clear messages that we understand and validate that they feel unsafe and threatened, alongside messages that we can provide the safety and security they need to allow them to feel confident enough to try new ways of interacting. To do this we need to start at the bottom.

We have seen that traumatised children have poor capacity to regulate their own somatic (bodily) feeling states and emotional responses; they can be quickly aroused if exposed to over-stimulation of their sensori-motor systems. We therefore need to consider both the external and internal physical environment in our homes and find ways to reduce sensory stimulation (at brainstem and limbic levels). Fewer toys and fewer choices are important ways of creating a less stimulating and thus safer external environment (brainstem). Close proximity to, and attention from, calm, capable adults are crucial to reducing emotional stress and helping traumatised children remain, or become, calm (mid-storey limbic areas). In addition, we must help our children distinguish between 'then' and 'now', offering accepting messages that we know it will take time for them to recognise this (encouraging cortical connections). Together these strategies help integrate children's sensori-motor, socio-emotional and cognitive systems, reflecting bottom-up neurobiological sequences.

Opportunities for change are a vital aspect of developmental reparenting. While it is important to recognise why, for example, angry children may hit their sibling, we also need to help them practise managing their feelings more appropriately. It helps nobody, not least the aggressive child, to have their hurtful behaviour go unchallenged. Not stepping in and validating the victimised children's feelings makes them feel 'unheard' and potentially increases tension between siblings. Moreover, it allows angry children to feel frighteningly powerful and out of control, which increases the underlying fear they are 'showing us' through their behaviour. Nobody benefits from this situation, parents included.

To help our children become secure adults able to develop healthy, positive relationships and increasingly happy, comfortable lives (resilience and wellbeing), we must show them safer ways of interacting. Accepting the powerful feelings that underpin their actions and empathising volubly avoids plunging them into shame, supports them to let go of old survival patterns, and enables change. In doing so we need to recognise our own 'knee-jerk' responses, practise monitoring and managing our arousal levels and make enough time to look after ourselves: a simple enough task for super-parents! The same fundamental principles apply to children who seem 'too good', 'shut-down', 'manipulative', 'oppositional' or 'attention-seeking'.

Fundamentally, developmental reparenting is about safety, security and predictability. Our children may rarely have felt safe or secure before coming home to us, having survived chaotic, terrifying family circumstances. They will almost certainly have a different concept of what safety and security means from ours. We may strengthen our sense of security by sharing our worries with trusted others; our children may only feel safe when coping by themselves. This epitomises the difference between secure and compromised attachments and forms a cornerstone of developmental reparenting. We cannot offer the safety, security and predictability essential to the development of secure attachments unless we understand the distorted perceptions that make safe, consistent, 'in charge' parents seem so terrifying to our children. These survival-based misperceptions can continue to drive them to recreate the 'safety of the familiar': the very chaos and mistrust that created their developmental attachment difficulties initially! Thinking *Alice Through the Looking Glass*, Kafka and *Catch-22* rolled into one can be very helpful to us as therapeutic parents.

Therefore 'safety, security, predictability and trust' mean much more than ensuring that our home is child-friendly and that we meet our children's physical needs well. We need to remember that our children's MN ◖ patterning can lead to difficulties understanding the intentions behind our actions. For example, when we say 'no' to an inappropriate request, we may be coming from a benign perspective, recognising that this is an unsafe option for them. Unless we are aware of our children's 'mirror distortions' and find ways of creating a common language to communicate our intentions clearly, in advance of our actions, we are likely to perpetuate their misperceptions and may be perceived as critical, sarcastic or abusive. As therapeutic parents we must work towards helping children feel both physically and emotionally safe enough to let go of their 'survival-based' beliefs and responses.

WHAT DO CHILDREN NEED?

- to feel safe
- to feel understood
- to feel they matter and belong
- to learn to self-regulate and to be themselves
- to feel calm and relaxed in their bodies and minds
- in essence, to feel.

WHAT DO WE MEAN BY SAFE?

- safe in their bodies
- safe in their families
- safely contained/co-regulated
- safe to love and be loved
- safe to explore their world
- safe in the knowledge that there will always be someone there for them.

Developmental reparenting means recognising our children's unique qualities and communicating these so that they 'hear' our positive messages. Since children learn from success not failure they need endless practice at 'getting things right' and hearing praise they can accept. Given their fragile sense of self-worth, we are often working with 'mirror-images' here. When we make global comments like 'good girl' this contradicts internalised beliefs such as 'I am bad' and can cause acting out ('this is what I'm really like') or feelings like 'if they knew what I'm really like they wouldn't love me'. More focused, lower-key statements, for example *Wow! You found your shoes. Nice one!*, may slip under the radar. Moreover, if we can set children up to avoid 'failure' by making simple, non-challenging requests and fun opportunities to 'get it right', even asking them to do what they want to do anyway, we create 'win-win' situations. Then, feeling somewhat better about themselves, children can begin to let their guard down and take in essential, positive messages that they are 'good enough', deserve praise and can take us at our word.

As developmental, or therapeutic, parents we should start by understanding our children's histories and how they continue to impact on them in the present: in turn this will inform our understanding of the developmental trauma issues that underlie their current behaviour. We also need to recognise that parenting traumatised children is likely to be stressful and can 'push the buttons' of the most stable and secure parents to the point where we feel a sense of failure as parents, as couples or as individuals. Hence a vital part of developmental reparenting is to look at our own attachment histories alongside those of our children. This should be an ongoing process rather than a one-off event, in the same way that understanding the processes that underlie our children's behaviour needs to become integral to our moment-by-moment relationships with them.

Being therapeutic parents means looking at our children's needs and finding ways to meet them; it also means creating opportunities to take care of ourselves. In doing so, we demonstrate the sense of self-worth we want to create in our children and provide role models our children might emulate. This challenges a commonly held view that thinking of ourselves is selfish: we prefer to reframe it as 'looking after ourselves so that we can better look after our children'.

Using the term 'practising' gives the message to us and our children that learning a new skill takes time and that we all make mistakes when attempting unfamiliar tasks. Practising our developmental reparenting skills is a learning curve where mistakes can lead to new ways of seeing ourselves and our children and new insights into how best to help them. Indeed making mistakes is an essential part of being therapeutic parents. Being able to apologise to our children when we have become angry is a potent way of not only demonstrating how to manage angry feelings appropriately but also of communicating that we do not have to be perfect to be 'good enough', a message that is especially important for children whose experiences leave them feeling they are a mistake and that making mistakes only confirms this. In fact mistakes also provide wonderful opportunities for 'repair'. Dan Hughes (2000, 2006) and Alan Schore (2001b) emphasise that intrinsic to creating healthy attachments is reconnection to our children immediately after experiences of misattunement.

Children who suffered early abuse and neglect are consumed by feelings of shame that overwhelm their ability to recognise and practise pro-social behaviours, since they see themselves as intrinsically 'bad' and worthless. They struggle to accept responsibility for their mistakes, while at the same time being highly sensitive to criticism. This juxtaposition is very difficult for parents. We need to find ways to help our children assume responsibility for their behaviours as a springboard to making changes, while simultaneously ensuring we do not damage their fragile sense of self-worth. We must help our children recognise their essential goodness and that, when we address difficulties with them, we are discussing a particular behaviour rather than their worth as human beings. Otherwise they will continue to 'disown' parts of themselves, be they the 'unacceptable' or 'acceptable' ones, and will be unable to make positive changes.

Developmental reparenting takes into consideration the impact their early experiences have on all aspects of children's functioning: their neurobiological systems, the ensuing developmental trauma issues, their attachment patterns, sensorimotor needs, special dietary requirements, paediatric difficulties, EF and any specific psycho-social and therapeutic considerations that may be identified. It is most effective when it does not function in isolation: for maximum effect it should be reflected in school, social situations and any therapeutic and adoption support work provided for our families. Integrated working that places caregivers at the centre of the healing process creates the optimal environment for positive change within our families.

In Chapter 17, 'Taking Care of Ourselves', we explore the stresses and strains of therapeutic parenting, including secondary trauma. We consider the impact of our own formative childhood experiences on our expectations, beliefs, self-image and parenting styles. Even the best of us cannot face the challenges our hurt children bring to our families alone; we need all the support and guidance we can get from our families, friends, communities and informed professionals. Knowing ourselves and our children will allow us to identify what we need and feel confident in making informed choices when asking for help. We are our children's best advocate; we are best placed to identify their needs and, with good supports, to meet them effectively. We may need to remind ourselves of this daily!

WHAT DO PARENTS NEED?
Information:

- to know what was done to their child
- to understand what this did to their child
- to make sense of their child's behaviour
- Understanding of the neurobiological underpinnings of their children's behaviour.

Access:

- to specialist advice, support and counselling
- to a network of integrated services – for as long as they are needed.

PARENTING PATTERNS

- Parents tend to make sense of their children's behaviour in terms of their own experiences of being parented.
- Parent–child misattunements will occur, however secure parents' attachment patterns are.
- Parents need understanding and support to identify and explore inevitable vulnerabilities and 'triggers'.
- Supportive 'adult attachment figures' can empower parents to become sensitive, secure attachment figures for troubled, traumatised children.
- Parent mentors are well placed to fulfil this role: providing therapeutic supervision for therapeutic parents.

Summary

Developmental reparenting aims to provide:

- a developmentally based loving guide to parenting children and helping them change and heal
- greater understanding of, and empathy for, children's difficulties
- reduction in misperceptions, mismatches, conflict and stress

- nurture and structure that allows children to learn to feel loved, secure and 'held'

- opportunities for children to learn to trust that we are 'there for them' and can meet their needs

- the family infrastructure that allows children to change and manage their lives in healthier ways

- support for us to look at ourselves and any difficulties we may bring to our therapeutic parenting

- the confidence to be effective therapeutic parents and to commit ourselves to the long haul.

Chapter 4

Information
The Need to Know – Understanding Our Children's Past to Understand their Present

As we know, therapeutic (developmental) reparenting draws on the fundamental principle that children's early experiences influence how they perceive, understand and relate to the world around them. Early trauma, particularly within families, significantly impacts children's bodies, brains and minds, affecting their perceptions and beliefs about parent-figures. Babies with loving, nurturing parents develop neurobiological 'hardwiring' that promotes feelings of safety and self-worth and MN ◯ systems that allow them to 'read' parents' intentions in light of their positive experiences. Conversely babies whose early care is abusive, neglectful or abandoning are 'hardwired' with belief systems that adults are untrustworthy, that the world is unsafe and that they do not deserve to be loved or kept safe. Therefore they are likely to respond with circumspection to attempts by new families to offer them security and stability.

If children 'read' our loving actions as potentially abusive, their responses will be fear-based: expecting danger at every turn. In this environment children cannot relax, meaning their poorly developed capacity to self-soothe and regulate their emotions is further compromised. Since they cannot afford to filter out incoming data for fear of missing signs of danger, they frequently experience sensory overload in the mid-storey, limbic, areas and their perceptions become increasingly linked to negative emotional memories 🏛. Processing of fear-based stimuli will continue to take priority. Consequently, children's only recourse may be to shut down their sensory and emotional systems using the dissociative responses of fight, flight or freeze. Their behaviour may be typified by anger and aggression, running away, physical or emotional withdrawal, 'going into their own world' or emotionally 'shutting down'.

To get an idea of what this feels like, imagine spending time with a friend in a noisy, crowded place. How difficult would it be to hear and make sense of what was being said or to feel heard? How much more difficult would it be if we lacked the capacity to concentrate on that friendly voice (filtering out unnecessary aural stimuli), instead hearing every voice at the same intensity, whilst simultaneously being bombarded by all the other sights, smells and movement around us? Imagine further that people were talking about us: some offering praise and positive messages, some seemingly intent on hurting us. How could we work out which of these messages to attend to in order to help us feel safe? How would we know how to respond appropriately? This is the confusing world our children inhabit and which they need help to make sense of and cope with.

We must start by understanding the fundamental issues affecting our children and recognise the situations that create particular difficulties for them. To do so we need as much information as possible about their histories, since their early experiences form the developmental building blocks of their bodies, brains and minds: establishing the 'wiring' that links their senses, perceptions and responses. Becoming aware of our children's early experiences allows us to recognise and understand situations in the present that may trigger trauma-responses that evolved to ensure their survival in the past. We can then work to avoid these triggers, limit trauma-responses and help our children accept they are no longer in constant danger.

To do this we need to obtain as much information as possible about the following:

- Children's early life experiences, particularly the traumas they suffered in the most formative three years of life, including pre-birth.

- The reasons for our children being looked after and how this was undertaken.

- The number and duration of all placements and moves, bearing in mind that children may have experienced many more separations than are documented: for example, being passed 'from pillar to post' within the chaotic world of drug-abusing birth parents.

- The reasons for each move, informally within birth families or formally within the looked after system.

- Full descriptions of children's behaviour in previous placements and nursery or school settings.

- The nature and extent of contact our children had with birth family members whilst being looked after. The timing and content of their 'goodbye contact' may be an especially important piece of information. This may have given our children messages that we are merely a 'holding placement' until they return to their 'real' family, preventing them from attaching to us or feeling safe enough to relinquish their early survival behaviours.

Access to all this information is vital if we are to make sense of our children's view of the world and their continuing responses to it, communicate effectively with them and provide an environment they can experience as safe and nurturing. For example, children left alone for long periods may feel as if they are being neglected again if we leave them for even a short time, responding with fear, anger or withdrawal. Being aware of their early experiences, we can more readily validate their feelings and help them learn they are now safe. Similarly, it is important to have a shared understanding of how our children communicate their distress. Gaining accurate information about their behaviour in previous placements allows us to recognise how our children communicate their fears. Ensuring our children 'know that we know' how they communicate their distress helps create a shared 'language of trauma' as a step towards developing a shared 'language of love'.

If we recognise our children's behaviour as a vital form of non-verbal communication, we can avoid blaming them for their actions and find a more positive approach that embraces the underlying issues. For example, empathy and shared understanding of why our children take things that do not belong to them, alongside shared practice at 'doing it differently', gradually helps our children communicate more appropriately and effectively. Making children aware that we understand why they 'steal' helps them 'feel felt' and more able to accept support from us to reduce the ongoing negative effects of their behaviour on their self-perceptions and their perceptions of others. We, and our children, will feel less anger, rejection and shame 😕; we can more readily find the 'silver lining' in our children and help them find this in themselves too.

Our children's histories provide the essential 'dictionary' (Archer and Gordon 2006) from which their puzzling behaviours can be 'decoded' and the foundation on which we can build good relationships. Children who 'know that their parents know' as much as possible about their background and ways of expressing their feelings through behaviour begin from a firmer baseline than children who are unsure their parents are able to accept them 'warts and all'. Fearing that we would not love them if we knew the bad things that happened to them, children are likely to 'test' our commitment to them, unconsciously provoking us to abandon them 'sooner rather than later'.

Finding opportunities to share the 'behavioural meanings' in our 'dictionary' creates an atmosphere of increased honesty and openness: instead of anger, rejection, withdrawal or 'compulsive compliance' (our children's first language) we can develop a language of mutual love and trust. Together we can compile a family 'dictionary' based on honesty, openness, security, loving care and understanding. Gradually, as our children begin to internalise this new language, the neurobiological patterns they developed through living with trauma will be altered to patterns founded on love, trust and self-worth, providing the firmest basis possible for changing their unacceptable behaviours. Children who have learned to trust we love them and will keep them safe learn to love and take good care of themselves. They develop the behavioural language that reflects this, establish MN systems that accurately reflect our intentions, and acquire a sound sense of OP 🐾, OSP, OC ⓒ and OSC.

Our dictionary allows us to reflect on what their early traumatic experiences *did* to our children in terms of bottom-up development. As we shall explore in more detail in the next chapter, 'Laying the Foundations', sounds and smells can be potent sensory triggers. These may seem harmless until we locate them in children's histories and understand their meaning in terms of 'survival' responses. Whilst it may be easy to recognise that the smell of alcohol could trigger overwhelming sensory experiences reflecting abuse and neglect and producing feelings of dysregulation and panic, it can be harder to realise that a particular perfume, or a raised voice, could trigger equally extreme reactions.

Movement and body position can also be potent triggers, creating sensory overload and fundamental dysregulation. This may make sense to us where children were physically abused and startle at sudden unexpected movements; it may be less clear when children respond negatively to cuddles, lying down, car rides or wobbly chairs. Recalling the principle that all children's behaviour has meaning and that we can locate this in the dictionary of their past will help us make sense of children's seemingly random reactions.

Children who have been sexually abused, neglected or abandoned may have triggers associated with bath or bed times that make these events especially fraught in our families. While our children need to learn that touch and cuddles from safe adults are vital to their recovery process, we often need to proceed at a slow pace, yet remain confident that we are on the right track. Children who struggle to accept physical affection may respond positively to a Post-it note on their pillow: a simple *'missed you, hope you had a good day'* can be enough. A smiley face inside a heart offers a loving message to children who cannot read; for older children text messages can tell them we are thinking about them when they are out of earshot and remind them of our love. They also act as transitional objects (TOs) that encourage OP and gradually allow our children to recognise our positive feelings and intentions. Eventually new sensori-motor and MN circuits will develop, allowing them to perceive and accept touch, cuddles and hugs as signs of affection rather than precursors to further abuse.

At the limbic level, the feelings generated by sensory overload are linked to overwhelming emotional responses. Children who have been maltreated, whose brainstems communicate messages of danger 'upwards', continue to react with trauma-responses learned early in life. How they do so depends on the particular patterns they evolved to gain some sense of 'control' over their chaotic environment. We readily recognise crying as signalling distress, conveying children's underlying fears. It is often not equally clear that fear underpins the behaviour of aggressive children or youngsters who are compliant or silent. Yet fear lies at the root of all these reactions. Using our behavioural dictionary allows us to make essential links between past and present and manage our children's sensori-emotional environment better for them and with them.

When children are becoming dysregulated, remaining calm and in control allows us to calm out-of-control children. Lowering our voice may be ineffective where 'matching affect', by speaking louder and with emotion yet maintaining self-control, can help us reconnect to our children. We are then well placed to 'bring them down' to more comfortable arousal levels. Getting 'in synch' this way allows co-regulation to kick in and we can help our children practise finding their comfort zone. The trick is not to match distress with distress, but to match intensity of feeling, whilst making it clear that we can contain those feelings safely, for example, saying excitedly to a child having a 'wobbly': '*Wow! I can really hear how angry you're feeling. Let's jump up and down!*'

Understanding our children's histories not only helps us know which situations are likely to be distressing, it also helps us know how best to help them manage their overpowering feelings. For example, children who struggle with changes in routine may have histories of neglect where parents' turbulent lifestyles created enduring fears of hurt or abandonment. Minimising changes in routine and staying aware of the difficulties our children experience when things change helps reduce these adverse effects. We might say '*I know this is difficult for you but we can't go to the cinema as promised. I've just heard Granny is coming round. Let's see what we can do to make this easier for you. Get your diary out!*' Such statements validate children's struggles, show that we understand *and* that we can work together to help them cope.

Historical issues can also impact the way children handle separations from us, for example when they go to school or bed or we go out without them. Children who respond with anger, rejection, manipulation or 'shut-down' are communicating feelings of intense fear and rejection. Bearing this in mind helps us manage our feelings of frustration or rejection and informs how we can work to help our children cope better. Preparing a snack before we leave, containing a hidden 'love you' note, for them to be given later, conveys vital messages that we care for them, are 'holding them in mind' and are still there for them. Acknowledging how hard they find separations and wondering aloud how they will let us know how they feel communicates that we can make sense of, and handle, whatever behaviour they throw our way: potentially reducing the need to 'act out' or 'act in'.

Simultaneously, we should be aware of our own histories, reflecting on the ways in which our 'story' mirrors, or differs from, our children's, and exploring how our communications with them have been influenced by our experiences. We discuss this in greater depth in later chapters.

Summary

It is vital that we obtain as much information about children's early histories as possible. We need to know what happened to them and what it did to them in order to create the basic dictionary through which their behavioural language can be understood. Learning our children's language provides the tools to reduce the sensory and emotional overload triggered by current events that 'speaks' to our children about their traumatic past. We can then create a less stressful physical and socio-emotional environment within which we can help them 'rewire' body–brain–mind connections and introduce them to the unspoken and spoken languages of safety, trust and love that form the cornerstones of effective developmental reparenting. We also need to explore the ways we ourselves learned to communicate our feelings and consider whether we should adjust our communication patterns to better meet the needs of our children.

Chapter 5

Laying the Foundations

Co-regulation for Self-regulation

Alongside our extended knitting metaphor, in Chapter 1 we introduced the concept of the three-storey, semi-detached house to represent the structure of the brain and explore its developmental sequences.

The bottom storey (basement) represents the brainstem, which begins to function in the womb and is responsible for basic life-sustaining processes such as heart and breathing rates, determining levels of wakefulness and sleep, and initiating 'fight, flight or freeze' responses. The middle storey (main living area) comprises the limbic areas responsible for appraising meaning and organising sensations and emotions, attachment, OP and memory creation. The top storey (studio) represents the maturing 'thinking' brain that allows reason, negotiation and social and moral values to influence the more reflex emotional and behavioural responses of the two lower storeys.

However, unlike a typical 'semi', the brain establishes important inter-connections between its two halves, alongside the complex web of connections across, and between, the three storeys. We might visualise this in terms of shared 'public amenities': a co-operative system where wiring (electricity and telecommunications) and pipelines (water and gas) are utilised communally. In addition, key brain structures, such as the amygdala, hippocampus, orbito-prefrontal cortex (OFC) and Broca's area (primarily responsible for expressive language), develop at significantly different rates within the two halves, allowing increased specialisation of function. In our shared house this facilitates enhanced efficiency: where, for example, having one larger 'rumpus room' accessible to all residents and a smaller one for quieter activities, or a bathroom with a sauna in one half and a walk-in shower in the other, allows for greater adaptability and flexibility.

Many of us are familiar with the parable of the two houses built upon sand or rock. Whilst the first lacked the solid foundations it needed to withstand the elements, the house built on solid rock remained firmly intact. In our building metaphor these firm foundations, necessary not only for well-functioning brains but also sound bodies and minds, represent the co-regulation (re-regulation) provided by 'good enough' parents and the self-regulation that is created from these dynamic, regulatory relationships during children's first thousand days of life including the pre-birth period. These neurobiological regulatory processes begin in the bottom-storey brainstem, move upwards through the limbic areas and finally achieve maturity in the top-storey neocortex.

We only need to observe wriggling, screaming babies to recognise that they are not born with the capacity to regulate their sensory and emotional feelings. They lack the capacity to move independently or control their environment: instead depending on their caregivers for life-giving food, shelter and protection. To acquire basic self-care and self-regulation human infants require access to reliable, shared monitoring and modulation of responses and feelings, through consistent co-regulation (re-regulation) to help them practise finding their 'comfort zones'. This vital process can only be provided by parents or other significant caregivers, takes place over an extended period during youngsters' earliest years of life.

Babies can only experience co-regulation within sensitive, dynamic, two-way relationships where parental facial expressions, touch, 'baby talk' and exaggerated body language reflect their own movements, sensations and feelings, helping them recognise them as their own, name them, make sense of them and manage them. Through these parent–child dialogues infants acquire increasing self-awareness and control over their bodies and minds: self-regulation. Thus it is parental attachment figures that provide the nurture, organised structure and secure environment that allows young children to build the structurally sound and functional body–brain systems that are best suited to the world around them. Without this, children lack the neurobiological 'hardware' and complex 'wiring' that enables them to organise and regulate themselves well.

As therapeutic parents we must begin our developmental reparenting with an in-depth structural inspection of our children's foundation systems (histories), to see how they measure up to 'building regulations' and 'environmental controls'. It can be helpful to seek the guidance of professional 'surveyors', such as parent mentors or developmentally informed therapists and social workers, with the specialist knowledge and experience to identify potential structural weaknesses at key foundation levels: for example, due to early adversity, such as neglect or abuse, that can lead to poor internal regulation of external sensations (like sounds and smells) and internal sensations (such as from muscles and the gut). These difficulties are often apparent in children's volatile emotional and behavioural responses, or their lack of awareness of sensations such as pain or hunger. Underpinning these difficulties there are likely to be functional 'faults', at the brainstem level, in children's capacity to monitor, modulate and calibrate their heart and respiration rates, sleep and wakefulness, and nascent sensory processing systems: all of which play a major role in promoting 'survival', resilience and wellbeing.

We can then apply our knowledge of 'building regulations' to put in place the solid foundations and 'environmental controls' that allow children to build more solid body and brain structures and 'rewire' their poorly integrated systems from 'bottom up'. These are the essential prerequisites for the development of secure attachments, OP and OC, healthy MN circuits, healthy relationships, resilience and wellbeing: providing the foundations and scaffolding of structure and nurture upon which therapeutic reparenting principles are built. We can think of 'building regulations' primarily in terms of structure and 'environmental controls' as representing nurture.

It is clearly important to consider ways in which we can provide a 'safe container' for our children, such as establishing consistent patterns of response, rhythms, routines and 'house rules' ('building regulations') and the optimal physical and emotional milieu within which they can thrive ('environmental controls'). In essence, as parents we must become the co-regulatory secure base from which our youngsters can develop: the consistent 'safe house' within which they can begin to feel 'held' and valued, allowing them to explore within safe limits and to acquire self-confidence and competence.

Turning to 'environmental controls', these will include the furniture and fittings of our homes: soft furnishings, wallpaper patterns and paintwork colours, lighting, odours, levels of background and sudden, occasional noise, the availability and use of electronic equipment and even the general 'clutter' of our personal possessions. In addition, consideration of the emotional milieu requires us to reflect on our patterns of handling and expressing our own emotions and the feelings other family members or friends may bring to our homes.

We saw in Part 1 how the ability to learn to self-calm starts in the womb and that foetuses who have a calm and relaxed atmosphere in which to develop are likely to be calm, relaxed babies. They learn from repeated interactive experiences how to use their parents as vital 'regulators' to calm them when aroused, and become 'wired up' accordingly. Conversely, babies exposed to distress, such as parental violence or depression, in the womb are unlikely to experience sufficient calm and relaxation. Instead they become 'wired up' to remain in high states of arousal (Schore 1994; D'Andrea *et al.* 2012) in order to survive the continuing stress they anticipate on entering the world. Due to increased 'baseline' stress hormone levels they are likely to remain unregulated with high heart and respiration rates, and tensed bodies. A smaller group learn to 'shut down', appearing unusually unresponsive and 'flat' or with a weak muscle tone. Over time these response patterns and associated physical sensations become consolidated into children's perceptions of 'what the world is like', 'who I am' and 'what I do', so that, in effect, they may struggle to access any other way of feeling or being.

Poorly regulated children need help to identify, name and manage their feelings long beyond the time when their more securely attached peers have learned to regulate themselves: 'think toddler' is the watchword here. We may have children who are chronologically ten years of age but whose ability to regulate has not moved into, or beyond, the toddler stage of development. As therapeutic parents this may mean managing our ten-year-olds as if they were babies or toddlers, while at the same time recognising their chronological needs and responding with age-appropriate strategies. This might mean providing increased supervision and support in any environment or situation where we recognise our children may struggle. It is likely to mean changing our expectations of their capacity to undertake tasks that we would expect to be easy for similar-aged children with less traumatic backgrounds.

Our task may be made more difficult since our children's abilities are not fixed; at times they may seem to manage in age-appropriate ways, whilst at others they may struggle. This can lead to the perception, in ourselves or others, that they are being 'lazy', 'oppositional' or 'stupid'. We must remind ourselves, and explain clearly to other people, that what looks like 'won't do' is a case of temporary 'can't do' and respond appropriately to their current functional, rather than their chronological, age.

Building regulations

We can think of 'building regulations' in relation to the concrete structures that surround our children, providing them with a stable 'safe house' within which they feel 'at home' and to which they can return whenever they need reassurance and comfort. Initially this will be a literal 'return and check-in' process, allowing our children to reconnect and become re-regulated. Gradually this leads to the inner construction of OP 🌫: when children take for granted that we are always 'there for them', and 'in their corner'. Whilst at one level maltreated children may 'know in their heads' that their house is still there when they cannot see it, their 'faulty wiring' can mean they do not 'know this in their bodies' (Bomber 2007). The body sensations they experience can trigger memories of previous abandonments, losses or placement moves that 'short-circuit' conscious awareness, pressing 'hard-wired panic buttons' and undermining the safe foundations we have been building with them. For these children 'out of sight' is quite literally 'out of mind'.

Recognising these 'structural and functional weaknesses', it makes sense that, for example, when our children come home to us we do not move house for some considerable time. However tempting it may be to look for a bigger house with, perhaps, a bigger garden, our children are likely to feel destabilised and out of their already precarious 'comfort zone'. It may also be advisable to stick to our existing décor: 'shabby' beats 'showy' in inner-comfort terms. (In similar vein, taking short breaks from home can wobble children's foundations – even if we are with them all the time, as we explore in Chapter 13, 'Making Changes, Managing Changes'.) If a house move is unavoidable it can help our children feel 'we are all moving together' if, for example, we pack our clothes in the same container as theirs, rather than separately, talk about 'when we are in our new home' and display photographs of both old and new houses prominently.

In our experience, 'our house', to poorly regulated children of whatever age, is the cornerstone upon which we can help them build attachment security: a real place that they can continually touch, feel, smell and move about in. They may become unexpectedly distressed when away from home or show reluctance to 'go out to play' or on school trips, since this involves the perception of loss of their safe space. If we remain understanding in these situations and let our children know it is OK to have these fears, we can help them practise managing their distress. We have also found that it can help to identify a special 'safe place' to which children can retreat in times of stress. This might be the corner under the stairs or beneath the kitchen table: a small 'nest' space providing physical as well as emotional security. Initially we may need to help our children find their safe place, encourage them to go there, and stay there with them, when we spot that they are becoming upset. Familiar story books and a favourite 'blankie' to touch and smell can make their 'hidey hole' even more comforting.

Although OP begins with the gradual recognition that 'things' (objects) remain when out of view, fundamentally it depends on our predictability and consistency as co-regulating caregivers. Hence our enduring physical presence, alongside the predictability of our actions and emotions, provides the foundation upon which our children build secure new lives. Therapeutic parents are specially placed to offer children the closeness, solidity and 'feel-ability' to create the new relationship connections that will, in turn, alter old response patterns, repair 'wiring circuits' and develop better functioning bodies, brains and minds. The more physical dependability we provide and the more physical dependence we encourage in the short to medium term, the more independent our children can become. When we find ourselves acting in counter-intuitive ways, such as finding and putting on our children's shoes for them, when their peers can manage these tasks competently, we should recognise that we are 'filling in the experiential and developmental gaps' in our children's lives: creating opportunities for rebuilding their structural foundations.

Environmental controls

This brings us nicely to 'environmental controls'. Since as caregivers we are the prime regulators of our children's environment, both physically and emotionally, we should begin by considering our home environment in 'bottom up' terms: asking ourselves whether the level of stimulation is too great for our children's under-developed core regulatory systems (bottom-storey level) 🏠 . For example, as caring parents, we may wish to provide a huge choice of toys and experiences for our children, assuming this will help them grow and develop, particularly if we know they have previously been neglected. However, this 'catch-up sensory diet' often leads to children pulling out or wrecking every toy, recreating the chaos of their past experiences, and becoming so over-stimulated that they play in stereotypical, 'tantruming toddler' ways. Alternatively they may appear incapable of engaging in any meaningful play whatsoever. In our experience it is better to adopt the principle of 'the fewer toys the better the learning environment'.

Our aim is always to avoid sensory overload whether seen, heard, touched, smelled, tasted or experienced as movement. It takes babies years to learn about, and make sense of, everything around them, to filter out 'irrelevant' information and 'set their physiological and emotional thermostats' for maximum comfort. Like new-born infants, maltreated children may still startle at loud noises, find the tastes and textures of new foods challenging, or become upset by unfamiliar odours or unexpected movements. Just as 'good enough' parents intuitively take control of the sensory environment for their babies and toddlers, we as therapeutic parents should explore ways of managing our children's environment and help them establish their vital regulatory circuits. In essence, the 'bottom up' approach means creating safe space, alongside support and encouragement for them to practise becoming, and remaining, calm and relaxed.

For example, we need to think about the sounds in our homes and whether these form part of the optimal milieu for our children's fragile sense of wellbeing. Interestingly, while silence might seem the ultimate way to experience peace and tranquillity, this may prove too much for children whose inner worlds are chaotic and fear-driven. Here the judicial use of calming music may help. At other times we might try out different types of music and monitor their impact: louder music could work when engaging in more boisterous activities, whilst calmer music would be more appropriate at night-time. We also need to be aware of the noises we ourselves create, as we move about and chatter, and the volume and tenor of the television programmes we are watching, particularly when children are in bed. It is important to remember that whispering or trying to move about quietly can be as distressing to traumatised children as too much, or violent, noise; they may be lying awake anticipating the inevitable next step: the rows, the slamming doors or the creaking stairs as their abuser approaches their room.

Smells can be equally, if not more, provocative. The smell of frying chips may be over-arousing to children who have waited with an aching belly for their parents to return home late at night with the only meal of the day. Whilst the odour of alcohol needs little explanation in terms of children's distress, that of cigarettes may also bring with it memories of being burnt or the accompanying aroma of parental drug use and the terror of a frightening or passed-out parent. On the other hand the smell of urine may feel so familiar that it can be a source of comfort however unpleasant it may be to us. We can try to alter the 'nasal environment' in our homes by, for example, placing a cut lime or lemon on a saucer in the living area, baking bread, or trying out calming essential oils in a safely placed burner. It can be even more effective to apply these as relaxing massage oils: offering a therapeutic cocktail of soothing, deep touch, warming sensations and olfactory experiences that speak directly to the 'bottom and middle storeys' of the brain.

Touch is highly pleasurable to most of us. At times it can make us feel special, give us a warm feeling inside and relax our bodies and minds; at others it can bring excitement or put us on our guard that we may be in danger. Whilst we may have learned to process and manage these disparate feelings, our children may find them hard to comprehend: some find any touch distressing, others show little or no reaction. Touch can become a particularly sensitive issue in relation to abused children. Adoptive parents and foster carers are often offered advice around 'safe touch' and counselled to avoid close contact, or to wait for their children to take the lead in physical engagement, in order to prevent triggering distressing memories, or accusations, of abuse. This can have the unforeseen and unfortunate consequence of perpetuating 'unspoken messages' children receive from their abusers: that they are tainted, unlovable and untouchable. It also denies children the tactile sensations they missed in infancy that are known to release oxytocin, creating feelings of shared pleasure (Roth 2010) and establishing positive neurobiological feedback circuits in their bodies, brains and minds.

True 'safe touch' allows children to practise connecting directly with us in very literal ways. In engaging in physical touching interactions we create 'joint circuitry' which allows children to 'get the feel' of touch and 'get the message' not only that they are wonderful and lovable but also that they exist and are a real part of our families and our world. Dan Hughes (2009) emphasises that children need touch to develop secure attachments. Moreover he suggests that, where touch is an issue, we contract with our children an agreed number of touches from us each day. He encourages parents to use up their 'hug ration' early in the day and spend the remainder acting sad that they cannot have more. This humorous approach can touch parts others cannot reach and stimulate requests for more! We can also make use of children's MNSs ◖ by being very obvious in touching others: for example, exaggerated cuddles between ourselves and friends or partners will activate children's mirror neurons and begin to build new circuits. We are connecting them both to the outside world and to their inside world, establishing new 'procedural' (non-verbal) memories. We might call this 'mental rehearsal', 'walking' with our children 'through the part' until they can 'walk the walk' for themselves.

Since the vestibular system begins to be 'turned on' in the womb, experiences at this time are pivotal to internal and external integration and regulation (Porges *et al.* 1996) and hence to the formation of the secure base that is at the heart of attachment. Sadly in chaotic and neglectful families, unborn babies may be exposed to too much movement (perhaps Mum was subjected to repeated shaking by an abusive partner) or too little sensory experience, such as in concealed pregnancies. These experiences adversely affect the development of the vestibular (balance) system, bodily and spatial awareness and vital connections to other sensory systems: children's sense of themselves and others, their position in the world and their connections to it are compromised.

Since children's balance systems are consolidated in the early months after birth, they remain vulnerable to sensory under- or over-load during this period. Maltreated children may be left lying for extended periods without being picked up, or strapped into baby carriers, bouncers or buggies, limiting their experience of being moved and of moving themselves. Others may have been pushed, pulled, whirled around or shaken so much that they may, quite literally, 'not know which way is up'. We need to be aware, on our children's behalf, of the upsetting effects in the present of, for example, wobbly chairs, uneven floors, mattresses with too much 'give', bunk beds, playground equipment or even rough-and-tumble play. We should also remind ourselves that a physically out-of-balance child is likely to be more readily thrown out of kilter by other environmental stimuli and less likely to find comfort in being picked up, being rocked or other physical contact. In fact these actions may destabilise them further.

Now let us consider the emotional environment within our homes: the metaphorical furniture, fittings and wallpaper of our living space. We might begin by asking ourselves whether our homes are calm spaces where clear boundaries have been established. For example, have our children learned to expect 'three square meals a day' yet? Do we usually have predictable mealtimes, where children recognise and know what kind of food they might expect – and how much? To children raised in chaotic families, where food was scarce or meals a case of 'grab what you can when you can', the availability and predictability of food can feel like 'life and death issues'. In human evolutionary terms this may indeed have been the case, causing their core systems, such as the brainstem, to trigger survival behaviours to obtain vital energy supplies. Reprogramming such a basic drive will take a great deal of time, energy and 'strategic planning' on our part.

In similar vein, we need to consider whether we have developed sufficiently clear, predictable bedtime routines. While these may be set aside occasionally, it is important to be as consistent as possible. Children who have suffered physical neglect are unlikely to have had anyone who routinely put them to bed; where they suffered emotional neglect, being sent to bed may have been experienced as punishment or rejection. For sexually abused children, bedtime may have been a time of anxiety and fear rather than of calm relaxation. Over and above this, since most of our children have had little opportunity to establish OP, part of their distress will relate to uncertainty that we will still be there in the morning, or indeed whether, when they are alone and upstairs in bed, we are there for them at all. All these factors may be coming into play when we encounter delaying tactics, resistance, repeated calls for attention, insistence on strange rituals or night-time wanderings: typical behavioural communications that the emotional environment is not conducive to relaxation and 'letting go'.

Moving upwards through our three-storey house, we turn more specifically to the limbic areas that form the next step in our process of 'environmental control'. Observing attuned parent–child interactions we can see the reciprocal nature of these relationships that represent the second foundation stone of co-regulation. Unfortunately, maltreated children do not have consistent experiences of creating this shared 'dialogue'. Instead they become attuned to their parents' fear-based states, tuned into recognising and dealing with parents' expectations, rather than expecting to be regulated by them. Consequently we are unlikely to receive the responses from our children that we might expect.

Smiles may prompt glares or avoidance of eye contact; cuddles being shrugged off or actively avoided; a gentle hand on the shoulder resulting in spitting, or a fist in our face; our attempts to comfort a crying child yield only stiffness and withdrawal.

Here we should remember that our children lacked opportunities for their bodies, brains and minds to make good connections between their needs and feelings and their parents' responses. They have been tuned to discord rather than harmony, 'tuned out' or 'turned off' rather than having rehearsed the attunement that would allow them to feel cared for and comforted. It is crucial to remind ourselves that our children's behaviour is not a rejection of us: it is the only way they know of communicating their inner feelings and beliefs. Holding in mind that our children are 'talking to us' rather than 'lashing out at us' enables us to step back from their behaviour and remain open and calm. Our mantra of *'What's this child saying to me?'* rather than 'What's this child doing to me?' sums this up. Repeated regularly it helps us develop the right mind-set for developmental reparenting and tune into what we cannot see and hear rather than what we can.

We understand it is hard to go on offering positive, loving care to rejecting children. Equally we have learned that this is the best way to help children experience the world as safe, and us as nurturing, ready and able to meet their needs. Hence it is essential that we begin by clearly identifying our own feeling states and how they change according to our environment. We are then in a better place to consider our children's emotional and behavioural states and provide the co-regulation they still need. Moreover it is vital that we consider who and what we are. Are we 'morning' or 'evening' people? Do we need a cup of tea or a shower before we face the world? What are the particular behaviours in our children that most upset or frustrate us? Becoming more aware of such issues helps us plan our interactions with our children in calmer and more receptive states, enabling us to remain nurturing even at times of stress. If we are not 'larks' we might prepare for the morning 'rush hour' the previous evening. Small things like ensuring school uniforms are ready and breakfast cereals set out in 'cling-filmed' bowls make a big difference: we will feel more in control of our environment and hence more able to provide a relaxed environment for our children.

Another 'emotional hot-spot' we need to consider is the 'school run'. Many children come out of school a little 'hyped up' and tired; this pattern is often magnified in our children, making home time very stressful all round. It can be extremely helpful to have a 'nurture break' for ourselves before we start the school run. Taking half an hour to have a cup of coffee, read a book or go for a walk is much more effective than continuing with our workplace or household jobs and then dashing out of the door feeling stressed. We can also practise prioritising our tasks and 'letting go of stuff', rather than worrying that things have been left undone. Reminding ourselves that, like babies, our children can only be calmed by calm parents helps us see the importance of taking our time and exploring ways in which we can remain as calm and relaxed as possible.

Regulating emotions

Abusive, angry parents repeatedly leaving their children over-stimulated, and neglectful parents leaving their infants under-stimulated or over-stimulated over long periods, cannot provide the vital nurturing environment that promotes the development of self-regulation. Instead children remain in unregulated physical and emotional states, unable to self-calm or establish their 'comfort zone'. Such strong feeling states become trauma-linked via the amygdala in the brain's middle storey, especially in the right hemisphere. As a consequence, children continue to use emotionally driven behaviours, reflecting these powerful sensory states, that are often inappropriate to the social context, such as when playing with friends or at school.

By understanding that the 'bottom up' developmental attachment approach is the starting point in helping our children, we become more able to manage daily life for ourselves, and ultimately for them. However, initially at least, our children may be unable to use our calming influence, even when we offer them the nurturing experiences they need. Indeed their MNSs may be so 'programmed' to 'perceive' threat that they continue to be triggered into automatic trauma reactions by the slightest hint of uncertainty, unfamiliarity or change that reflects past distressing experiences.

Nevertheless, once we have found ways to help ourselves feel calmer and more relaxed, we can begin to consider ways to regulate our children more effectively. The most crucial element here is our own calm and accepting presence: offering healthy co-regulation for children who still struggle to self-regulate. Taking time to be with our children enables them to function better, even when later they are away from us. Of course no child can, or should, be calm all of the time. Babies need us to help them experience a range of emotions, to explore pleasurable feelings, like joy and excitement, and to accept and cope with over-excitement, frustration, fear and anger. Without safe practice in modulating and shifting their feeling states, children can get 'stuck' with strong physical sensations and emotions they cannot handle. It is up to us to 'mirror' and 'hold' these states: giving them the experience of 'moving up and down the feelings scale' safely and creating their own 'comfort zone'.

Children who have not had these experiences in their early lives tend to swing between emotional extremes. Some develop ways of changing their feeling state by, say, cranking up their arousal until they 'hit the roof' (sometimes taking us with them) and then 'dropping to the floor'. Others distance themselves by, for example, using television or computer games, eating or self-harm, to escape their overwhelming emotions. Many swing from one extreme to the other, with little intervening 'middle ground'. These simultaneously rigid yet chaotic behaviour patterns are terrifying for children, and often for us and our families. It may take years of shared practice before our children can manage fluid state changes and create the free-flowing river of wellbeing (Siegel 2010) that will bring them peace of body and mind and the resilience to 'bounce back' into healthy shape.

Taking a developmental approach, we must adopt the interaction patterns that come naturally to good enough parents of infants and 'go through the emotions' with them. Naturally this will be far easier if we establish a calm emotional environment, so that extremes are less likely to be reached and our children are more likely to succeed in establishing a comfortable baseline of feelings. We must examine our 'emotional thermostats' and reset them to 'warm' if they seem 'too cool' or 'too hot'. An added bonus here is that this milieu will feel more comfortable to us, lowering our stress levels and ensuring we are more emotionally sensitive and responsive when the need inevitably arises.

The cortical (top storey) level of the brain also plays a vital part in the development of self-regulation 🏠. We know that children who had inconsistent care as babies do not develop MN circuits that allow them to reflect on, understand or anticipate the intentions behind their own actions, let alone the thoughts and actions of others. Instead, abused children establish MN connections that reflect previous distressing experiences, meaning they interpret our intentions as potentially threatening. Talking to our children about '*why we are going to do what we do*' and letting them know we understand that they may not be able to work this out for themselves helps them alter their MN firing patterns. These, in turn, connect up to and influence other parts of their neurobiological systems, giving them greater awareness and control over their core brainstem and limbic socio-emotional functioning.

Like all neural pathways, MN 'wiring' depends on previous 'firing': the more our children experienced painful, frightening or shame-inducing events the more activity there will have been in the relevant MNS and the stronger will be its influence on future behaviour. Their responses and expectations are preferentially 'wired up' to anticipate, react to and perceive threat in the actions and intentions of other people. We must be mindful of this when we are with our children, so that we, in turn, can use our MN circuits to identify and predict their likely responses and step in immediately. Our facial expressions, body language and tone of voice are pivotal to 'breaking the circuit', so that new, healthier information can be 'heard' and 'seen', encouraging new MN pathways to begin 'firing and wiring' together. We may need to check ourselves out in a virtual mirror first!

The timing of our interventions is crucial. Talking to children about our intentions before we interact or intervene in situations, whilst they are relatively calm, is more helpful than trying to explain our intentions after we have acted and triggered our children into a dysregulated state, since at this point they will be acting out of their sensori-motor and emotional systems and will have little access to their thinking brains. They are then quite literally unable to 'hear' what we are saying, and instead of setting in train new, healthier patterns of neural firing we reinforce the unhelpful old patterns and set them, and ourselves, up for failure. Of course, if we identify feelings in ourselves that could create fearful perceptions and expectations in our children, this is the time to walk away, letting our children know we need time to re-regulate before we engage with them. Since they are tuned to non-verbal messages, they are not easily fooled by verbal 'cover-ups' and need to see we can recognise and modulate our own feelings and actions appropriately.

More generally, 'talking as we go' is fundamental to building internal connections throughout the body, brain and mind. Good enough parents intuitively chatter to their babies as part of their moment-to-moment interactions with them, even though they do not expect them to understand spoken language or reply verbally. It is the rhythms of our non-verbal communication, our sensory and emotional body language, that creates the attachment dialogue with infants at the mid-storey level and facilitates a gradual developmental shift from primarily non-verbal to verbal communication. Recent MN research using brain scans shows that areas in monkey brains that light up when observing others' gestures are the same areas (predominantly in the left cortical hemisphere) responsible for interpreting and generating spoken language in humans (Rizolatti and Sinigaglia 2007). In pairing verbal with non-verbal language in mundane interactions with our children we 'wire up' their MNSs, allowing them to interpret, anticipate and reflect on our actions and intentions. Using developmental reparenting principles we can re-route neural circuits throughout children's semi-detached brains and create more 'joined up' bodies and minds.

Finally, continuing our semi-detached house metaphor, we should ask ourselves where in the house our children are at any given moment and, simultaneously, where we are when we are trying to communicate with them. If we are in the study (cortical mode) and our children are in the basement (brainstem mode) they are unlikely to hear us, let alone understand us, or take conscious control of and for themselves. Instead we need to join our children in the 'basement' and gradually help them move up through, and across, the house towards the study. It is by this step-by-step movement between floors and between areas of our shared home that our children will begin to lay the foundations of their inner world, establishing the springboard to them moving out, when the time is right, to live comfortably in their own homes (bodies), secure in the knowledge that 'Mum/ Dad is there' for continued support in times of need.

Chapter 6

Rocking and Rolling

Creating Physical and Emotional Balance

Throughout our writing we emphasise the fundamental importance of balance and organisation in children's early experiences in order to develop balance and organisation in their bodies, brains and minds throughout their lifespan. We established that neurobiological development is 'bottom up': the 'input' to the 'bottom storey' of the 'semi-detached' brain providing the foundation for our 'semi-detached house' 🏚. Within the brainstem ('basement') the vestibular system forms, both literally and metaphorically, 'the organ of balance', connecting directly to the inner ear. Here three fluid-filled 'semi-circular canals' containing extremely sensitive hairs detect miniscule changes related to body position, movement and position relative to the environment (Goddard 1996): telling us 'where our bodies are at' and 'which way is up'.

Neural connections develop on a 'use it or lose it' basis, where 'neurons that fire together, wire together', determined by the quality of our earliest attachment experiences, particularly during the first thousand days from conception. In the womb, amniotic fluid cushions babies from extreme external movement, whilst allowing them to change position, to achieve maximum comfort and acquire a burgeoning repertoire of basic movements. From the early months of pregnancy this provides invaluable input to the developing vestibular system (Reebye and Stalker 2008), preparing babies for the challenges of the outside world. However, the amniotic fluid cannot protect babies from violent external impact or extreme movement that could occur where mothers live in violent relationships or, perhaps, when they engage in repeated frenetic behaviour, such as over-vigorous exercising or wild dancing. Difficulties can also arise where mothers' movements are over-inhibited, for example where extended bed-rest is required due to threatened miscarriage, or where tight-fitting clothes are worn to conceal weight-gain in unrecognised or unwanted pregnancies.

The impact of exposure to too much, or too little, sensori-motor information to the vestibular system is not confined to the womb. Traumatic experiences during birth are known to affect the neurobiological organisation of balance and movement systems (Goddard 1996): very rapid, slow, unmanaged or complicated deliveries can also affect children's motor development. Subsequently, as we know, babies need endless experiences of being picked up, nursed, rocked and carried by consistent, loving caregivers to feel safe: an underlying sense of physical security is vital to the development of our sense of emotional security.

Sadly, many hurt children were raised in neglectful or abusive birth families: left unattended in cots, or strapped in carrying seats or buggies, for extended periods. As they began to become more mobile, their activities may have been discouraged or over-restricted by depressed or over-anxious parents. As a result of sensory under-stimulation they may 'shut down', often becoming floppy or apathetic. This lack of responsiveness or activity can be misinterpreted as 'contentment' ('good baby') or 'rejection' ('bad baby'), leading to further neglect, by omission or commission, or to abuse. Other youngsters attempt to find ways of stimulation, through rocking, head-banging or becoming increasingly over-active, often developing chronic muscular tension in their necks and limbs. This, too, often generates anger in caregivers, exacerbating their poor care.

Conversely, children may have had distressing experiences of over-stimulation, such as being whirled round, swung wildly or jiggled rapidly by caregivers misguidedly attempting to engage with, or pacify, them. Only too frequently they have been dragged, bounced or thrown around by out-of-control family members. In such circumstances, children's awareness of, and capacity to achieve, physical balance is compromised, affecting their co-ordination and ability to feel physically at ease and safe in the world. Where too little stimulation is available to enable appropriate 'wiring and firing', neurons are not 'switched on', nor are good, functional connections established. Too much incoming information overloads youngsters' 'wiring' processes, causing temporary 'meltdown' and throwing their sensitive systems 'out of kilter'. Consequently children remain on 'red alert' for further dysregulating sensori-motor input: their bodies prepared for fight, flight and freeze responses, since their early experiences of co-regulation have been inadequate.

Since the vestibular system is also associated with auditory and visual perceptual processing (Reeby and Stalker 2008), global neurobiological integration can be adversely affected; developmental difficulties such as dyspraxia, dyslexia, sensory integration and speech and language disorders, and executive function difficulties, can result. Frequently traumatised children's difficulties do not end there. If their vestibular system, informing the relationship with the physical world, is compromised, relationships in the social world are also affected. Imagine how hard it would be for children on permanent red alert to cope with simple nurturing interactions such as hugging. Our actions may be enough to challenge their precarious physical equilibrium, triggering positional insecurity. Their response may be to push away, become floppy or stiff, or wriggle about. If we respond with irritation or dismay this causes further 'faulty connections' in the mid-storey emotional brain, strengthening negative perceptions of caregivers. Through these distressing experiences, our loving intentions become interpreted by their distorted MNSs 🔍 as confirmation that all parent-figures are ultimately hurtful.

Our children often develop quite 'organised' ways of controlling their sensory input themselves, to the exclusion of others: resisting our attempts to get close. We can recognise this in 'hyperactive' children who are constantly on the go, moving, touching everything, creating noise to create a personal environment over which they feel some control. They 'thrive' on intense stimulation to provide the stimulation lacking in their birth families, or to recreate its familiar, 'comforting' chaos. Conversely, our 'quiet' children seek to avoid intense movement and other sensory input; they may resist joining in games or going outside. They can become distressed easily, and as they grow up they may appear 'lazy', 'dreamy', 'loners' or 'couch potatoes'. In fact, they too are desperately trying to limit the sensory and motor input that informs their emotional states and threatens to overwhelm their sensitive systems.

Our job, as therapeutic parents, is to 'feed' our children a 'sensory diet' that takes full account of their individual, underlying needs. Children who appear unable to recognise when they are full, seem obsessed with food or eat inappropriately need our help and support to acquire healthier eating patterns, as do our poor and 'fussy' eaters. In both cases, we are helping them practise new, and better, ways of managing their input and creating fresh, positive associations between food consumption and nurturing care. Rather than 'food–fear' connections we encourage 'food–comfort' connections, establishing new and improved neurobiological 'wiring systems', using the principles of developmental or therapeutic reparenting. The same concept holds for children with sensori-motor difficulties: they need us to provide a 'custom-built diet' of movement and sensory experience that allows them to create healthier neurobiological wiring systems through adjusting their intake and output.

Our aim is to reset the balance of their sensory systems, offering them moment-by-moment opportunities for new experiences that improve their somato-sensory (bodily) perceptions and enhance their body–brain–mind connections. Sharing these activities we provide essential co-regulation that was a vital missing ingredient in their early sensori-motor diet. We should start with the kinds of activities we would naturally provide for very young children, finding creative age-appropriate ways to slip these in to our daily routines. On our 'special menu' are the oxytocin-inducing cuddles and gentle movement of the early months, the rough-and-tumble play of toddlerhood, and the more organised, fun activities like cycling, swimming, trampolining and the team games of school age.

We often need to start by helping our children 'learn to play' before they can 'play to learn'. The watchword of all our interactions should be 'hand-in-hand': where simple, playful acts of togetherness gradually become transformed into physical and social practice for life. Our children will make better progress if we avoid an over-stimulating diet with too much choice and if we make small step-wise changes that do not threaten to overwhelm them. This holds true whether youngsters appear under- or over-reactive, or 'flip-flop' between these two responses. Whilst 'less' and 'slower' may be self-evident concepts for hyper-sensitive children, who avoid intense sensations, it holds equally true for those who seemingly 'can't get enough' stimulation and constantly attempt to create their own. For both groups, their precarious neurobiological equilibrium is all too easily disturbed by change that threatens their basic physical and psychological security.

Way to go

In Chapter 4, 'Information: The Need to Know', we explored how children's histories provide the key to understanding them in the here and now. We discussed how children express their needs, predominantly through behaviour, rather than spoken language, and that the way we can make sense of their 'behavioural language' is by looking back at their early experiences. We emphasised that we should reflect not only on what happened to our children, but also on what it 'did' to them, in terms of their neurobiological development and attachment patterns. This applies as much to physical as to socio-emotional behaviour.

Clearly, therefore, our 'going-back-to-go-forward menu' should start with exploring ways of 'revisiting' our children's early histories from bottom up. Gentle rocking is vital for the healthy development of infants' vestibular systems and the integration of their motor and sensory systems, and must occur within consistent, caregiving relationships. If we know that our children were over- or under-stimulated, and continue to struggle in this area, the 'starter' in their 'diet' should take the form of shared 'rocking experiences'. Below are some ideas to get us going and providing a jumping-off point, to inspire us to be creative with our children. Many more can be found in *First Steps in Parenting the Child Who Hurts: Tiddlers and Toddlers* (Archer 1999a).

Action rhymes such as 'Row the Boat' and 'Ring-a-Ring-a-Roses' come to mind: preferably enjoyed body-to-body or hand-in-hand. However, if children are uncomfortable with touch and closeness, we could begin by using a rocking chair or horse, where we provide the 'kinetic energy'. 'Swooshing about' in the bath could be fun: after preparing ourselves in full rain gear! We could invent singing games which involve leaning forwards and backwards, practise the Chuckle Brothers' 'to-me-to-you' scenario, play 'Simon Says', or pretend to be 'trees swaying in the wind'. Over time we can introduce our youngsters to the delights of playing on swings (slowly at first) or sitting astride gently swaying branches.

Good rocking experiences are as important for youngsters who are over-active as those who appear uncomfortable with changes in body position or active movement. Since the most effective ways of soothing crying, flailing babies or 'tantrum-ing' toddlers use gentle body language, rhythm and tone of voice, the same holds for 'wound-up' children. Whilst for under-active children we are aiming to 'fire and wire new circuits', for over-active ones we are working to replace 'old circuits' with healthier ones. We could think of ourselves as 'generators' or 'regulators': in either case attempting to control input and output. So with children who are forever jiggling, spinning, bustling or bouncing to provide self-stimulation the principles remain the same, although we need different techniques.

We might begin by 'inviting' ourselves to join in our children's frenetic activities: remembering to be playful and simultaneously holding on to our capacity for self-regulation. We can then begin to slow down or redirect their movements using our bodies, our voices and our breathing. Singing is invaluable here. No matter what we sound like, this rhythmic information goes into the non-verbal right side of the 'semi-detached' brain, where it can be processed by the sensori-motor and emotional systems, even when the (left) language and thinking brain has 'shut down'. It is therefore much more effective than pleas to 'calm down': allowing children to feel safer in, and more in control of, their bodies. This, in turn, forms the basis for their secure base and sense of wellbeing. However, since our youngsters may have clung to their behaviour patterns for years, as their 'safety net', it can take time to alter them. Indeed, practice may not make perfect but the dividends are certainly worthwhile.

With a little imagination, many of these ideas can be adapted for older children. A garden swing may allow both rocking and 'acceptable' closeness with teenagers, in time becoming a place where they can feel safe enough to explore feelings in ways that seem impossible otherwise. Other ideas could include wobble or skate boards, balance balls, surfing, rowing or even tug-of-war (folding sheets could fit in here – playing and learning (and whistling) while you work!). Why not try a steam train journey (often much less distressing to the vestibular system than cars)? And let us not forget Wii Fit (or similar) options: there are many that will appeal to even the most truculent teen.

Once we feel that our children are finding their 'balance' through rocking, we can begin expanding their 'sensory diet' and help them feel increasingly safe in their bodies. We might think about the rolling, bouncing and jumping games we enjoyed as children and introduce these at our children's pace. Action and singing rhymes, like 'Bouncing Up and Down on a Big Red Tractor', 'Wheels on the Bus' and 'Jumping Jacks', can offer a great start. We can wrap children in blankets and roll them slowly around the room, or roll with them down gentle grassy slopes. Paddling in the sea can encourage stepping and leaping, whilst swimming pools provide excellent opportunities for a broad range of movements and acceptable close physical presence.

Trampolines appeal to children of all ages: at first children may need us to hold their hands and bounce with them for security or to have the trampoline to themselves so they feel more in control of the movement. Then if we stand alongside as 'coaches', perhaps singing or clapping out the rhythm of their bouncing, we become part of the activity and provide essential co-regulation. Trips to the 'swings park' can provide wonderful moving-fun areas, avoiding busy times, so that over-active children do not hurt others accidentally and under-active ones do not feel intimidated. Older children can benefit from fun fairs and Disneyland, once they have developed a sense of danger and responsibility! Meanwhile, Wii and Kinetix action and dancing games could be just the thing.

An essential part of the sensori-motor diet must be rough-and-tumble (RAT) play. Parents usually introduce such games when babies become more mobile, as they move into toddlerhood. RAT or rough-housing play (Panksepp 1998) has many beneficial effects for both brain (notably the vestibular system) and body and simultaneously encourages socialisation. Panksepp (1998) claims that play is 'one of the major brain sources of joy': its primary feature being touch. Clearly we can all have fun with this one – except, initially, for movement and touch-sensitive children. Thankfully we can introduce endless opportunities that will entice the most avoidant youngsters into RAT play. Pillows and cushions can be used as 'buffers' or 'weapons', water wallowed in, streams jumped, trees climbed, holes dug. We can play hop-scotch, skip with ropes, twirl like ballerinas, ride dodgem cars, swing on monkey-bars, run three-legged races – the list is as huge as our capacity to be creative. Team games will become more important once our children have had sufficient practice rough-housing with us.

Summary

As therapeutic or developmental parents we need to:

- be in the 'right' mood or find the 'right' mood
- understand our children's early histories
- remember that 'bottom up' is the right way up
- be mindful that learning to play is playing to learn
- take our time: slower is faster and more is less
- control the physical and emotional environment
- give it time: practice is essential
- lead the way: hand in hand
- be sensitive and creative
- recharge our batteries regularly
- have as much fun as possible!

Chapter 7

Seeing Eye to Eye

Our organs of touch, sound, smell and taste allow us to build up a partial picture of the outside world and can generate important physical, emotional and thought associations. These sensations and eye contact can all alter our feeling states dramatically, bringing us comfort, joy and excitement or discomfort, pain and shame. Being able to produce and respond to sound has led to our capacity to produce beautiful music, to detect sound sources before they become visible, to share our thoughts through conversation and become social beings. However, our eyes play a unique role in enabling us to engage, communicate and socialise with others: to perceive their intentions (Baron-Cohen 1999), to create mental images of them, and of ourselves through their eyes, to express ourselves and reciprocate.

It is difficult to over-estimate the importance of eye contact in the parent–child relationship. Gazing with love into the eyes of their new-born babies, parents convey messages of love, safety and security, simultaneously communicating that they are unique, special and valued (Trevarthen 2001). These non-verbal communications, although often accompanied by 'baby talk', are experienced primarily through body sensations and emotional feelings, creating the environment for healthy neurobiological connections and the building of well-functioning MNSs ◯. Conversely, absence of eye contact, or the gaze of angry or frightened caregivers, conveys distressing messages to babies that they are unworthy of love and cannot depend on their caregivers for security or comfort. In research involving 'still faces', where parents were asked to show interest in their babies and then withdraw attention for 60 seconds, the babies reacted almost immediately with tears, followed by despair (Tronick *et al.* 1975). If these distressing experiences occur repeatedly, they trigger distinct neuron 'firing' patterns and 'wire up' unhealthy neurobiological connections, including the 'firing' and 'wiring' of MN circuits.

At a recent training event we attended, participants were divided into pairs. Half were given notes asking them to spend two minutes describing a pleasant experience, their partners instructed to show interest for ten seconds and then withdraw eye contact. Almost immediately the talkers felt uncomfortable and struggled to complete their task, drying up and being unable to continue. They began to feel their partners were uninterested and feelings of anger followed, alongside the desire to shout and ask them to pay attention. If adults with reasonably secure attachments and sufficient experiences of positive interactions can experience such disturbing emotions so quickly, consider how much more profound will be the impact upon babies with limited experiences of comfort, security and self-awareness on which to draw and whose neurobiological connections are still being formed. We could try this exercise with a friend and consider how we might feel if we were totally dependent on that person, they were the most important figure in our life, it happened time and again, and we had insufficient positive feedback to over-ride the negativity we experience.

Infants' experiences in the womb inform the senses of balance (the 'sixth' sense), touch, smell and vision; however, these senses are not equally well developed at birth; nor do they have equal importance. Whilst balance and touch are essential during the birth process, smell and vision are vital, in evolutionary terms, in allowing infants to identify their mothers immediately after birth in order to seek safety, comfort and nutrition from them: all crucial to survival. Newborns pay greatest attention to parental faces (Frank, Vul and Johnson 2009), in particular to their eyes

(Maurer 1993). Whilst their capacity to focus is generally weak, it appears that the focal length of 'babes-in-arms' is just right to meet their caregivers' gaze. It may be that it is the contrast between the face and the eyes that attracts infants' attention: that the eyes appear to 'pop out of the head' of those who are being observed and who, in turn, are observing them. By six months (Papousek and Papousek 1984) babies spend two to three times longer watching faces that are looking at them than at those looking away. Since brain development is 'experience-dependent', it can be no coincidence that this allows babies to establish two-way communication channels with others, thereby laying down vital neurobiological intra and inter-connections.

The amygdala in the right limbic (mid-storey) hemisphere is intrinsically involved in processing information from the eyes (Schore 1994): assessing its emotional significance and laying down non-verbal, or body, memories in the earliest months. Such memories, also described as procedural or implicit, are not retrievable through conscious awareness but recreate feeling states that directly influence babies' and children's behavioural responses. These reactions can be thought of as beneath consciousness and 'reflex' and may be triggered by a partial similarity between the current feeling and the memory contributing to the resultant feeling or behavioural state. Infants who have predominantly positive early 'eye-to-eye' interactions with their caregivers will, over time, be 'wired' to expect positive, pleasurable experiences and learn to cope, in later life, with discomfort and absence of interest from others with fewer distressing feelings and behaviours. They experience greater wellbeing and face the challenges of life with greater equanimity and resilience. Appropriately, the acronym devised by Siegel (2010) to describe wellbeing is FACES: that is, individuals who experience wellbeing show high levels of Flexibility, Acceptance, Coherence, Empathy and Stability.

Loving looks and smiles from parents create a cascade of pleasurable feelings in babies (Roth 2010). We see this almost from birth in the smiles and giggles these simple facial gestures generate. It is the dilated pupils of caregivers' eyes that infants 'read': followed by the unconscious mirroring of the positive arousal they perceive, raising their heart rate and releasing neuro-bio-chemicals such as oxytocin, endorphins and dopamine (Schore 1994). These chemical messengers not only produce a 'feel-good factor', they also stimulate the release of glucose, which actively promotes brain growth (Schore 1994). So the more smiles and positive gazing babies receive from us, the more pleasure, joy and excitement they feel and the better performing their brains become. Of course, regulation of arousal is also essential, as it is in every area of our lives. Youngsters are highly dependent on their caregivers for co-regulation in the early years, and sufficient, good quality, eye-mediated arousal regulation gives babies a head start: typically they are able to make and break eye contact appropriately and manage stimulating input within comfortable levels. Just think of the way they draw us into games of 'peekaboo' and let us know when they have had enough!

When discussing object permanence and constancy we explore the importance of learning that things and people are still there when they cannot be detected through the 'five senses', particularly through the eyes. This is evident in the making and breaking of mutual eye contact through games like 'peekaboo' that provide essential 'firing' practice for the 'wiring' of positive neurobiological circuits ☁. Through these, and similar, experiences youngsters gradually learn not only to regulate their sensory and emotional feelings but also to see themselves mirrored in their parents' eyes: to see, and learn the meaning of, their feelings (Siegel 2010). Simultaneously, in looking into their parents' eyes, children begin to 'feel' that they exist and are part of the wider world ◖◯. This consolidates developmental attachments and creates trust that they are 'held in mind' (Siegel 1999), even when they cannot check this directly through 'seeing eye to eye'.

Young children who are not exposed to parents' loving gaze and smiles receive insufficient positive feedback via mutual eye contact to 'wire up' positive arousal circuits; they cannot gain self-worth, acquire functioning regulatory systems or use other people's eyes as reliable sources of information about themselves and others (Roth 2010). Many of us are familiar with children who are distressed by sharp glances, or struggle to make or keep eye contact; their MN circuits are 'hardwired' to anticipate hurtful communications and dysregulation, including the triggering of overwhelming shame ⊡⧉. A key element of shame (Schore 1994) is the effort made to 'escape the gaze of the world', to avoid the critical or threatening perceptions of others. Children may look down or turn away (de Waal 1992), hide or take off; they feel disconnected and isolated and their arousal systems shut down. Conversely, in 'shame-rage', children take control of distressing situations by rapidly escalating their arousal and making threatening, or defiant, eye contact.

We can consider these contradictory responses in terms of the electrical wiring in our 'semi-detached' brain ⌂: with the loss of positive eye-to-eye contact triggering either 'short-circuits' or 'power-surges'. Returning power to a domestic wiring system requires us to check the fuse boxes and replace blown fuses, or reset the trip switch: merely flicking an individual 'on' switch yields nothing but frustration. Similarly, in order to 'resume normal service' in our children we need to check ourselves out as the essential power source, recalibrate our own emotional settings and make our restored positive energy supply available to restart our children's circuits. It is helpful to have a 'head torch' to hand and to practise finding it 'in the dark', when we need it most yet have greatest difficulty in seeing our children's needs and being their power source. Using our 'emergency power supply' we can 'find' our enlightened 'sensible head' and reconnect our children's 'broken circuits'. With sufficient repetition, we encourage the development of healthier wiring in our children, with better internal connections and less sensitive trip switches.

Both eye contact avoidance and overpowering eye contact create discomfort in all those involved, leading to negative consequences. We may perceive our children as 'sulking' if they resist looking at us, or as 'rude' and 'aggressive' if they glare or stare. Unfortunately this reinforces our children's feelings of isolation, worthlessness and shame and prevents them learning from their mistakes. The natural 'shame socialisation' interactions between caregivers and infants that begin in toddlerhood

(Schore 1994) allow young children to learn basic social rules, so that they can fit into, and play their part in, their community. Consequently children who miss out on mutual positive eye contact in babyhood and experience overpowering feelings of shame are in 'double-double jeopardy': they feel unloved and alienated, they cannot regulate their feeling states, they do not read other people's intentions well and they fail to grasp social rules. In addition they risk alienating the people best placed to help them: their parents. Their capacity to 'see eye to eye' with those around them is indeed compromised.

Another familiar behaviour may be our children's tendency to be 'in our faces', commanding our attention through fair means or foul. Others attempt to be inconspicuous, preferring to remain 'out of the line of sight', or make their presence felt through being ever-present, 'helpful' and 'willing to please'. We can understand these behaviour patterns in terms of children's early neglect and abuse and hence insufficient experience of feeling themselves reflected positively in caregivers' eyes. Not only do our children have little sense of their own bodily and emotional feeling states, they have not consistently experienced 'feeling seen' or 'held in mind' when outside caregivers' direct sight. Nor have they had consistent opportunities to practise 'checking out', through eye-to-eye contact, the range of well-regulated parental emotions, positive and negative, that help them 'read minds' (Siegel 2010) and predict intentions accurately. Since 'good enough' two-way communication and anticipation systems have not been set in place, our children are 'working in the dark'.

Since their very existence depends on feedback from others, children may go to great lengths to 'be seen in the spotlight'; often they have finely honed skills in 'making a scene' and 'attention seeking' in order to get what they need (Bomber 2007). To them 'out of sight' is literally 'out of mind', so that even being cast in the role of 'the bad child' feels better than not being seen at all. Other youngsters actively seek to remain 'in the shadows' or develop ways of staying close and playing the part of the good child, to obtain the smiles and looks of acceptance they do not feel they deserve by rights. How many of us, as children, experienced distress at being sent to our rooms for 'showing off' or 'being rude'? Conversely, how many times did we offer Mum a cup of tea before asking for something, offer our friends sweets if they would walk home with us, or work extra hard in school so that teachers would praise us? We all develop strategies to get our wants and needs met: most of us using a broad repertoire of 'acceptable' interactions with others and using 'in your face' behaviours only *in extremis*. For maltreated children their behavioural 'choices' are more limited and persistent.

A major element of therapeutic parenting is developmental 'reparenting'; that is, recognising where our children missed out developmentally and providing them with consistent opportunities to 'make good' their disorganised patterns through shared positive experiences. For children whose immediate, over-riding need is for recognition, approval and acceptance, the intensity, frequency and duration of their behaviour patterns provide us with opportunities to recognise their real meaning and, with experience, to 'read' them: alerting us to the covert needs beneath our children's overt interactions.

Bearing in mind babies' need for mutual eye contact and communication (Gratier and Trevarthern 2008), we can explore ways of letting our children and young people know we are 'seeing' and 'holding them in mind', so they feel less driven to engage in counter-productive negative behaviours. In order to help children 'see eye to eye' we need, metaphorically, to get down to their eye level, just as we might join toddlers on the floor to play. Simultaneously we should remind ourselves that our children are likely to have poor skills in modulating eye contact, and hence regulating their feelings. As the brain is an 'anticipation machine', their brains, bodies and minds are wired up to expect the rejection, abandonment, criticism and pain that infused their earliest experiences. To these youngsters, an unguarded or untimely word, gesture or glance from us triggers anticipation of further negative interactions and generates overwhelming 'mid-storey', emotionally driven reactions not mediated by their 'top storey' thinking brains.

Consequently, it is vital we remain vigilant to where we ourselves are 'coming from' and take time to consider our visual communications carefully before acting. It may help to visualise ourselves picking up a new-born baby: approaching slowly, smiling, making eye contact, moving in open, non-threatening ways and speaking lovingly and with pleasure. Alternatively, visualise meeting our boss for the first time: we would be on 'our best behaviour', again approaching carefully, smiling and making just enough eye contact, using a measured tone of voice and gestures indicating respect. This may be a far cry from the off-hand way we might greet a partner after a brief separation, or the over-exuberant hugs, raised voice and teasing banter when meeting old friends. Here, 'we know that they know' that we have 'seen' them and care about them and they too intuitively understand our actions and interpret them appropriately. We cannot afford to make similar assumptions with our children, any more than we would with an injured animal. When approached and looked at, 'hurt animals' immediately go on the defensive, growling, glaring and baring their teeth, or conversely cowering, lowering their eyes and shaking with fear. These could be appropriate images to hold in mind when approaching and communicating with our hurt children.

Summary

- Eye contact is vital for babies' attachment and development. In the earliest months it is a source of comfort and pleasure and helps, directly, to build better brains and, indirectly, to establish healthy, integrated neurobiological circuits.

- Gazing into caregivers' eyes gives vital messages to infants that they are lovable and special, sowing the seeds of self-worth. Eye-to-eye contact provides 'psycho-bio-feedback', allowing babies and children to see themselves reflected in a 'virtual mirror': to see who they are and what they are feeling.

- From a very early age babies can regulate the amount of stimulation they receive, through making and breaking eye contact. Since infants require almost constant co-regulation of their body, brain and mind systems this indicates just how significant eye-to-eye connections are.

- Since eyes are 'the windows of the soul', they are the means through which we begin to interpret both our own and other people's feelings, thoughts and intentions, communicate non-verbally and hence learn to 'see eye to eye' and form meaningful relationships.

- Neglected and abused children have too few consistent, positive experiences of shared eye contact to develop these essential life skills. Consequently, they cannot acquire sufficient practice of managing eye contact, since it was often absent, overwhelming or unpredictable. This significantly limits opportunities for youngsters to practise rudimentary self-regulation, 'feel good' and build healthy brain circuits.

- Maltreated babies and toddlers do not receive the unspoken messages that they are unique, wonderful and deserving of loving care: instead internalising messages that they are 'bad' from adults who themselves lack self-regulation. This creates the 'frightened or frightening' caregiving environment that is highly predictive of disorganised developmental attachments.

- Being seen, quite literally, becomes a major preoccupation for traumatised children: they constantly strive to control both the circumstances and extent of their 'visability'.

- Children's perceptions and expectations of themselves and others are distorted by hurtful early experiences. These distortions continue to affect their beliefs and responses within our families: creating insecurity and fear rather than security and trust. They fail to see eye to eye.

An eye to the future

Having come this far, how can we translate our growing awareness of our children's negative perceptions into positive action? How can we give them messages that carry just the right balance of interest and yet are not over-intrusive or overpowering? How can we develop mutual eye contact from which our youngsters can learn about themselves through our eyes and become more able to 'read' them and make better sense of our intentions? What are the therapeutic reparenting principles we can introduce to help them begin to 'see eye to eye' with the inhabitants of their social world? Below we provide a five-stage plan of action. We should keep sight of the fact that parents are the real experts on their own children and, once familiar with the basic concepts, they can, with growing confidence, create their own family 'knitting patterns'.

Check in and check out[1]

Stage 1: checking ourselves out

- Check out how we feel physically, emotionally, cognitively.

- Identify whether we are functioning primarily from our bottom, middle or top-storey brain, sensing whether we are breathing too quickly, feeling too hot or cold, hungry or thirsty, wobbly. Explore our feelings, observing whether we are upset, angry, powerless or scared.

- Using our awareness of 'top down' controls, make conscious efforts to re-regulate ourselves from the bottom up. Adjust our breathing, nurturing ourselves: dealing with our feelings sensibly we can switch on our thinking brain circuits.

---

1 The 'check in and check out' outline in Appendix 2 is the basic template. The one here and in some other chapters have been specifically tailored to the subject matter as they are innovative concepts with which some readers may be unfamiliar.

Stage 2: practising by ourselves

- Practise making eye contact with partners or friends, checking out the feelings this generates in them and in us. This works equally well using a mirror.

- Experiment with the facial expressions, gestures and tone of voice that feel most comfortable, whilst remembering that smiling with our eyes has the single most powerful effect.

- Try out these exercises both when we feel relaxed and when we feel stressed, to get a feel for how our reactions vary depending on our circumstances.

- Take into consideration our unique family circumstances, such as whether we are on our own or whether we have other children who may also need our help during times of stress.

- Establish ways of getting some additional help if we, or our other children, need it. Test these arrangements out in non-stressful situations.

Stage 3: checking out our children

- Observe how they are 'making us feel', physically and emotionally.

- Use this information to work out whether they are mostly functioning out of their bottom, middle or top-storey brains.

- Check in on ourselves again, in case we need to re-regulate ourselves.

- Use what we know about bottom-up development to identify where our children most need our help. If in doubt, start at the bottom and work up.

Stage 4: practising with our children

We need consciously to work on encouraging all aspects of eye communication in our moment-to-moment family interactions. Simple actions like passing a piece of toast offer great opportunities to build vital social, emotional and cognitive connections. In addition here are some simple things we can do on a frequent and consistent basis:

- 'Notice' our children and let them know we have noticed them – smiling, winking, waving, laughing *with* them, putting our hand on their shoulder, 'high-fiving', giving them the 'thumbs up'.

- Comment on what our children are doing: '*I can see...*' – being careful to avoid sounding critical or as if we are laughing *at* them.

- If we cannot see them, 'check in' verbally from time to time – a quick call is enough to reconnect. With older children, a short text, 'smiley' icon or photo could be good.

- Show interest in our children and in what interests them. This is a vital tool in helping them to 'feel seen' and gain a sense of self-competence and self-worth.

- Shared attention is essential to the development of inter-communication: encouraging this need not be obvious. Reading comics together, cutting shapes from biscuit dough, playing board games, throwing and catching balls and asking to be 'shown' how to use the TV remote or adjust our mobile are examples of how we can encourage this.

- Suggest shared activities, such as bird or plane spotting, collecting and swapping cards, watching sports or pop bands: again providing a common visual focus.

- Devising games that 'accidentally' involve eye contact can create many opportunities to connect. Play is the ideal environment for learning, and 'working through the eyes' increases feelings of comfort and pleasure whilst growing brain cells and their connections. One of the most obvious playful interactions is 'peekaboo' – adding age-appropriate 'tweaks' to engage older children and keeping the 'disappearing' times very short. For some children we may need to hide our faces only partially, to reduce their distress, remaining vigilant as this may not be very obvious.

- Introduce games like 'Pass it on': where a wink is passed on from player to player – 'over-doing' our expressions and collapsing into helpless giggles.

- Look in the bathroom mirror together whilst teeth are being cleaned, or faces washed, grimacing, grinning, gaping, groaning, using our whole face and grossly exaggerated movements.

- Have a go at mutual face painting – chocolate could be fun! For older children we might experiment with make-up together, 'doing nails', false tattoos or spiking or streaking hair.

- Once we are comfortable with adjusting our eyes and feelings to a suitably comfortable setting in 'normal circumstances', identify one or two 'tricky' situations where we might try out 'seeing eye to eye' with our children.

Stage 5: dealing with difficult situations

- Take time to assess the situation and how best to approach it.

- 'Think toddler' – working out our children's functional age *at that moment* and treating them as we would a child of that age. If in doubt, go lower.

- 'Think hurt animal' – checking out their current emotional state and adjusting our 'approach' accordingly.

- Attempt to make *some* eye contact whilst staying aware of our children's difficulties in this area; on the other hand, do not *force* eye, or physical, contact, as either may trigger fight, flight, freeze or shame reactions.

- Provide simple, loving, accepting, verbal messages to accompany simple, loving, accepting, non-verbal messages through our eyes, facial expressions and body language.

- Speak calmly and gently, showing acceptance of our children for who and what they are *at that moment*, staying aware that they are so sensitised to perceived threat and shame that we may inadvertently trigger powerful, negative responses by 'looking too hard'.

- Meet our children's basic nurturing needs, for example through cuddles (where safe), shared stories or TV programmes, snacks. This allows 'shared looking' and simultaneously encourages calming, 'feel good' biochemical messengers, such as endorphins and dopamine, to circulate.

- Suggest physical activities we have previously identified that work for our children to help them burn off over-arousing biochemical messengers, such as cortisol and adrenalin, circulating through their bodies. Nervous energy has to go somewhere, and introducing regular 'burn-off sessions' can begin to 'rewire' trigger-happy systems.

- Say what we see, empathise and gradually use our own bodies and *expressions* to co-regulate our children and alter the emotional climate for the better.

- Initially, match our communications to what we see before moving our children 'up' or 'down' the arousal scale and, once in their 'comfort zone', into their top-storey thinking brain.

- Extend what we have seen to other difficult situations.

Chapter 8

Object Permanence and Object Constancy

We defined object permanence and object constancy in Chapter 1, exploring briefly how inconsistent, neglectful and abusive caregiving compromises the development of these two key concepts. Below we discuss the potential impact of adverse early developmental attachment experiences on our children's current behaviour and suggest some useful reparenting strategies.

Children with poorly developed OP ☁ struggle to keep things safe or to find items, such as shoes, coats and sports kit, once they have been put down. Their unconscious 'thinking' could be expressed as: 'was it ever there?', 'how can I expect to find anything?' or 'anyway it will have gone by now'. They may not think this consciously, or state it out loud; if asked, the majority would probably say they know things and people are still around when they are not in view. Even if they have little trouble finding items that are hidden, or change in shape or form, the cognitive awareness they have begun to develop is often overlaid by 'gut feelings' of emptiness and loss that might be seen, fleetingly, in changes in their breathing, twitching, scratching or fidgeting, burping or slight flushing of their face or neck (van Gulden 2005).

Where objects or people are more significant, we might observe a sudden rush of temper, defiance, dejection or confusion: subtle signs that sensory and emotional areas of the mid-storey brain have been triggered by a sense of absence or loss that our children neither recognise nor understand. So their statements that they know things are there are inconsistent with the implicit, non-verbal, 'body' memories, stored in the amygdala and 'hardwired' to 'reflexive' reactions, below conscious awareness, that directly influence their behaviour.

In addition, the more mature, explicit memory system, involving the mid-storey hippocampus and directly 'wired' to the cognitive and verbal areas of the top-storey 'thinking' brain, may tell them that the object or person is still there. Having had insufficient opportunities to 'wire together' their separate memory circuits into an integrated system during their formative years, hurt children lack a 'joined up' view of the world: their minds and bodies give them contradictory messages 🏠. The clear disparity between children's feelings and responses ('unknown knowns') and their conscious awareness ('known knowns') that people and objects will reappear can be highly confusing and distressing. This is particularly relevant in respect of even a temporary absence of important people (or objects) in the present because it reflects the absence of adequate caregiving from earlier attachment figures. In effect any present emotionally charged feeling of loss can trigger powerful feelings of abandonment and loss from the past.

We can check this out for ourselves using a simple exercise described by Holly van Gulden (YouTube 2012). Holly asks attendees at presentations to place an item of little significance beneath their seats and leave it there for a short time before retrieving it. Participants have no difficulties with this task. However, their response is quite different when they are asked to repeat the process with something that has special meaning for them. Holly describes meeting a good deal of resistance to this request and that when participants place objects on the floor under their chairs they tend to glance down surreptitiously to check their items are still there. Trying this exercise for ourselves and with friends can help us make more sense of the sometimes contradictory feelings and thoughts we experience and more able to imagine the extent of distress generated by the perceived threat of loss in children whose cognitive development remains immature.

Many of us will be familiar with children who become upset if we are just a few minutes late meeting them from school, or coming home after work. Met by anger or sullenness, our initial response might be to ignore them, wonder why they are upset, give rational explanations for why we were delayed or tell them they are over-reacting. With increased awareness of the underlying reasons for our children's difficulties, we can practise responding in ways that are more sensitive to their needs, empathising with their difficulties and apologising for getting it wrong. We might say '*I was thinking about you and wishing I could let you know I was on my way*' and '*I'll do my level best not to be late again*'. We can also help them practise 'getting it' that we are always there for them in spirit by saying '*Remember you're in my heart even when I'm not with you.*'

We can also create a broader range of 'controlled' situations where we encourage both of their memory systems to 'fire' simultaneously and begin to 'wire together' more healthily: for example, talking aloud about our thoughts, feelings and actions when we lose and find items. Sharing our insights with our children in simple, clear language and being prepared for an extended practice period will help them 'get it'. We can create mantras such as '*I know it's here somewhere*' when we cannot find something, speaking aloud in a firm, calm voice. Similarly, if we ask our children, for example, to find their shoes and they are unable to do so we should remind ourselves this may be an OP issue. We might say: '*I think they're probably under your bed. Let's go and look for them together.*' A swift response provides direct brain connections: linking the item, the belief that it still exists, and the action of locating it.

Putting experiences into words helps children recognise and interpret their confusing feelings and behaviours and encourages new 'wiring' connections, particularly in the top-storey, cognitive, areas. 'Good enough' parents of babies and toddlers do this without thinking: using language way before they expect their youngsters to recognise or understand their words. Together they co-create associations between voice patterns, sensations, emotional feelings and actions through the simultaneous 'firing and wiring' of discrete brain areas, including MNSs ◖. Over time this use of language enables children to develop 'symbolic', logical reasoning (top-storey) brain functions, using conscious memories linked to words and events in time and space. In doing so, cause and effect thinking, OP and OC are strengthened, allowing them to reflect on current situations more coherently, and to anticipate outcomes, using knowledge gained from their experiences. Children are able to feel safer, more confident and competent to manage their relationships and their lives comfortably. Reflecting aloud about our thoughts, feelings and actions offers children opportunities to make sense of our thoughts and feelings and hence of their own thoughts, feelings and actions.

By spontaneously instigating 'lost and found' play, such as 'peekaboo', 'where's (teddy) gone?' and 'jack-in-the-box', drawing attention to infants' food 'going in through the tunnel' and pointing to, or rubbing, their tummies to indicate where it has gone ('*Wow, I can see your tummy's full now*') we can consolidate the concept of 'lost and found', even when things are transformed during the process. We can expand this for older children, using more appropriate terms like 'digestion' or 'going to the toilet'. For even school-age children, games such as 'hide and seek' should begin with caregivers hiding just part of themselves, a face, arm or foot, under a blanket and then 'discovering' the 'lost' part with a great flourish. This reflects the toddler stage when children are often seen 'hiding' themselves, behind curtains for example, oblivious to the fact that their head or feet are protruding. At this developmental stage they believe that if they cannot see us, we cannot see them. Parents should play along with this initially, gradually helping their youngsters learn that they do not, in fact, 'disappear' when they are out of sight. Hence, slowly but surely, children given playful learning opportunities can consolidate the 'rules' of OP and begin to generalise the concept to other areas of their lives. Adapting such games for use with older children who are still operating at the toddler stage of object permanence allows us to help them develop their memory systems and lays the foundations for the consolidation of OC ⓒ: the concept that a particular object or person remains the same whatever their appearance.

Over time, these experiences allow children to make sense of changes in more significant items. The gradual generalisation of awareness allows children to know that 'Granny is Granny', whether she is sleeping or singing nursery rhymes, that 'my sweeties' are still 'my sweeties' when Mummy has put them away 'for later', or if Suzy borrows my hairbrush it will be the same when she returns it (hopefully!). They are able to recognise that they, too, are the same whatever they are doing and however they are feeling. So, for example, when they feel upset or 'bad' they can increasingly remember (with prompting!) that they do sometimes feel happy and have even been known to be 'good'. For some children these are totally alien concepts, since they have not previously had caregivers who 'contained' their 'big feelings' or helped them move from one feeling or behavioural state to another or made them feel good about themselves. They may see themselves in one dimension only, or 'forget' what they did at a different time or in a different state of being. Here we need to remind ourselves of these misperceptions and be available to remind our children. We should also try to create numerous opportunities for our children to experience themselves in different ways, especially positive ones! We might record such times, in a special diary, through photos, or on our mobile phones: when they are, say, laughing, cuddling the dog or helping bake bread. Talking to our children about our own mixed feelings can help: reflecting that certain events make us feel both excited and scared, such as horror movies.

Since it takes time for children's thinking to move from 'concrete' to 'symbolic', the more 'evidence' we provide, the more we can stimulate and integrate healthy neural connections, and move them from bottom and mid-storey to top-storey functioning. Moreover, once children develop a strong sense of security and trust in the reliability and predictability of their environment and themselves, they acquire the resilience to 'bounce back' from adversity, such as the temporary loss of a valued person or object. They can 'hold on to' that object 'symbolically', knowing that it continues to exist independently: allowing them to function more independently. They will also 'know', and become able to regulate, their feelings and actions. For children who faced inconsistency, unpredictability and loss of caregivers in their early years, the world seemed very different: instead of security and trust in others there were expectations of threat, loss and chaos. Consequently they still do not 'get' that their ever-evolving world has order and consistency, that things 'stay the same' even when they appear to have changed (van Gulden 2005). Having a family calendar detailing regular appointments and activities prominently displayed and referring to this regularly can help children develop a sense of order and predictability that will encourage a stronger sense of consistency in their lives with us.

Developmental reparenting provides moment-to-moment opportunities for our children to develop the joint concepts of OP and OC that are vital to help them develop the secure, healthy attachment relationships, perceptions and expectations that will enable them to function better and more fully in the world.

Way to go

First 'Check in and check out' (see Appendix 2). Then we can consider activities based on the three basic steps outlined below.

Step 1: objects

Play 'hide it and seek' games little and often and move on to person-hiding games only when we feel our children are 'getting it'. Start by searching together, giving plenty of clues, cues and support. Exaggerate pleasure at finding hidden objects. Reduce the level of support as children practise looking and finding.

VARIATIONS

- Child hides object; we seek (with exaggerated, audible 'wonderings', identification of clues).

- 'Hunt the Sweetie' (finder keeps the trophy!).

- 'Hunt the Sound' (hiding radio/CD player, with familiar tunes, or wind-up timer that ticks loudly and goes off almost immediately).

- 'Hunt the Smell' (concealing cut onion, favourite soap, something you wear regularly (unwashed)). Use odours children already know and like.

- 'Make a Trail' (like Hansel and Gretel) to find the way back – beginning in one room, gradually extending range.

- 'Bran Tub' – hiding several solid objects to be found and identified, *before* they are lifted out.

- 'Jack in the Box' (using toy or playing in person-size box).

- 'Post Box' and posting toys (using containers with transparent sides).

- 'Yo-yo' – symbolic of 'going and always coming back': reinforcing message verbally.

- Push child on swing or roundabout (as above).

- Puppet 'peekaboo' – hiding puppet behind (visibly at first), returning swiftly with gusto! Use unimportant objects at first: it is easier to tolerate absence.

- 'I-mail' – asking your child to draw a picture or write a brief message to self. Place in self-addressed envelope. Then, acting as post-person, leave room, knock and push letter under the door.

- Biting into bananas (apples, biscuits), chewing and swallowing, then patting stomach: 'feeling' the food inside; children doing the same. Asking where the food's gone and, if not squeamish, exploring the outcome!

GOOD BOOKS
Lift-flap books (e.g. *Where's Spot?*; *Elmer and the Lost Teddy*; *I Want My Dummy/Potty*) are useful for this step. (See 'Selection of Good Books for Children'.)

Step 2: people
Once Step 1 is firmly fixed, introduce concealment of body parts – using see-through fabrics initially.

- Starting by hiding parts of self only, gradually hiding increasingly large portions and making it lots of fun. Keeping children close (preferably touching), perhaps asking them to do the covering up. Gradually introducing hidden *parts* of face – eyes are particularly important for young children, so watch for any distress.

- Once whole body can be 'found', moving on to hiding self within room (e.g. behind curtain, toes protruding, rustling, or wearing special perfume); slowly extending 'seeking' range.

- Children struggling with OP cannot wait to be found, so keeping minimum delay between hiding, seeking and finding. As we sense their capacity to stay 'invisible', slowly extending our 'seeking time'.

- Introducing blindfold games: only when certain that children 'get it so far' and can tolerate being unable to see out or see you; standing just out of range and wearing a bell, whistling or chewing mints can help children manage short 'absences'.

- Holding on to the end of a long ribbon whilst hiding can maintain a degree of continuing 'there-ness'.

- Identifying/creating objects that remind children of self when not there (e.g. photographs of you, with them), mounted on key-ring or fridge magnet.

- Making sure children know we carry their photograph with us at all times: involving them in taking the snaps and being very 'obvious' about checking they are still there.

- Providing item (hankie, scarf, dirty socks) smelling of self and encouraging children to keep these 'transitional objects' with them.

GOOD BOOKS

Books which can be helpful here include *Where the Wild Things Are*; *I Want My Mummy*; *My Family*; *Where's Wally?*; *Whose Nose?*; and *Whose Feet?* (See 'Selection of Good Books for Children'.)

Step 3: child (self)

Developmentally this cannot occur until Steps 1 and 2 are soundly established: it may take months before children are ready.

- Beginning by concealing only *parts* of children's bodies (face is more problematic as 'seeing is believing').

- Introducing variations using other senses: 'smelling out' children, listening for breathing or movements, 'feeling' with fingers or toes (not for touch-sensitive children).

- Drawing round children's bodies, colouring in, sticking pieces of fabric or paper (with lots of help) to 'flesh it out'. Talking about each body part and its role/connection to others.

- Encouraging play with tunnels, dens, tents: initially together, then remaining audible/visible/touchable as children 'go it alone', maybe offering one end of long elastic, whilst hanging on to the other end.

- Tin-can whispers – talking to each other through cans joined by string, or using mobile phones with photos.

- Playing with mirrors or shadows, emphasising 'it's still me' (encouraging OC).

GOOD BOOKS

As above, *Where the Wild Things Are* is useful here. We also recommend *My Book About Me*; *The OK Book*; *The Underwear Book*; and *This is My Hair*. (See 'Selection of Good Books for Children'.)

IDEAS FOR OLDER CHILDREN

- Lending children something with no extrinsic value but lots of intrinsic 'us' value.

- Providing laminated photo-key ring, wipe-able message bag label or other age-appropriate 'transitional objects'.

- A printed photograph is especially helpful, keeping copies as replacements of lost or damaged ones.

- Playing with a 'yo-yo': as metaphor for always being in contact even when apart – and always coming back.

- Throwing a frisbee/boomerang.

- Throwing balls into bushes to be searched for and found.

- Customising 'Bear Factory' teddies: pre-recording your message.

- Playing 'Pairs' memory game.

- Playing ongoing 'O and Xs' game (O = hug; X = kiss: to be redeemed by winner).

- Jigsaws can also be left out so family members can pop pieces in as they pass.

- Giving exaggerated reminders, for example 'see you soon' at each separation, however brief; using egg-timer to make time tangible and more bearable.

- Trying never to be late: if unavoidable, acknowledging, empathising with how distressing this feels.

- Leaving short messages (or e.g. chocolate hearts) for children to 'find' when separated – or popping into school bag.

- Using calendar (with family photos) so children can see what's happening, such as shared mealtimes.

- At bedtime, providing 'transitional objects', photos, recorded messages/songs, promising to return after a few minutes and consistently doing so.

- Supplying mobile phone: texting or sending photos to keep in touch.

- Using family photo as screensaver on PCs; tweeting if comfortable with this.

- Providing children with photographs of our workplace; including pictures of ourselves with our children displayed in our workspace.

Chapter 9

Talking, Telling, Timing

The following are typical conversations that might occur in our homes on a daily basis:

Scenario 1

'Why did you hit your brother?'

'I didn't.'

'I saw you do it.'

'Well he hit me first.'

'That's not true. I saw what happened.'

'It's not fair, you always take his side.'

This is frequently followed by children going into a rage and storming out of the room, leaving us feeling angry and bewildered at how such simple interactions escalated into major arguments.

Scenario 2

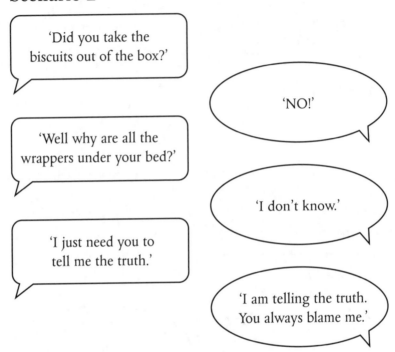

This is often followed by a 'No, I don't'/'Yes, you do' dialogue, leaving us and our children trying to justify our positions and feeling misunderstood and defensive. Moreover we fail to resolve the situation.

Scenario 3

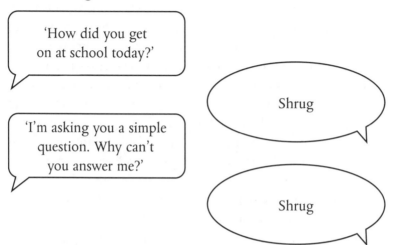

This is followed, again, by us feeling a sense of frustration and failure. This scenario is likely to feel hurtful because we desperately want to be good parents, able to create an environment where our children feel relaxed enough to talk to us and share their experiences and worries. Yet, here we are, with our children refusing to share simple things like their school day, whilst other children seem happy to greet their parents and engage with them avidly. We may also feel that teachers and fellow parents are observing, and perhaps judging, us, knocking our self-confidence still further.

If any of these conversations strike home, we should remind ourselves that we are not alone in experiencing rejection, insolence, tantrums or even violence. Feelings of frustration, anger, disappointment and failure are only too common, and understandable, in our families, experiences that are shared by many parents of hurt children who faced anger, criticism, threats, violence, ridicule or rejection in their birth families. Open discussion and truth may also have been at a premium there. In our first example we may initially have felt annoyed, in the second, mildly frustrated, and in the third, pleased to see our children and interested in their day, then hurt by their rejection.

It is hard to think that such natural feelings might be interpreted by our children as rage, fury or interrogation: yet this is what is likely to underlie their responses. Rather than 'lying', trying to make us angry or dismissing us, our children are letting us know the fear that such apparently mundane interactions generate in them.

Earlier we explored how children's brains, including their MN ◌ systems, develop in light of their early experiences and consequently affect their thinking and feelings in quite different ways from those of children who had 'good enough' parenting experiences. We discussed how it was important to consider which storey of the brain our children are 'coming from' at any moment: taking a bottom-storey 'basement' default position if we are uncertain. We also considered how our children are frequently dysregulated and need our calm, co-regulating presence to manage their feelings. Only then can they move towards their top storey, to access their language and thinking brain and respond more appropriately.

Reflecting on this allows us to appreciate how our communications can be misinterpreted by children whose ability to 'read' facial expressions, emotions and the intention behind words and actions has been compromised by early neglect and abuse. It allows us to understand that they cannot for the moment 'know (or speak) their own minds', consider how we might help our children make sense of what is going on, and improve communications between us. Here the 'trick' is to think as much about *when* to intervene with our children as about *what* to communicate. Reminding ourselves that our children's brains have been 'hardwired' to anticipate hurt, and to use survival-based responses, let us revisit the conversations highlighted above.

In Scenario 1 our children would have anticipated that their actions, if discovered, were likely to lead to negative responses from caregivers. In the past this may have included physical or verbal abuse or rejection, as parents over-reacted to their children's actions. An awareness of these influential, early experiences is crucial, so that we recognise that small triggers from us mirroring the parental response they have come to expect can catapult children into a state of fear and confusion. We can then begin to make sense of the denial that is often children's first response, since accepting responsibility for their actions has potentially terrifying consequences. In effect we are trying to engage with our children at a cortical level (the study) when they are stuck somewhere between brainstem (basement) and mid-storey (ground floor) 'survival mode' . Their only recourse may be to shout 'louder and longer' in a distorted attempt to be heard and understood.

Often children repeat patterns of behaviour common to their families of origin: where parents denied the reality of their behaviour, even when confronted with the 'truth'. In these situations our children learned that threatening interactions were part and parcel of family life and were frequently accompanied by angry denials. Such patterns of interaction become 'hardwired' into our children's body–mind–brain systems, meaning they repeat them in current situations that mirror, even to a minor degree, their early experiences. In effect, our children learn that denial is an appropriate response to difficult situations and their MN circuits are organised in the expectation that owning their actions can lead to serious, negative responses from caregivers. Therefore they often misread our intentions, unconsciously interpreting our mild annoyance, frustration or questions as malevolent: responding from fear-based states and unable to access the 'mindfulness' needed to 'read' the situation and use 'top down', cognitive, controls.

We should also consider the emotional impact of suggesting our children take responsibility for their actions, bearing in mind that they are frequently 'catapulted' into shame-based responses that reinforce their negative self-worth. They will have received potent messages in their birth families that they were responsible for being neglected, abused or abandoned: for example, hearing parents say 'look what you made me do' as a rationale for their abuse. So not only did our children have to cope with the constant fear of being abused, they also had to accept responsibility for adult behaviour they could neither impact nor change. Faced with this dilemma, children internalise beliefs that they are intrinsically helpless, bad and worthless: feelings that are the precursors of shame-based responses ⊡⟨. They did not receive the 'shame socialisation' that occurs in toddlerhood within 'good enough' families, which allows them to experience, and learn to manage, tolerable levels of guilt. Without this essential practice in self-agency, they cannot begin to accept responsibility for their actions when challenged. Instead they continue to respond with anger or defiance (Schore 1994) or 'freeze' under the burden of perceived shame.

Food issues, common in children who suffered neglect, may also be important aspects in our second dialogue. Having received inadequate or unpredictable supplies of food in their early years, and often learning to fend for themselves, they are unused to having their needs met by others. Children's ongoing fear of 'never having enough' can lead to them 'taking matters into their own hands'. Issues of OC ⟨○ are also relevant. Since our children have weak 'inter-state' connections, at that moment their right hand may truly not know what their left hand has been doing. They may be unable to recognise that the biscuits they took from the tin an hour ago have any connection with the biscuit crumbs or wrappers that adorn their bed now. Taken literally, our children may not be lying when they deny eating the biscuits, since 'then' they were not in the same state of being as they are 'now'. Combined with desperate attempts to avoid experiencing shame ('I don't want it to be me, that would be too painful, therefore it wasn't me'), this is a potent combination that can end in full-scale denial or patent fabrication, as children struggle to come up with stories that seem reasonable to them.

The third situation may appear quite different from the previous two until we consider what our children may be feeling on coming out of school. They have spent a day without us, facing a stressful environment where they may have become dysregulated, or tried valiantly to 'behave'. As we have seen, our children frequently struggle with OP and consequently feel that 'out of sight' means 'out of mind'. It can be hard for them to have any real sense of connection with us when we are absent; they may also, unconsciously, blame us for 'abandoning' them. Children who have had multiple caregivers may have little expectation that the adult who took them to school will be the same one who greets them at the end of the day. Moreover the mummy who took them to school (waving goodbye) may not feel like the mummy waiting for them at the school gate, smiling and with open arms, or wearing a different coat. It may also be hard for them to make the state change from school pupil to family member (OC). With all these muddles whirling around inside, it is not surprising that responding to seemingly simple questions may be too hard to handle.

Perhaps most importantly we need to remember that, although it has non-verbal aspects such as tone of voice and rhythm, which are 'read' at limbic ('ground') and brainstem ('basement') levels, spoken language is a largely cortical, thinking activity. It is therefore most effective when both we and our children are 'in the study' of our semi-detached brain. If we or they are 'elsewhere', non-verbal means of communication are likely to have greater impact: in such situations it is the tone and rhythm of our voice (prosody) and our body language that children will tune into. We may be using 'empathy' words yet conveying, through prosody, looks or body stance, our frustration, anger, blame or even disgust: our children then get 'stuck in the lift' somewhere between the 'basement' and 'study'⌂.

The implications for therapeutic parenting are profound. Starting from the twin premises that children's behaviour is the only 'language' at their disposal and that their behavioural language makes sense in light of their histories, we should be mindful of the reality of our children's experiences and the enduring effects this has on them. We must understand not only what was done to our children but also what it did to them, not as a simple, one-off exercise but as essential data that allow us to reflect on the meaning underlying our children's responses during our everyday interactions with them.

We have considered how our children's ability to regulate their bodies and emotions has been impacted by their early experiences and how they continue to need our calming presence to become, and to remain, calm. Hence we need to examine our own feelings alongside those of our children and ask ourselves whether we are engaging with our children in calm, regulated ways. Similarly we need to recognise when our expectations of the outcome of such discussions are likely to be affected by previous difficult interactions. In Scenario 1, knowing that we are dealing with an incident of negative sibling interactions, our own MN circuits may be 'gearing up' to face our children's over-reactions, putting us 'on edge' and ready to 'fight', 'flee' or 'freeze'. It is important to 'know' our own inner feelings and likely reactions when considering ways to interact effectively with our children.

Now let us explore the impact our own histories can have on our current interactions with our children. As children we may have been told that, if we were 'naughty', 'telling lies' compounded the issue, leaving us with a clear message that 'telling lies' was an absolute 'no-no'. However, if we were raised by parents who, by and large, met our needs, our experiences were very different from those of our children. Repeatedly being lied to, and hearing parental dissimulation about events, means they learned that telling lies was the 'norm'. They have often 'learned' that this was a way to protect themselves from further abuse. Their relation to truth-telling may therefore be quite different from ours. Exhortations to 'tell the truth' may both be asking the impossible and counter-productive for our children. They may be in such fear-based states that they cannot know how to respond, respond defensively or try to create stories they think might 'fit'. Whilst 'after the event' reconstruction is an accepted part of 'normal' memory, for children with developmental gaps that weaken cause and effect thinking, combined with fear-based high arousal and loose memory connections, this may indeed be their 'best guess'. So we need to recognise that 'truth-telling' should be our goal in helping our children heal, rather than our starting point.

Furthermore, children who were forced to deny their lived experiences of mistreatment are likely to have body feelings (non-verbal memories) that are at odds with their 'remembered' verbal memories. Their feelings of pain, hurt and rejection were frequently denied by caregivers who minimised their own behaviour using statements like 'it wasn't that bad' or 'it was an accident'. This leads to children having difficulty connecting actions and words, since the data are held in separate 'storage systems', resulting in their current struggles to make connections between what they did (then) and what they are feeling and saying (now). Again they are not consciously lying; their bodies and thinking abilities are 'out of synch' and they are 'best-guessing' as to what actually happened.

Holding all these issues in mind allows us to consider ways in which we can communicate with our children productively. In doing so, we need to consider the timing of our verbal interactions to reduce children's fear-based responses. Since talking involves predominantly cortical, left brain ('study') activity, we must practise ways of lowering children's arousal (right brain, 'basement' and mid-storey) to allow them to move up into their 'studies' where they can 'hear' us – and time our discussions accordingly.

For our children to engage with, and hear, us they must be able to:

- recognise and use us as a secure base

- accept our help to co-regulate and avoid being overwhelmed by sensori-emotional input

- learn to manage fear and shame-based responses

- 'read' our facial expressions and body language and grasp our true intentions through functional MN circuits

- 'hear' and make sense of what we have to say

- access their left, top-storey 'thinking' brain ('study')

- know, accept and make sense of their past histories

- get in touch with and accept all of themselves, including their innermost 'fear-based' child (OC).

To facilitate this we must be able to:

- be calm and regulated, so that we can provide co-regulation
- stay alert and emotionally available to help children recognise and deal with their emotions
- show we are predictable and that our children can trust us
- create quiet, confidential times to talk
- choose our words carefully and match these to our tone and body language
- remain aware of our children's histories and trigger points
- share, in simple terms, what we know about 'then' and how this impinges on our children 'now'
- understand that 'lies' may be children's way of keeping themselves safe or their 'best guess'
- help our children work out 'what really happened' – our 'best guess' is often pretty close
- show we accept our children for all of themselves and remain non-judgemental
- explore and practise ways of 'doing things differently'
- keep it short and sweet.

Translating this into practice and revisiting Scenario 1 concerning sibling rivalry, our dialogue might go something like this:

'I know it's hard for you when you hit your brother and I ask you what happened.'

(increasing our children's ability to engage cortically)

'I wonder if you're forgetting that I won't hit you.'

(reducing mirror neuron firing)

'I guess talking about it makes you feel really bad about yourself.'

(recognising shame-based feelings)

'I can understand that.'

(giving the message we understand why they struggle, in light of their history)

'I want to help you with all these big feelings.'

(showing empathy)

'When we've done that maybe we can think about how you can make things up to your brother.'

(recognising that there are consequences for behaviour and showing we are ready to help them manage these)

Then, later on, when both we and our children are calm:

> *'I know you want to get on with your brother. My guess is your birth family didn't help you manage this. Guess what? This is something I can help you with. You're such a great kid, I'm sure we can work this out together. You might need some practice to get it right, so I'll keep an eye on how you get on with your brother while you're practising.'*

(giving the message that we can help
and that change is possible)

We should, of course, have thought through the strategies we offer our children in advance, taking time to do so between the incident and our conversation and perhaps contacting a supportive friend or mentor for advice.

We could formulate a similar conversation regarding the biscuit-taking (Scenario 2). This may seem a less pressing issue than sibling aggression, so we might take more time planning and creating time to talk when we are feeling well regulated:

> *'I need to talk to you about the biscuits that are going walk-about. I know how hard this'll be for you.'*

(increasing our children's
ability to engage cortically)

> *'How about if I gave you a cuddle to let you know I love you and it's just your behaviour we need to sort out.'*

(reducing fear and shame-
based feelings, showing
empathy, reducing MN firing)

'I know it's hard for you and I really understand. I know you didn't get enough food when you were living with your birth mother. You must have felt so hungry at times and I guess you still get these feelings sometimes, even though there's always enough food in this house.'

'But it wasn't me.'

(giving the message we understand why they struggle in light of their history, demonstrating empathy, reinforcing OP and OC and reducing MN firing)

'I really want to help you with this and wonder if [the strategy we devised in advance] might help?'

'Why don't we practise now? We can check in each day and see how you're feeling. I know it's going to take time for you to feel safe with us and I guess you'll go on letting me know when you don't by eating the biscuits. When that happens I'll give you cuddles to let you know you're safe and that you'll always have enough.'

(showing empathy, consolidating OSC and giving messages that we can help our children manage their feelings and begin to feel safe and secure)

Scenario 3 lends itself to even greater possibilities for prior preparation. It is helpful to work out practice scenarios for ourselves, based on our understanding of ourselves, our children's histories and our current difficulties. Perhaps we could begin by working out a bubble scenario in relation to Scenario 3.

'Hi there. I really missed you today and was sooo looking forward to home time.'

'Hi there. Can I have a cuddle to let you know how much I missed you?'

'Now what was that snack we prepared for after school time? Yes! It was…'

On a broader front, our sample conversations raise a number of key issues:

1. Children's behaviour on the outside signals what they are feeling inside. They tend to show predictable responses to familiar situations, helping us recognise the situations with which they will most struggle. This allows us to prepare our children, in anticipation of potentially difficult situations.

2. Talking to our children in advance enables us to help them 'feel felt and understood'. Simultaneously we begin to help them 'read' situations differently. When they are able to reflect on and recognise our true intentions, we reduce the firing of their trauma-based MN circuits. Over time this alters our children's 'firing and wiring' pattern, allowing them to respond in ways that reflect the safe and loving environment we are striving to provide.

3. Being open about children's history allows them to process their experiences and make sense of their past. Over time this reduces their trauma triggers, helping them feel safer and more secure at home and making it easier for them to build secure attachments. In demonstrating empathy for their struggles we communicate to our children that we are 'there for them', that they are no longer alone and can trust us to help them. By promoting their healthy dependence on us we move them towards healthy independence.

4. Providing opportunities to discuss and practise alternative ways of responding means that our children need not remain 'stuck' in re-enactments of their early history. It provides a forum in which they can feel good about themselves, gradually reducing their shame-based reactions and conveying messages that, with our support, they can make better choices. In doing so we are building the foundations upon which our children can develop into self-confident adults, able to feel good about themselves and sustain lasting relationships, strengthening their wellbeing and resilience. It may also help us feel better about ourselves as parents.

5. Last but not least, we need to remain on our guard against asking the 'why' question: reminding ourselves that, if our children knew 'why', they would not be doing what they do. Rather than asking children 'why' questions we need to provide 'why' answers, saying for example:

   - '*I wonder why that happened/you did that/said that?*' Then without pausing for an answer, '*I wonder if it's because you were scared/hungry/muddled/angry?*'

   - '*My guess is that you're telling me that because you can't quite remember what happened and you're scared you'll get into trouble/we won't love you/we'll hurt you/we'll send you away?*'

- *'Lots of children who were treated badly when they were little feel they can't trust grown-ups to be fair or listen to them. They've had to learn to "forget" what happened and then make stuff up. I think that's why it's hard for you to handle this.'*

- *'D'you know what? I think you so much don't want it to be you who hit your brother/ate the biscuits, 'cos it makes you feel bad, that you can't say it was you. Don't worry, I can usually work out what's going on and help you work it out too.'*

Chapter 10

Loose Connections

In their early days, babies experience the world as an ever-changing sequence of discrete events and themselves as a series of disjointed sensory states over which they have little control. They are vulnerable to unpredictable, external and internal, state changes and totally reliant on their caregivers to regulate their physical and emotional environment and help them move from one feeling and behavioural state of being to another. As we discuss throughout our book, feedback from significant caregivers allows infants to make sense of what they see, hear, touch, smell, taste and feel, from sensory information coming from the outside world and from within their bodies. It is only gradually through ongoing co-regulation and two-way communication that they begin to recognise that objects and people still exist when they are not immediately apparent (OP) 🐛.

From this, young children subsequently infer that they too continue to be, irrespective of whether or not they feel observed directly – object self-permanence (OSP). Not until the concept of OP and OSP become established can youngsters learn about the changing states of objects or people, using their maturing mirror neuron systems (MNSs). Through repeated consistent experiences, they come to realise that, for example, teddy is still teddy whether clothed or undressed, wrapped in a blanket or thrown on the floor (OC) (○. Subsequently, they recognise that people stay the same, whatever their appearance or mood, and begin to extend this awareness to their own states of being – object self-constancy (OSC). Each state of being is characterised by a particular constellation of sensations, emotions, memories, beliefs, behaviours and thoughts that are 'wired together'. The 'firing' of one element is likely to lead to the immediate firing of the entire neurobiological circuit that underpins that specific state of being.

Thinking back to infants' perceptions of experiences and themselves as discrete 'chunks', and how these become connected over time through consistent feedback from attachment figures, it is hardly surprising that the degree of 'being joined up' is frequently much less in our children. Without a sound concept of OSC (○ how can we expect them to seem 'together', react consistently, move appropriately from one state of being to another, remember accurately, or know their own minds? Our children's body–brain–mind systems lack regulation, organisation and integration: as a consequence they live poorly regulated, disorganised and poorly integrated lives. So, when our children's mood swings seem unfathomable or scary, we should remind ourselves that, like babies, they are unable *at that moment* to make smooth transitions between different states of being and that they are feeling far more scared or confused than we are.

Difficulties in making smooth state transitions is particularly likely when children are already in high arousal, since during extreme feelings they remain 'stuck' in their bottom or mid-storey brains and have extremely limited access to 'top-down control' ▦. Over time, many 'learn' to escape these powerful feeling states through dissociative strategies, such as cranking their feelings up further and then 'exploding', perhaps through provoking arguments, destroying furniture or possessions, physical aggression, or self-harm. This is likely to involve the triggering of 'feel good' neurochemical messengers, such as endorphins. Consequently they are able to 'come down' into a more comfortable state and begin to reconnect with us. Conversely we may find ourselves continuing to feel wound up, as if we are 'holding' all the emotion our children have 'left behind' and sometimes they are 'choosing' the timing of their outbursts to upset us and gain control. Luckily, as 'good enough' adults we can develop 'top down' strategies to re-regulate ourselves and remind ourselves of the 'scared baby/child inside' behind these survival responses. Subsequently we can make ourselves available to help them move towards more regulated, comfortable states of being without them becoming overwhelmed and 'out of it'.

Other children take a more classic dissociative route: immediately 'shutting down' or 'zoning out', withdrawing from us physically or emotionally, and often appearing comfortable in 'their own little world'. In reality they feel as isolated, scared and helpless as their 'acting out' counterparts. In physiologically 'shutdown' states, where their awareness and energy resources are unavailable, they cannot re-regulate or reconnect with us. The feelings of frustration, helplessness or rejection we ourselves experience here are a valuable indicator of the distress our children are experiencing simultaneously. Unlike them, however, as 'good enough' adults we can re-regulate, reconnect to our 'thinking' brains and use our understanding and empathy to 'get alongside' our children and reduce their fear, isolation and hopelessness. Reconnecting and drawing on our energy, they can be re-energised, change states and 'come back' into the world. If physical closeness (especially good for releasing the 'feel good' neurochemical oxytocin) is impossible, we can use our body language and tone of voice to reduce the painful 'distance' between us.

For our children, these polarised responses often become their norm. The loss or transience of their caregivers, the inconsistency, unreliability and emotional volatility of care and the over- or under-stimulation to which they were exposed created a chaotic and potentially overwhelming environment. There were limited opportunities for our children to gain a sense of order, permanence and constancy on which to build their perceptions and expectations of themselves and others. If significant people, homes and possessions disappeared or changed inexplicably in the past, seemingly at the drop of a hat, how can they trust that people and things will not do so now? If their own feelings, behaviours and thinking were not 'joined up' how can they become coherent, connected, confident individuals able to recognise, make sense of, trust and build sound connections with others?

Where infants and young children face such adversity, their state-dependent 'wiring circuits' remain to a greater or lesser extent in 'closed loops', disconnected from each other. Moreover, within any 'closed circuit' state of being, further 'disconnections' can occur. The acronym SEAM is useful to make sense of these intra-state 'loose connections': theoretically and in practical terms for us as therapeutic parents. SEAM refers to the Sensations, Emotions, Actions and Mindfulness that comprise any given state of being. Where these elements are well-enough connected, children can feel and act in 'joined up' ways suited to the conditions of that moment. They can integrate and interpret their own body feelings, emotions and behaviour thoughtfully and reflectively, drawing on past experience, in particular memories that are recalled linguistically, logically and consciously. They are able to be mindful of, to sense, empathise with, respond to and reflect on the actions, and their perceptions, of other people.

However, children functioning predominantly out of their bottom and mid-storey brains are frequently disconnected from their top-storey (mindful) brain. Their memories tend to be strongly emotionally weighted, and retrieved through sensori-emotional, 'body' memories and 'unconscious' behavioural responses. Removing (dissociating) Mindfulness from the SEAM acronym leaves us, perhaps appropriately, with SEA (Sensations, Emotions, Actions), since our children often appear 'all at sea': directionless and floundering. They need us, as therapeutic parents, to bring them 'home and dry', 'stitch their SEAMs together' and 'join them up'.

Exploring 'loose connections' more closely in terms of dissociation and applying SEAM, we can recognise the potential for dissociative disconnections between individual elements within a single state of being at any given moment. For example, weak associations ('loose connections') within a state might involve dissociation of sensory information both from outside and within the body. Our children may respond confusingly to pain and discomfort: seemingly oblivious, for example, of accidental injuries or stomach upsets. Some also seem unable to discriminate between major and minor hurts, or to know when they are hungry or satiated. We can link these 'dis-associations' to children's early experiences of neglect or abuse. Perhaps they experienced unrelieved hunger or inconsistent nurturing and did not 'wire up' the links between discomfort and effective relief, or were shaken or hit by caregivers who then minimised or denied their actions and their children's feelings. Exposure to chronic or repeated pain is barely tolerable at any age; in infants and young children it is unbearable. The body responds by releasing pain-relieving neurochemicals (endorphins) that diminish or numb the pain. Over time this survival response can become habitual, meaning that hurts experienced now may be 'shut off' or dissociated from awareness, at least temporarily.

Applying the concept of dissociation, both inter-state and intra-state (SEAM), helps us make sense of many situations we experience with our children, such as their tendency to forget, 'lose' or 'take' things, find 'telling the truth' difficult, ignore pain or take risks. For example, if children are in a different behavioural or feeling state from their state of being when they put an item down, or their conscious memory system remains immature, they will struggle to locate items, especially under pressure. This increases feelings of distress and shame and further weakens inter-state recall and intra-state, mindful, connections. Consequently their actions can appear incoherent, 'lazy' or 'controlling' and generate negative responses in us, such as anger, rejection, powerlessness or attempts to 'control' them at all costs. These responses confirm our children's perceptions and expectations of us as unsafe and deny them opportunities to re-regulate, reconnect and rewire their MN ♀ circuits.

Other children may appear to have learned a particular skill, only to act as if they do not know what to do at other times, either because they are in a separate state of being or lack good access to their mindful (thinking and reflecting) brain. This is often perceived as 'won't do', leading to critical remarks or irritation from others and to children failing to learn from their experiences. Recognising these as 'can't do' situations, we can use our insight, empathy and gentle support to encourage the strengthening of 'loose connections' and promote feelings of confidence and competence in our children. Although aggressive, oppositional-defiant, lying and stealing and 'shut-down' behaviours are best understood as part of our 'joined up' understanding of developmental 'loose connections', we should also hold in mind the powerful feelings they frequently provoke in us and our communities, together with the longer-term consequences for our children's acceptance and wellbeing in society at large. It is therefore vital that we consider these further. In Chapter 11, 'The Child Within the Child', we discuss some of these 'acting out' and 'acting in' dynamics; we explore the issue of 'stealing and lying' separately in Chapter 12, 'Taking, Borrowing and Difficulties with the Truth'.

Summary

We have explored the effect of attachment-trauma on children's capacity to move 'seamlessly' from state to state according to the situation at any given time and to demonstrate the ongoing effects of weaknesses in awareness of, and access to, all 'parts' of themselves on their perceptions and behaviour. We considered how early experiences influence the degree to which integration takes place and how many of our children lacked sufficient opportunities to become 'joined up'. As a consequence they develop neurobiological 'short circuits' biased towards 'bottom up' responses, rather than 'top down', mindful consideration. Many do not develop the capacity for smooth state-to-state changes according to circumstance and 'swing' abruptly from one feeling and behavioural state to another. Moreover, within any given state of being, children may not have full access to all parts of that state. For example, children may 'know' their painful early history and recount this as if they have no feelings about it, yet tell us in their body movements or behaviour that they are distressed. As for so many of our children's developmental-attachment difficulties, with our help and suitable therapeutic 'knitting patterns', we can 'join them up' into healthier, more complete human beings. In turn, this helps them feel more connected to their physical, socio-emotional and cognitive world and hence to us, their communities and the world they inhabit.

Below we explore the basic principles through which we can begin to unravel their muddles, identify functional 'gaps' and design new and better patterns from which we can 'knit our kids'.

Check in and check out
Stage 1: checking ourselves out

- Check out how we feel physically, emotionally, cognitively at any given time and how we behave as a consequence. Although we may recognise some 'loose connections' in our make-up that make us the only-too-human beings we are, on the whole we are probably 'joined up' enough to do well in most situations.

- Identify whether, at that moment, we are functioning primarily from our bottom, middle or top-storey brain.

- Sense whether we are breathing too quickly, feeling too hot or cold, hungry or thirsty or 'wobbly'.

- Explore our feelings, observing whether we are upset, angry, powerless or scared and being consciously aware of our thoughts and interpretations of people and circumstances.

Stage 2: practising by ourselves

- Use 'top down' awareness to notice and, where necessary, regulate our inter-state 'switches'.

- Encourage 'inter-state self-talk' between separate parts of ourselves. If they seem at odds with each other: remember that commonplace sayings like 'pull yourself together' tell us how 'normal' these minor disjunctions are.

- Check out our memories to illustrate this concept: for example, do we 'forget' what we went upstairs for, only to remember again when we return to the place we started from?

- Recognise any intra-state (SEAM) disconnections we experience, like suddenly realising we are cold and stiff only when we put down an enthralling book. We can then make better sense of our children's seemingly unfathomable responses, or lack of response.

- Explore these ideas when we feel relaxed, so that when stressed we can be mindful of them and respond appropriately.

Stage 3: checking out our children

- Observe how our children 'make' us feel, physically and emotionally, think and react, when we 'tune in' to them.

- Check ourselves out again, in case we need to re-regulate and reconnect ourselves once more.

- Use the information we gain from 'tuning into' them to work out where our children's 'loose connections' lie.

- Remind ourselves of our children's early histories to gain insights into their disconnections and resultant behaviours.

- Integrate this awareness to identify where they most need our help.

- Find healthy ways of connecting with our children and 'retuning' them to our better-regulated neurobiological systems, to help them become more organised and connected internally.

- Remind ourselves that we are the experts on our children and are best placed to create the best 'knitting patterns' for them.

- Be aware of potentially difficult situations and be prepared to deal with them. Having a well-rehearsed plan can sometimes be enough to reduce the likelihood of difficulties arising.

Stage 4: practising with our children

We need to stay consciously aware of our own moment-to-moment interactions. Simple actions like mentioning our state-to-state transitions and 'talking to ourselves' out loud can help children identify these inter-connections and normalise them. In addition here are some simple things we can do on a frequent and consistent basis:

- 'Notice' our children's behaviour as a matter of course and comment on what we see, being careful to avoid sounding critical or as if we are making fun of them.

- 'Notice' our own changing states, feelings and behaviours and verbalise these aloud, to begin to lay down 'connections' for our children.

- Play games that strengthen OP and OC. Building up these linked concepts helps children 'get' that things and people are always consistent whatever the situation. Not only is this highly reassuring, it also allows them to learn that they, too, are one and the same.

- Model 'parts talk'. We might debate with ourselves, aloud, what food to prepare for dinner: *'I'd like fish pie'; 'Well, that's hard work and I haven't got time'; 'But it's good for us'; 'I know, but it'll have to be pasta again'; 'You're just being lazy!'; 'No I'm not, I'm being realistic.'* We may find that we have already been doing this silently and quite unconsciously.

- Demonstrate, in exaggerated ways, our own responses and how we deal with them appropriately. If we lose something we might shake our head in disbelief or confusion, saying aloud '*I feel so stupid not being able to remember*', followed by '*Let's see, I know I had it somewhere. Hmmm, where was I when I put it down?*' or '*I know, I'll walk backwards through my mind until I remember*' (like Big Bird in *Sesame Street*).

- Affirming volubly that the item will be there demonstrates how we can change our feelings and displays confidence that we *will* locate the item. This can become the 'cement' that begins to bind children's developmental building blocks together.

- Point out when, for example, the car has stalled, or it has rained on our washing, that we are angry yet can still maintain 'top down' control. We might 'ham this up', saying something like: '*Wow, my angry part was really loud there, I'd better find my calm and sensible parts. Getting angry won't sort this out.*'

- Remind ourselves that 'safe' actions, such as dancing around, jumping up and down, or shouting loudly, burn off the neurochemicals of over-arousal (e.g. adrenalin) and 'get us back in balance'. That goes for our children too!

- Play games using puppets or stuffed toys. Take it in turns to act out scenes involving a particular emotion, talking about how it feels and how we might move to another feeling. This allows children to explore strong feelings at a safe distance and for us to 'slip in some practice' in playful ways: always the best way to learn!

- Help our children identify pain if they seem 'not to feel' it. We might say 'Ow' for them, followed by 'That must have hurt, let me rub it better/put a plaster on it.' We are not creating hypochondriacs; rather we are joining up sensations that have been disociated. After a period of, perhaps intense, 'nursing' responses, connections will be made between hurts and receiving comfort from us: laying down new procedural memories (involving MN circuits) and establishing new response patterns for our children.

- Seize 'minor opportunities', such as our children's tearfulness at breaking a favourite toy or bumping their knee, to name aloud their sad, or upset, parts and provide comfort to 'help us find your happy, or comfy, parts again'.

- Validating 'where they are coming from' first is vital before children can feel comforted and reassured enough to engage with us. Until they 'feel felt and understood' they cannot make changes in, and join up, the way they feel, act and make sense of themselves.

Stage 5: dealing with difficult situations

- Take time to assess the situation and how best to approach it.

- Consider our other children and whether they are likely to become upset and need our help to deal with what is going on.

- 'Think toddler' – working out at what age our children are functioning at that moment, spotting the 'loose connections' and handling them as we would a child of that age. If in doubt, go 'lower and slower'.

- Speak calmly and gently and show acceptance of our children for all of who and what they are *at that moment*, staying aware that they are highly sensitive to perceived threat or shame, or associations or memories that caused them to dissociate initially. Remain vigilant, to avoid inadvertently triggering further powerful, negative responses.

- Say what we see, empathising and using 'parts talk' to begin to re-regulate and reconnect our children. Even rage-filled children can be encouraged to 'find' their 'quieter' or 'calmer' parts if we work with sufficient confidence. Faced with opposition, or denial that such parts exist, we can say with assurance: '*I know they're in there, because I've seen them. Let's find them together.*'

- Match our communications to what we see before moving our children 'up' or 'down' the arousal scale using 'parts talk'. Once in their 'comfort zone', they can start to join up separate states and begin to engage their top-storey thinking brain.

- Find ways of reconnecting with 'zoned out', 'switched off' children. Providing simple, loving, accepting, verbal messages to accompany similar non-verbal messages through our eyes, facial expressions, body language and touch puts them 'back in touch' with us and with themselves.

- Extend what we have learned to other difficult situations.

Chapter 11

The Child Within the Child

We are probably familiar with the idea of 'getting in touch with our inner child': looking at the childlike qualities that become overlaid over time as we develop into adults. Alongside the concept of 'loose connections', or separate states, this will help us consider 'the child within the child'. Thinking about how each of us has several 'parts' (Archer 1999b) and how this has filtered into everyday speech ('I was in two minds', 'I was beside myself', 'He was in a state', 'Pull yourself together'), we have discussed how children who faced early adversity, such as abandonment, neglect and abuse, have insufficient opportunities to become 'joined up' and practise moving comfortably from state to state. We now explore these concepts in greater detail in respect of 'angry', 'oppositional' and 'too good' children. Whilst we focus on children at the 'far end' of the 'loose connections' spectrum, most of our children struggle to some degree with these issues, and hence every parent and child will benefit from understanding the underlying issues and implementing the basic principles of developmental reparenting outlined here.

It is easier to accept fear as the underlying feeling in children presenting as vulnerable and anxious than in 'bad' (angry, aggressive, destructive, oppositional) youngsters, even more so in 'good' (too-good, caretaking, compliant) ones. Yet all these children are equally fearful deep down: their behaviours are adaptive, 'trauma-normal' responses to early adversity, usually intra-familial maltreatment. As in every situation, we should consider children's actions in light of their lived experiences, to make sense of 'now' in terms of 'then'. Our children were raised in chaotic environments where caregivers behaved in 'out of control' ways and provided insufficient opportunities for them to feel safe, have their needs met, recognise and manage their feelings, feel 'in control', make internal and external connections, and form healthy relationships. Children left feeling isolated, needy, scared and helpless carry with them the perceptions, expectations and beliefs of the 'scared and hurting child within' when they come home to us. Their 'scared, hurting child' part may be clearly visible to us or remain for the most part concealed under protective layers of 'bad' or 'good', or volatile moods and behaviours. Like Matrioshka dolls (painted wooden dolls that 'nest' inside each other), there may be layers of separate states (parts) overlaying each other that become 'available' to our children only in specific circumstances, such as when we ask them to do something, rather than readily through conscious choice.

'Acting out', angry and oppositional children characteristically show us their 'controlling', aggressive, hurtful, awkward, stubborn or rejecting parts, driven by the 'fight' survival response. Their overt, angry or destructive behaviours evolved, unconsciously, to provide a sense of control over their terrifying, unpredictable lives: often mimicking the hurtful, powerful figures in their early lives. The predominant survival response of other children is 'flight': we might see active 'running away', or a tendency to keep to themselves and avoid interactions with us, perhaps through excessive TV watching or computer playing, 'sulking', sullenness or self-harm. They, too, are driven by fear, the need to gain a sense of control over the frightening, incomprehensible world they perceive and are desperately trying to get their needs met, unsure that we can be there for them.

These 'bad' parts help children manage their fear of rejection by making the 'inevitable' happen 'their way', by acting as 'bad' as they feel, or by rejecting us first. For both 'fight' and 'flight' groups their 'bad' parts predominate in their relationships with us although they may present their more pleasant or vulnerable sides to extended family members, friends, teachers or social workers. At times we, too, can glimpse our children's 'better sides': invaluable in helping us recall that 'every child has a silver lining' and encouraging us to find their 'hidden parts within' during challenging times. We must remind ourselves that 'acting out' children should not be blamed for their 'anti-social' behaviour and need to feel accepted for all of themselves, yet we ignore their emotionally driven behavioural language at our peril.

'Acting in', good children tend to ignore or over-ride their own needs and feelings, attempting to control their environment by being 'good' (for example, smiling, being helpful, endeavouring to be obedient, or giving into siblings and peers). We may only occasionally see the 'scared, hurting child within' or recognise their overwhelming feelings of fear and helplessness and how unlovable they feel. Understandably we feel delighted that we have such 'lovely' children and are likely to praise them directly and sing their praises to others. On the other hand, when they do 'slip out of character', becoming angry or 'difficult', we may show we are disappointed in them, or shocked at their behaviour. Responding in these ways reinforces our children's world view that they are only acceptable when they are 'good', yet their deepest, unspoken fear is that if we only knew what they were really like we would reject them. Indeed our caregiving and praise are likely to make them more fearful of eventual hurts and losses, since to them it is so patently 'false'. 'Good' children's occasional lapses in 'self-control' reinforce this perspective: since it is the 'scared, hurting and "bad" child within the child' that is actually in control.

At times both 'acting out' and 'acting in' children may also show the 'freeze' behaviours they evolved to stay safe when they experienced terror, abandonment, helplessness and hopelessness. Some children 'go quiet', repeat actions over and over, twirl around, doodle obsessively, stare into space, or hurt themselves seemingly without feeling pain; others may 'go off on one' or 'trash their rooms'. The behavioural messages are the same: they need help to 'reconnect' from their dissociative states and 'find themselves again'. Tempting as it is to 'leave them to get over it', we need to take the initiative and find ways of getting in touch with our children, if not physically then emotionally and verbally. If we imagine them in a 'sensori-emotional bubble', our aim is to join them in their 'bubble state' rather than waiting for it to deflate over time, or trying to puncture it. Remaining mindful of the 'scared, hurting child within' and demonstrating through our non-verbal and verbalised behaviour that we are 'with them' (and they with us/held in mind), we begin to rewire both their MN circuits and their 'loose connections'. Our attempts to get in touch with, and accept, 'all of them' allow our children to be aware of, and gain top-down control over, all of themselves 'good', 'bad' and 'indifferent', reinforcing OSC ⊂○.

Managing the 'bad' aggressive child

It is never too early to begin helping our children develop healthier ways of relating to themselves and to us. Toddlers who hit us or their siblings need just as clear messages that this is unacceptable as older children. Too often we find ways of managing our children's behaviour, particularly when young, by dismissing it as a 'phase', or 'ignoring the negatives' and 'accentuating the positives'. We may speak of children 'having a wobbly', or 'losing it' when they punch, kick or threaten us, trying to reduce the fear we would feel if we 'saw' their behaviour for what it is, or could become, and the impact it would have on the sense of wellbeing within our family homes. As our children, and the actual threat, grow we may feel ashamed of our vulnerability and helplessness to control them. Recognising early on that by 'doing nothing' we allow our children to practise being violent and abusive and to become more 'stuck' in destructive states of being leaves us better placed to help them develop healthier ways of knowing, and dealing with, their feeling and 'doing' states.

Aggressive children feel neither safe nor powerful, coming as they do from their 'bad' self-image, so the more we respond with understanding and firmness, creating opportunities for them to find other parts of themselves and practise 'state shifts', the healthier and safer they, and our families, become. Acknowledging, but not accepting, children's anti-social behaviour may feel like rejecting them, since it conflicts with the positive, loving messages we wish to give. However, the opposite is true: loving parents provide safety, co-regulation and containment (nurture and structure) for their children. The secure base (and OP) 🌣 we create forms the platform from which we can encourage them to explore their inner and outer worlds. We can help them 'find' their 'silver lining' parts, allowing them to see beyond their 'protective shells', and practise being all of themselves: including 'bad' and 'good' (OSC).

Some of us feel that living with angry children is like existing in a state of war: a war zone that nobody else sees; moreover, we feel we should present our family situation as a state of peace. Here, we are ourselves developing a dissociative response that 'normalises' our children's behaviour and allows us, in periods of relative calm, to deny the reality that this 'peace' is only a 'temporary ceasefire'. We can liken this to the impact of early maltreatment on our children. Like them, the 'flight' response often feels unavailable: it would mean giving up on our children, distancing ourselves from them, or drifting into depression. We know the 'fight' response, in which we might respond to our children's behaviour with shouting or smacking, is unacceptable, yet we can occasionally 'lose it', or take it out on ourselves or others. Frequently the 'freeze' response may seem the only viable alternative.

Often we come to fear our children's aggression but, being unable to articulate it, protect ourselves from further abuse or share this with others, we learn to 'switch off' (dissociate). We may appear flat and emotionless, or 'put on our happy face' and laugh at situations most people would find frightening. We may feel that we provoked the situation, that it was 'our fault', or feel blamed by other people, even within our families.

Our sense of shame compounds our feelings of isolation, helplessness and lack of self-worth, mirroring and reinforcing our children's feelings and their need to feel 'in control' 🖂. It is then hard for us to remember that 'Oppression dehumanises the oppressor as it hurts the oppressed' (Mandela 2006) and take positive steps to bring about positive changes.

Abused children feel they have no-one to talk to and often lack the language to articulate what is happening to them. They believe the abuse occurred because they were 'bad babies' or 'bad children'. They gave up trying to make sense of a world that was confusing and frightening, retreating into their own, more bearable, world. As parents we may respond in similar ways, particularly if we have histories of childhood neglect or abuse and have a heightened propensity for dissociation and self-blame. We may become 'stuck' in a 'helpless child' state, finding it difficult to shift to a more comfortable and 'adult' state of being where we could provide our children with the support and guidance they need. On the other hand, if we have explored these issues, our early experiences can give us greater insights into our children's inner world and let us 'hear' what is really happening. We can then provide 'good' role models and help them manage their 'bad child' within. Although our angry and aggressive children are likely to be operating from brainstem mode where words are not effective, they do need clear messages that violence is never OK, alongside suggestions for expressing anger in more appropriate ways. So, once we have provided safe containment, we can create 'time to talk' and look at these issues with them more fully.

Managing the 'bad' oppositional child

A common response to lack of respect, stubbornness, opposition or sulking is for us to try to impose our will on our children. After all, we were probably respectful and obedient to the adults in our lives and felt 'bad' if we failed to live up to their, or our own, expectations. If our reality as parents is very different we may find it hard to act as 'grown-ups' and maintain 'top down' controls.

Conversely, if we went through a period of rebellion in our teens, we may feel 'it did me no harm' and fail to recognise the real differences in frequency, intensity, duration and meaning of our children's challenging behaviour. Moreover, they may be pleasant and co-operative with other people, increasing our frustration, 'stuck-ness' and self-blame. Sadly, responding in ways that mirror our children's powerful 'bad' self-states reinforces their fears, increases their attempts to feel in control, and perpetuates their unhelpful survival responses. Furthermore we are not in a fit state to engage with them, help them move into more regulated states, or practise new ways of being.

Conversely we may respond by letting unacceptable behaviours pass over us. This dissociative response brings temporary peace of mind but denies both our own and our children's reality. Acting as if everything is fine may convince others and ourselves (albeit temporarily) but does nothing to convince our children of the need to change if they are to become acceptable members of society. It is vital we find ways of altering our own self-state, as a powerful role model to our children, and creating endless opportunities to set them up to succeed. Once we return to our adult state we can begin to work out which 'storey' our children are 'coming from', and at what age they are functioning, and respond accordingly 🏠. We would not ask toddlers to tidy their rooms single-handed: nor should we expect co-operation from children in their 'baby' or 'toddler' states, or who have 'zoned out' and have little access to their thinking brain.

Alongside their profound sense of being 'bad' our children are terrified of making mistakes since they feel they are 'mistakes': this can immediately plunge them into shame. Often they would rather face criticism and anger (responses with which they are only too familiar) by making no attempt to comply than try and fail. Here we might respond to our school-age children by saying 'I can see you're finding this hard right now – let's leave it until later' or offer to 'do it together, bit by bit'. At times we may feel discretion is the better part of valour and suggest without sarcasm or implied criticism that our children carry on doing what they are doing, or are likely to do (and if it looks like fun, join them). By creating these 'win-win' situations we encourage children to feel better about themselves, if only for that moment: helping them to see themselves as more than their 'bad child within'.

Managing the 'too good' child

If 'bad' children tend to make us feel 'bad', 'good' children tend to make us feel 'good'. We feel comfortable that our homes feel safe for our children and we are making a difference to their once troubled lives. The last thing we wish to consider is that they are being 'too good for their own good'. Yet, if our children have experienced poor early caregiving, they are unlikely to be acting from a 'good' place: instead they are terrified of being seen as the 'bad' children they believe themselves to be. They need our help to get in touch with all of themselves, to feel that their 'bad child within' is just as much part of them, yet not *all* of them, as their 'acting good' selves. They also need acceptance and support to handle making mistakes without 'being a mistake', since if we cannot connect ('associate') with our children's less acceptable parts we perpetuate their inner sense of worthlessness and their tendency to dissociate.

As with parenting 'bad' children, if as children we were neglected or abused, we will have developed strategies that helped us survive. Many of us will have a strongly developed 'good child within', people who choose to be kind, pleasing and take care of others, and put ourselves last. If we have not been able to get in touch with our 'dark' side we mirror our 'too good' children's world view and may respond negatively to any hints of 'bad' behaviour. We are unlikely to find it easy to accept that we should encourage our children to practise being 'naughty' or model such behaviour ourselves. However, if we have worked on our issues we will know that they need our 'permission' to be all of themselves: to choose to be 'good' rather than to feel they must do so at all costs.

Talking to their 'selves'

Below we provide some suggestions for 'getting in touch with' our children's 'bad' and 'too good' parts. We discussed talking in more detail in Chapter 9, 'Talking, Telling, Timing', suggesting that it is generally more helpful to delay discussions until 'things have calmed down'. However, the suggestions below are an exception to the rule, since they are designed to help children move into more comfortable states as soon as possible and build OC. Before we begin we should first revisit the 'Check in and check out' section in Chapter 10, 'Loose Connections', to get ourselves 'in a fit state' to provide the therapeutic parenting our children need (see pp.167–178).

Angry and oppositional children

It helps to prepare and practise simple, affirming comments we can make to our children when they, and we, are stressed or in danger of 'getting in a state'. Once familiar with them, we can use them with confidence in many situations.

- *'I know it's hard when I say "no" and you're showing me this by swearing at/punching me. In our family we try to work things out without hurting each other. I guess we all need more practice.'*

- *'We want this house to feel safe for all of us and show our anger in ways so people don't get hurt. So let's both try jumping up and down and shouting "I DON'T LIKE THIS".'*

- *'I love you too much to let you go on practising the angry ways people showed their feelings in your birth family.'*

'*I b~~~~~ love you*', shouted at the top of our voice, with a big grin on our face, can also get in touch with many 'out of it' children: it meets them 'where they are' and helps us reconnect and re-regulate. Using 'parts talk' (Bomber 2007; van Gulden 2010) we might say: '*Wow! Your angry/stubborn part(s) are really loud today. Let's find your "quiet/gentle" part(s) and give them a chance too.*' (For younger children it may feel right to playfully 'search' their bodies for the 'missing' states.) We should also validate why children's defensive states came into being: '*I know it helped you feel safe/in control to get angry/refuse to co-operate when you were little. Now maybe we can practise letting other parts of you take safe control.*'

Often children's 'good' parts are vehemently denied (beware of using the terms 'good'/'bad' directly at all costs). We could say: '*I know they're there, I've seen them before. You remember when…?*' This can be amazingly effective in moving children from one state to another, particularly if accompanied by mobile phone photos of 'good times'.

We can often use playfulness and humour to bring children back into their bodies ('I do exist') and then move them into more acceptable and comfortable states, almost without them noticing. Asking angry or oppositional children to '*have a minute of swearing*' is, counter-intuitively, a great 'state-shifter'. In fact children tend to run out of 'rude words' quite soon and collapse into giggles. In parallel with 'defusing' stressful situations, using 'play' neurobiological circuits to replace 'fear' circuits encourages valuable 'rewiring' and begins to alter MN circuits.

Examples of an anger contract outlining family rules and expectations and a poster showing ways of handling feelings (the 'Muir Family Plan') for display in prominent (but discreet) places can be found in Appendix 1. These can provide 'concrete' ways of reminding our children how to recognise and cope with their angry feelings.

While we do not advocate 'time out' for our children, we may need to reinforce the message that we are not prepared to be victims by removing ourselves from our children if remaining with them will lead to physical aggression. Conversely we do advocate the judicious use of 'parental time out' using such phrases as: '*I need to get myself together again, so I'm going to my room. I'll be back as soon as I've calmed down so that I can help you calm down too.*' This is not rejecting our children; it is rejecting behaviour that is not helpful for them to demonstrate while modelling good self-regulation and 'state shifting' and also keeping ourselves safe. However, wherever possible, taking safe control immediately is more preferable – particularly for younger children.

'Good' children

The essence of developing 'all of' good children is to create opportunities for them to 'dare' to be 'naughty' and 'make mistakes'. Whilst this can, and should, be great fun for all concerned, it requires preparation and practice. We need to find ways of 'slipping up' ourselves in humorous ways, role-modelling for our children how to handle these without 'falling apart'. We might pretend to pick up the 'wrong keys' or pass the cereal when asked for milk. We can then allow our children to draw our attention to this 'silly mistake' and then look dismayed, burst into mock tears or apologise dramatically. Similarly when we do 'mess up' we can 'retrieve' the situation by 'hamming up' our dismay and giggling at ourselves. Few children can resist the invitation to join in!

We might try saying something like '*Oh, no! I've spilled the milk! What am I going to do? What a wally!*', then immediately follow this with a change of outlook: '*Never mind. I'll get the sponge and mop it up. No worries!*' or '*What a silly billy I am. All fingers and thumbs. I need some help to do this properly.*'

Since 'good' children often see us as all-powerful and all-knowing they will 'hear' that 'nobody is perfect', encouraging them to accept that they too only have to be 'good enough'. If it feels appropriate, we can also provide them with opportunities to step in and help us, connecting them to their 'capable' parts and further boosting their self-esteem.

It is essential, and potentially even greater fun, to play at being 'naughty' together. We might start by recounting some of our childish misdemeanours with relish. Again this runs counter to 'good' children's perceptions of us, giving them tacit permission to think or act that way too and developing OC. Having set the scene we can encourage our children to try 'rehearsing naughty roles' together. Initially, dressing for the part can make this feel 'safer'. We might:

- grab a set of 'devil's horns', saying '*Come on! Let's be little devils, throw these cushions on the floor and jump on them!*'

- go out in the garden clad in waterproofs, shouting '*I feel like being wicked just now, let's have a water fight!*'

- put on aprons and conspire to set the table together, placing a jumping plastic frog on the seat of a grown-up (not another child), saying '*Tee-hee. This'll be fun. Daddy/ Mummy/Granny will be surprised!*'

- seize a hat and shout '*Let's pretend to be cheeky monkeys*', with full-on monkey sounds and actions

- have an 'untidy' day tearing up newspapers with our children and throwing them around the room, shouting '*Wow, isn't this fun?*' Later we can have fun tidying up together.

Gradually we can 'move into reality' and extend our repertoire, asking for suggestions from our children and celebrating their mischievousness. We can also:

- greet our children warmly, saying '*How's my little imp today?*' or playfully asking '*And just what have you been up to today?*'

- invite 'good' children to '*let your "naughty" part come out to play*' – and playfully prod them as if searching them for it (if this feels safe and appropriate)

- make sure we welcome any spontaneous 'wicked' acts with glee, perhaps saying '*Wow! I'm proud of you. It took some courage to show me your mischievous/"wicked"/cheeky part. I hope you're proud too!*'

Family, friends and school staff are often happy to be co-opted into becoming excited when they see spontaneous 'misdemeanours', once they understand the reasoning. We need not fear that 'too good' children will suddenly become 'bad'; they do, however, need endless opportunities to be, and feel accepted for, all of themselves. Only then can they 'act naturally', make real choices in their responses and develop relationships based on equality.

Useful slogans to display at home

- Every child has a silver lining.

- Mistakes are nature's way of helping us to learn.

- Nobody's perfect – thank goodness!

- Good enough is good enough for me.

- In our family *everyone* is OK, even if they don't always act that way.

- All of me loves all of you.

Chapter 12

Taking, Borrowing and Difficulties with the Truth

'Stealing' and 'lying' are amongst the most difficult behaviours we have to deal with; understandably tending to push most parents' buttons. They frequently feel more incomprehensible than other behaviours and may persist for longer; often our children take things they do not need and their 'crazy lying' appears more inclined to get them into trouble than out of it. They are certainly issues that can be highly emotive and provoke almost universal disapproval.

For therapeutic parents, the first step is what should now be 'the old familiar story': we need to explore the origins of these 'anti-social' behaviours and understand them in terms of survival strategies relating to our children's early trauma histories. We are likely to have quite different relationships to 'stealing' and 'lying' from our children's, and it is vital we recall that we can best understand their behavioural language through their 'historical dictionary'. Abused children may learn that 'truth does not pay' and 'it's every man for himself': their relationship to 'the truth' is therefore tenuous and egocentric. Children who suffered neglect, unsure as to when or where their next meal would appear, may be driven to scrounge and hoard food to survive, affecting how they relate to foodstuffs years after the actual need has passed.

Since food is such a potent driver here, we begin by exploring these issues in terms of our SEAM acronym, alongside our usual bottom-up approach. In their early lives, sensations (bottom storey) dominate infants' lives; they underpin their relationships with their inner and outer worlds: the Sensation of hunger then informs their behaviour (Actions), mediated by Emotions (mid-storey functions). Where caregivers fail to meet their needs, powerful negative feelings (E), such as fear, helplessness and abandonment, become 'hardwired' to children's bodily feelings (S) of hunger. Consequently the behaviours (A) that are triggered also become 'hardwired' into their developing neurobiological systems. If their 'survival' strategies, however apparently bizarre, had not been effective, our children would not be here now, showing and telling us what they need through their current behaviour. It is only through being mindful of and addressing their sensory, emotional and behavioural needs that we can 'rewire' their bottom and middle storeys 🏠 and connect them up to their top-storey thinking brains to reflect on and moderate their responses (Mindfulness).

Bear in mind, too, that existing traumatic hardwiring means that any part of a single element (S, E or A) can trigger hot-wired connections to any other element. So, for example, if our children feel mildly hungry on waking during the night and have no idea how long it will be until breakfast, they may panic, go onto 'auto-pilot' (bottom and middle-storey responses) and head downstairs to raid the fridge. Although at other times they are aware that they should ask before helping themselves, at that moment, in that particular state, they cannot reflect and make good choices. Nightly reminders are unlikely to alter this pattern, nor are morning 'naggings'. However, talking over the underlying issues and agreeing to leave a reliable supply of simple, sustaining food, such as bread or bananas (serotonin rich), can gradually resolve the problem at every level.

Moving on, sweet foods like chocolate and sugary drinks may have helped our children manage abuse and feelings of rejection and shame. Caregivers may have offered sweets after physically or sexually abusing them as 'rewards' for not telling and, perhaps, to make themselves feel better. Chaotic parents often use both 'carrot' and 'stick' to try to control their children's behaviour: though the 'carrots' are usually sweet and sticky. Where early connections between feeding (milk sugars), comfort and cuddles were poor, sensori-emotional links to 'good' foods are likely to be weak and those to 'bad' comfort foods strengthened. Since sweet, fat and sugar-laden foods then became associated with feeling less bad both physically and emotionally, albeit temporarily, our children learn to 'self-medicate' in the absence of 'benefactors'. With these kinds of histories children can view food as 'compensation', feeling a sense of betrayal if denied unlimited access to sweet foods by 'good enough' parents trying to encourage healthy eating; others learn to 'act up' in expectation of bribes to 'be good'. From their perspective, borne out by their distorted MN circuits, we become the 'bad guys' depriving them of their basic rights and needs. No surprise then that 'stealing' food is likely to be a big issue in our families and that the preferred food tends to be calorific and sugary.

As children we were probably told that we could only have pudding if we ate our dinner: old habits die hard and many of us hear ourselves saying this to this day, reinforcing the message that sweet food is a reward! Furthermore, sweet foods have strong social connotations. Our culture promotes customs such as giving chocolates, sweet foods and, later, alcohol (also sugar-based), not only as rewards or signs of affection but also as solace when things feel bad; TV 'soaps' and adverts make heavy use of this. We tend to use sweet things as terms of endearment, such as 'honey', 'sugar' and 'sweetie', reinforcing our concept of sweet items as the ultimate 'comfort foods'. Clearly we must also bear in mind society's, alongside our own, relationship to food if we are to help our children change theirs.

Taking all of these issues into consideration we need to work hard to help our children build up sensori-emotional connections between sustenance and nurture by creating numerous opportunities linking shared cuddles and positive experiences with sweet things: recognising that '*sharing* and pairing' experiences make all the difference, we can remind ourselves that 'a *little* of what we fancy does us (all) good', whilst total abstinence can increase cravings and feelings of deprivation. If we feel we need an 'excuse', what better than 'because it's Tuesday'?!

Turning to 'lying', this, too, emanates from our children's histories, as a survival tool they continue to use when no longer needed. Avoiding overwhelming shame reactions is a potent reason for lying when confronted ⌖. This is central to our therapeutic reparenting approach. As discussed earlier, our children see themselves as innately 'bad' and responsible for their maltreatment. This can seem a 'safer' option to children than accepting that, as victims of abuse or neglect, they were helpless to alter events or relinquishing the belief that their parents were loving and 'there for them'. Making themselves key players it may feel possible, by becoming 'good', to stop the maltreatment and make their caregivers love them. Their survival strategy of accepting the blame, in order to reduce their terror, means our children have already had a great deal of practice in 'lying to themselves' (dissociation). Furthermore, abusers often deny their abusive behaviour, providing unhealthy role models and simultaneously denying children opportunities to explore their lived reality. 'Buying into' the lies of their abusers both increases children's illusory feelings of safety and the dissociation between what is done and what is said. Placed in such situations repeatedly it becomes difficult for children to distinguish truth from fiction, making our exhortations to 'tell the truth' well-nigh impossible.

Children learn to define themselves in terms of their behaviour. Rather than seeing themselves as essentially 'good children' who sometimes behave in inappropriate ways, our children define themselves as 'bad children' whose behaviour defines their essential being: 'what they do is who they are'.

Thus when asked why they stole a sweet (*doing* something 'bad') our children 'hear' us saying they *are* 'bad' children (*being* something 'bad'). Therefore, whilst the feelings aroused in children raised in good enough families, on being confronted with bad behaviour, is guilt, the feeling aroused in our children is shame (mid-storey response). Such feelings overwhelm children's capacity to discuss their behaviour and resolve it (top-storey function): instead they defend against this overwhelming emotion through denial or fabrication. To do otherwise would mean confirming their essential badness; telling the truth would place them in a psychologically unbearable position. Since society's stance is that telling the truth defines 'good children' and lying defines 'bad children', an admission of stealing raises a paradox: do the right thing and portray ourselves as 'bad', or lie or dissemble to appear 'good'. This is not easy for any of us to cope with, even if we can reflect on the conflict and find ways of rationalising it.

For example, being aware of convention, we might eat and praise our host's food even when it is mediocre or worse: not to do so would be rude and embarrassing. However, if the chicken piece we are given appears uncooked, we face a dilemma. We could choose to make an excuse (lie), such as saying we have toothache, or to eat around the chicken and hope our host will not notice (dissemble). Conversely we could choose to 'do the right thing' and put ourselves at risk. Not an easy choice! There is a way out of this for us, if we dare to be honest, since we might expect our host to react reasonably. For our children there is no such expectation of adults.

It is clear also that MN circuits play a big part in the way children respond to 'confrontations' with us. We may merely be asking about a situation we want clarified and about which we feel mild frustration; our children may interpret our approach as indicating anger and our intentions as potentially abusive, neglectful or rejecting. Confronted with these fears, children's only recourse may be to deny, act dumb or prevaricate.

There can also be an element of feeling 'in control' implicit in 'stealing' and 'lying' behaviours. 'Knowledge is power', and if children believe they know something that we do not (having poorly developed 'mindreading' capacities) they may feel less powerless and less vulnerable. Here, subtly letting children know that 'we know what they know but are not saying' avoids direct confrontations yet challenges their assumptions. Furthermore, by school age, children have 'practised' effective ways of 'controlling' the emotional environment, our responses and hence their lives using their 'learned survival skills'. Acting in ways that are likely to lead to anger and confrontation provides a feeling of inappropriate control: control that we can help them relinquish by reacting to their behaviour with understanding and empathy.

Difficulties with OP ☼ and OC also play a vital role in our children's ability to acknowledge the reality of their behaviour. If they have not fully learned that items exist when they cannot see, touch or smell them (OP), then what does it matter if an orange goes missing? It is only to be expected. Furthermore, as a consequence of poor OP, children have poorly developed OC and may struggle to recognise that the orange that was in the fruit bowl is the same orange they took and ate; nor can 'they know that we know' any different. This is central to our understanding of our children's 'lying' and 'stealing'. Integration of all of ourselves is the last step in the development of OSC and hence a global sense of, and control over, self. Although our children will usually have some awareness of 'what I did this morning', it is not as 'hardwired' as it is in us. Intra-state (SEAM) connections may be weak and inter-state links more so. For example, it may not 'feel' (in Sensori-Emotional terms) like 'I took the orange', so that links to the behaviour (A) 'taking the orange' and its recall become tenuous. Simply put, 'it wasn't the same "me" then as it is now'. It is up to us to 'let children know what they don't yet know', challenging their perceptions as we would a toddler, gently but firmly, to avoid catapulting them into further denial, humiliation or shame.

We are all familiar with toddlers who clutch their 'blankie' at all costs when they are under stress, in even temporary separations. Gradually, as they learn to 'take us with them in their heads', they begin to let these TOs go. Children who have not 'internalised' their caregivers as their secure base still need these tangible aids to OP: it therefore makes sense that many of our children 'borrow' items of ours to keep as permanent reminders of us. Alternatively, some children unconsciously learn to substitute material items for positive relationships with caregivers who were not consistently available. In this instance they may be more likely to take money, small electronic items such as ipods or mobile phones, or foods that 'fill them up' physically if not emotionally. For some children 'taking' not only allows them to carry us, and 'home', with them when they are away from us, they may unconsciously be willing us to carry them in our heads: searching for our purse or car keys we cannot forget the putative 'taker'. Seen in this light, 'borrowing' can be seen as a sign of our children's growing attachment to us!

Relevant too are the disconnections in children's perceptions of themselves and others. To make sense of a mother who seemed alternately scared and scary, who would meet their needs sometimes yet become abusive and neglectful at others is distressing. Often children cannot accept that these two aspects represent one and the same 'mummy' (OC) ⟨○. Hence they cannot hold in mind, on (mis)perceiving our anger or disappointment, that we are usually loving and accepting of them. They must respond to the 'angry mummy' they see by reverting to (bottom and mid-storey) strategies they learned to manage their early abuse and neglect, not the 'loving mummy' we are usually and will soon be again.

Many of these behaviours cause huge problems at school and in peer relationships. Implicit in children's friendship is the ability to trust their pals and know they will not let them down. Children who 'steal' or 'lie' unwittingly sabotage the very friendships they are desperately trying to build. For others, the 'taking' is merely a precursor to the 'giving' they believe will 'buy' them friendships and make them liked. Teachers often become frustrated and angry with children who 'lie' and 'steal' because it threatens the safety and atmosphere in the classroom. It not only affects the other children, it may also mean imposing rigid rules about possessions that disrupt the 'flow' of the class and dealing with irate parents complaining about losses or demanding punishments for the perpetrators.

We should remind ourselves that children who 'steal' and 'lie' are not happy children: they are 'coming from their scared child within' (bottom and mid-storey). We must therefore consider how best to help them address the issues underlying their need to 'steal' and 'lie', make family life easier and help our children manage life better socially. However, before addressing what 'stealing' and 'lying' mean to our children, we should reflect on what they mean to us. What messages were we given as children about these issues? Were we taught that stealing was wrong and that lying about misdemeanours compounded the 'crime': that lying was worse than our original action? If we had good enough parents these messages were not followed by dire consequences and hence we had no need to practise 'lying' or 'stealing' as survival strategies, a very different experience to our children's. It would be helpful to write down the messages we internalised as children to highlight these differences.

Earlier we explored how our children's histories informed what they internalised about stealing and lying. Setting down these messages alongside ours allows us to think about how we might have felt living our children's lives. It allows us to consider the differences between our 'dictionary' of stealing and lying and our children's, which in turn helps us put ourselves in our children's shoes and find effective ways to help them.

Becomingly consciously aware (top-storey function) of the differences reduces our feelings of anger and frustration (mid-storey) about their behaviour. It allows us to empathise openly with them, and encourages them to begin to develop empathy for, and accept, all of themselves. When our children are more able to make sense of their actions (top storey) we can work together to make real changes, beginning with their innermost beliefs. Continuing our food example, they can begin to comprehend what happened to them that made them feel and react in certain ways and why they still feel and do these things now. Gradually with our support and lots of practice at times when they can manage this (see Chapter 9) they can learn that they are now safe and that food will always be readily available. Although this may appear like 'top down' work, it is actually working upwards from the 'basement', identifying the Sensations and feelings (E) that drive their Actions. Once these become better regulated (through us) our children can better regulate them for themselves and develop 'top down', self-limiting, conscious controls (M). For example, we might say:

> *'I know when you lived in your birth family you were hungry at times and had to take food for yourself and your sister. You did really well to take care of both of you. I guess it's hard to know that in this house you don't need to take food to make sure you're fed. Let's think about ways I can help you know this. I know this'll be hard but together we can do things differently.'*

Engaging our children in working out ways to help them can be very positive. It implies that, with our support, things can change. Giving messages that we know it will be hard implies that we do not expect instant results and that they are likely to make mistakes. We can then empathise with their difficulties when they 'mess up' and praise them when they succeed. (Self-congratulation is allowed too!) The emphasis on praise, rather than failure, is vital because *not* 'lying' or 'stealing' are acts of *omission* rather than *commission* and it is often easier to notice 'slip-ups' than achievements. Yet children learn better from success than failure, so we must create, and stay alert for, every opportunity to offer congratulations. Perhaps we could add a reminder to our mobile phone to alert us several times each day to make and take every chance we can. Using texts to pass on our messages to our children can also prove invaluable!

Finding opportunities to praise our children is also important to begin altering their perspective of themselves as 'bad'. For best effect the praise needs to be for specific behaviours and immediate, rather than broad statements about how good they are or hours after the event. Global statements are often too much for children with low self-esteem since they are at odds with their self-perceptions. Delays attenuate the perceived links between 'then' and 'now' and cause and effect, and can lose their meaning and the impetus for change. Instead we should offer specific, targeted praise such as:

> *'Wow! That biscuit is still on the table. That must have been hard for you. Good job!'*

> *'You came home and told me you'd left your gym kit behind. No problem – we can pick it up tomorrow. Well remembered!'*

We can make our jobs much simpler by setting our children up to succeed:

> *'When I asked you if the sun was shining you said "yes". Thanks for being honest.'*

(Although even this could 'fail' sometimes with children in 'stroppy' moods.)

> *'I noticed you walked past that carrot without eating it. Well done!'*

(This is much easier if they do not like carrots and we know it.) It implies that we would expect the carrot to be where it was left, enhancing OP.

Creating opportunities to praise our children for not 'stealing' or 'lying' simultaneously helps with issues of self-esteem and family harmony: two for the price of one! Conversely we may notice that our children's 'lying' and 'stealing' increase at times when there are other family stresses. We can then use their behaviours as barometers to their inner world and help them do likewise:

> *'I've noticed you struggle with lying and stealing when you don't feel good about yourself or when you don't feel safe. Well done for showing me that. Perhaps we can figure out why you're feeling bad about yourself/wobbly today?'*

Our increasing awareness of MN systems provides us with invaluable insights into how we need to express ourselves when we raise difficult issues like 'lying' or 'stealing'. While anger and frustration is understandable, tackling incidents when we are angry (mid-storey response) is not the best approach. Not only are our children triggered by quite minor stimuli, they are also doing the best they can to show us what they need. Finding ways of dealing with our feelings *before* tackling an issue is vital. We do not need to deal with a 'stolen biscuit' immediately. We may need first to 'phone a friend' or have a cup of coffee, allowing us to feel calmer and more reflective (top storey). In much the same way we can take time to 'rant, relax and work out an appropriate response' if we discover items have gone missing whilst our child is out. Acknowledging (and expressing) our feelings to ourselves is a vital first step towards us 'getting it right'; we will also be in a better position to acknowledge these honestly to our children too, to minimise fear-based MN firing.

> *'We need to talk about something we both find difficult. You might think I look annoyed. I hope you're beginning to remember that my being annoyed doesn't mean I'll hurt you. Let's give it a go!'*

> *'I know it'll be hard for you to hear this. So first I want to tell you I love you, even when I don't like your behaviour. I guess that's hard for you to remember if you think I'm angry. We both need more practice at this. Let's have a big hug first.'*

We discussed OP earlier and gave an example of how we can strengthen 'loose connections'. We also explored how poor OC can lead to our children denying the obvious, such as those tell-tale biscuit crumbs. We can often use humour to 'let our children know that we know' that these are intrinsically linked and can 'tell us the story'. With practice our children can then learn to make these vital links for themselves and create their own coherent narratives. We might say:

> *'Hmmm! Bring me my magnifying glass Watson. Ah yes! These crumbs look/taste/smell like the ones in the tin. Interesting... I wonder...?'*

Or adopt the 'Inspector Clouseau' approach: making ourselves look stupid yet inadvertently working it out:

> *'Ah! Zee cat was sitting 'ere earlier, perhaps 'e ate it. I must interview 'im first. Errrrr, but 'e 'ates chocolate, it makes 'im sick. Let's see, 'oo else was around? Dad's out. Zat leaves you and me. I don't zink it was me, I was on the phone...'*

Summary

While issues of 'lying' and 'stealing' are inherently difficult, they can be tackled in a variety of direct and non-direct ways we can incorporate into our daily lives. There may be several reasons for our children's behaviour, so we may need to consider which aspect is most pressing to focus our energies most effectively. Initially this can be challenging, but with practice, armed with our children's behavioural 'dictionary' and trusting our gut feelings, it becomes increasingly possible. Remember that our children are adept at telling us what we need to know and finding ways of signalling when we get it wrong: we need to listen to them constantly. We should also view the challenge as a long-term project: our children may have had to practise 'lying' and 'stealing' for years. We cannot hope to alter their behaviour in a few months, nor should we lower our expectations that our children can become more honest and trustworthy eventually. We may, however, need to adjust our expectations of the speed at which we can achieve this, alongside our perceptions of our children's behaviour as innately 'bad' and of ourselves as 'bad' parents.

Check in and check out

See Appendix 2.

Chapter 13

Making Changes, Managing Changes

Making changes

Change is a challenge: an opportunity for growth and development that is both exciting and scary. However, for our children any transition, however small, can feel like a terrifying step too far. As therapeutic parents we cannot expect our children to consider changing until we make some changes ourselves. We might argue that how we have parented in the past has 'worked', 'if it's broke don't fix it', or that being asked to change implies we are not good enough and should not be doing the job. However, a good enough car mechanic would be failing in her job if she continued to use the same tools on new vehicles as she used on older models. Similarly, building up our developmental reparenting 'tool-box' means more than changing the way we feel and behave towards our children and ourselves: it involves changing our mind-set as well as our tool-set. As ever, we should start by understanding our children's history and how this affected, and continues to affect, their bodies, brains and understanding of relationships and the world. This means walking a while in their shoes to appreciate the fear base that continues to dominate their lives and exploring the most effective transition tools for them.

At a recent training event, participants were invited to complete a 'wall' of paper bricks on which to write what children need at each stage in their lives: from birth to two years, two to five years, five to ten years and ten years into adolescence. Working upwards from the earliest stage we explored which bricks were missing or damaged through abuse and neglect. As we went through this exercise the gaps in the wall became apparent, as did the fragility of the structure: highlighting the impact of early adversity during that period but also at all subsequent stages. The robustness of a wall is only as good as its structure: cracked or missing bricks create points of vulnerability. Similarly, children's emotional robustness is only as good as the consistency and evenness of their developmental 'building blocks'.

What the 'wall exercise' failed to highlight was that any structure must stand on firm foundations. These unseen foundations are crucial for the survival of the entire structure, so that it can withstand the ravages of wind, rain and cold. Our children's pre-birth and early experiences form the 'unseen foundations' upon which their resilience and wellbeing are predicated. So, like an archaeologist, we must painstakingly 'dig down to their experiential foundations' to identify the 'earthworks' that support their neurobiological 'bricks'. We will then have a more complete overview of structures that underpin our children's physical and emotional functioning, their understanding of the world and their place within it. Amending the wall tool, to include the foundations, allows us to examine what happened to our children alongside what is happening now. Feeling how 'wobbly' and unsupported they feel can provide us with a better mind-set to offer the secure base that will allow our children to rebuild their lives.

After taking time to 'walk in our children's shoes' we need to explore 'walking in our own childhood shoes'. Reflecting on our childhood experiences allows us to recognise how they shaped our neurobiological connections and hence our competencies and outlook on life. It offers us opportunities to consider the old familiar 'voices in our heads' from way back that influence our interpretation of our children's behaviour now. Many of us will have been given messages that answering back, not doing what we were told or taking things without asking, were 'major misdemeanours' that drew epithets such as 'rude', 'lazy', 'naughty' or 'dishonest'. Given that we tend to parent as we were parented, we are likely to find it hard to silence those voices. Yet it is only by 'turning down the volume' and 'changing the scripts' that we can recognise the intensity of fear and confusion that underpin our children's perceptions and responses.

Acknowledging that children's behaviour is the only language they have for letting us know their feelings, and changing our interpretation of their actions from 'won't do' to 'can't do', we can take the mind-set leap that allows us to become the therapeutic parents our children need us to be. Being able to ask the question 'What are our children trying to say to us?' rather than 'What are our children doing to us?' will be the signal that we have started the journey. Articulating the answer is the next crucial step, a step that embraces all our therapeutic principles and considers our children's difficulties *at any given moment* in terms of:

- whether they are experiencing the safety of a secure base

- their need for nurture and structure

- whether they are in brainstem, limbic or cortical mode

- their sensori-motor tolerance and discrimination

- their emotional age

- their functional level of OP and OC

- the extent to which their perceptions of our actions accurately reflect our intentions or are refracted through the distorting prism of fear-based MN systems

- the degree to which their shame-based feelings impact their self-perceptions

- their 'mindful', 'mentalising' and EF capacities.

Managing changes

If the steps to becoming therapeutic parents seem daunting, we should remind ourselves that we need not be perfect and that we can and should make mistakes in our parenting. Indeed, 'good enough' parenting requires us only to 'get it right' about 60 per cent of the time; Winnicott (1965) makes it clear that being an 'ordinary devoted mother' is 'good enough' and that the vast majority of parents fulfil that criterion. While parenting traumatised children is far more complex than parenting securely attached children, the 'good enough' rule still applies. We can use our inevitable mistakes and misattunements as part of the joint learning process. Indeed both are intrinsic to all parent–child relationships, for example when toddlers begin to explore their world, make 'mistakes' and feel misattuned with caregivers. These temporary disconnections, when 'repaired' immediately, help them learn to monitor and keep themselves safe and internalise important social expectations and rules.

Children naturally respond to the word 'no' with feelings of shame and abandonment plunging them into deep distress. 'Good enough' parents respond and immediately 'repair' this break in attachment, using touch and reassuring words to let their children know they are still loved, despite their actions. These interactions gradually help children recognise danger and learn the difference between 'right and wrong'. Moreover, 'feeling felt and understood', they can learn to 'feel' for other people: to gain empathy for others. Abused and neglected children are unlikely to have been socialised appropriately. Instead they experience toxic levels of shame and unresolved misattunements; they received powerful messages that their behavioural challenges reflect their intrinsic worthlessness. Consequently they are unable to distinguish between 'doing bad things' and 'being bad' and continue to react with the overwhelming distress of young toddlers. Armed with this developmental awareness, we can move from 'chronological age' responses to 'functional age responses' in responding to our children's misdemeanours, using the toddler socialisation 'remind and immediately repair' approach. We can also relax into 'good enough mode' and have great fun 'making and mending mistakes'.

Managing change becomes easier when we remember that day-to-day interactions with our children create the perfect arena to hone our 'good enough' therapeutic parenting skills and that altering our interactions in one scenario can lead to changes in several areas of difficulty. For example, when dropping off and picking up our children from school we can:

- give ourselves time and take our time: reducing our stress levels and making ourselves available to co-regulate our children's fears about separation and transitions

- hand them a small TO, such as a laminated key-fob displaying a recent family photograph, blow them a kiss and tell them we will be there when they come out of school, strengthening attachment connections and OP

- ensure we wear the same coat on both the morning and afternoon school runs, addressing issues around both OP (we do come back) and OC (we look the same)

- remark on how much we missed our children while they were at school, consolidating object self-permanence (OSP) that being 'held in mind' they too continue to exist

- simultaneously express our love and commitment to our children and let them know they are special and worthy of love: an essential precursor to reducing shame-based feelings

- arrive on time at school, to offer routine and structure and strengthen their trust that they can rely on us: slowly and gradually 'rewiring' their MN Ⓠ circuits

- use our solo journeys from and to school to assess our own feelings where our children are likely to be on the brainstem, limbic, cortical continuum, our own feelings, and how best to greet them

- be more aware of their needs, and 'if in doubt going low', we could offer a quick cuddle and a run in the park rather than asking how our children's day has been: altering their stress hormone levels and moving them upwards along the continuum

- have a snack ready for our children when they return home, which they helped choose before going out, reinforcing all these messages in a single interaction.

Invaluable opportunities to practise managing transitions abound at bedtime. We can use our heightened understanding of our children's histories to anticipate what for us can seem simple transitions, such as going to bed, that can threaten our children's fragile security. If our children lived with domestic violence they may have lain awake at night listening to raised voices and worrying about Mummy's safety and their own; if they were sexually abused they may have awaited their abuser's next visit with trepidation. Neglected children may have gone to bed hungry and afraid that their caregivers would be absent or 'out of it' on drugs or alcohol when they woke up. Moreover, since abusive and neglectful parents tend to be highly unpredictable, our children could never be certain whether they would be hurt or abandoned on any particular night, making every night terrifying. In all these instances bedtime would have been a time when they experienced great fear rather than the safety and relaxation normally associated with sleep.

We must therefore develop bedtime routines that reflect our children's unmet needs for nurture and structure, offering them the consistent good 'baby' experiences that were absent in their birth families and validating the deep-seated fears they may hide through 'delaying tactics', night-time wanderings or midnight fridge raids. Our emphasis should be on practising the 'thinking toddler' approach, acknowledging the discrepancies between our children's chronological and developmental ages that affect their current perceptions, beliefs and behaviour. Acting in consistently loving, empathic and calm ways conveys our understanding of our children's needs even before they are aware of them. Expecting them to 'act their age' and 'not be afraid of the dark' sends messages that we do not understand them and does not allow them to learn how they feel themselves. We also need to remember that every facial, vocal or body communication we make may trigger a defensive or offensive response before we have uttered a word. Recognising these issues and changing our mind-set helps reduce our children's trauma-based MN firing and helps them recognise that *now* is not the same as *then*.

Bearing this in mind, a good bedtime routine might involve:

- preparing our children for bed in advance, reminding them well beforehand and introducing 'wind down' time; calming music and shared stories provide the co-regulation and relaxation that television and computer games cannot

- setting up mutually pleasurable experiences of bath-time; we may have to be quite creative in doing this: for example, showering together in swimming costumes, or chatting through a closed door if children are older or have been sexually abused

- creating regular times for reading and singing to our children in their bedrooms and using this time to point out things they did well during the day

- mentioning our plans for the remainder of the evening, letting our children know that we still exist when we leave their room (OP)

- giving them our evening 'schedule'; this simultaneously helps them make sense of any sounds and movements they hear, encouraging their sense of safety and structure

- letting them know we will be thinking of them, and are looking forward to seeing them in the morning when they wake up; this reinforces OSP

- telling them we will pop back to see them in a few minutes this gives the message that we are indeed still there for them (OP) and simultaneously builds trust that we are reliable

- adding in cuddle-time, night-time drinks and massage-time; this directly calms their senses and encourages relaxing neurochemical messages to flow through their bodies: for example, warm milk raises serotonin levels

- providing an automatic switch-off CD player with soothing music or rhythmic stories for our children that relaxes them towards sleep: for best effect creating home recordings of ourselves reading or singing

- empathising with them by saying we know they struggle with going to bed and want to help them with their feelings, mentioning that we know that in the past bedtimes were often scary times for them. This helps them 'feel felt and understood' and makes sense for them of their feelings and behaviour

- apologising for this, saying, *'I'm sorry I wasn't there to help you feel safe at bedtimes when you were little. I know it'll take you some time to learn that you're safe here and for me to get it right, so let's practise together.'*

This bedtime routine epitomises our developmental reparenting principles and works on all the key areas of our children's difficulties. It may not be a routine that is possible to achieve immediately or every night. However, making sure we include some elements nightly is certainly possible, and vital. We can acknowledge to our children in advance when their routine needs to be changed and explain why. However, if, for example, we are ill or the family returns late from an outing, we should bear in mind that such circumstances can raise children's stress levels (cortisol) and make bedtime more arduous all round.

In making and maintaining change we should also consider making changes to our priorities and our support network. While we may not be able to afford help in our home, we could reduce the number of household tasks we need to perform: perhaps by relaxing our standards in dusting and vacuuming or by shopping on line. We can then create more time to play with our children, or for a well-deserved coffee break that allows us to wind down and relax. We may also need to practise asking for, and accepting offers of, help from friends and family. While our goal may be for all our family and friends to understand our children's special needs and engage with them using developmental reparenting principles, this may not be possible in practice. However, we may have friends we can meet for coffee and chats avoiding child-related topics or for a swim, massage or walk. Such activities can give us back a sense of ourselves as valued individuals outside our role as parents: an important part of helping us feel good enough about ourselves to weather the storms of parenting our traumatised children.

Our two examples of common family activities can help us to consider other ways in which we can put developmental reparenting principles into practice in other day-to-day activities with our children. Gradually, as we work on our approach to parenting, we will acquire the mind-set to ensure that developmental reparenting becomes our natural, normal way of being with our children. We may even begin to recognise that this approach is invaluable in our interactions with our wider family and friendship networks. Whilst developmental reparenting principles are crucial in parenting traumatised children, they are not tools exclusive to this environment; they can improve our relationships within any social setting.

Check in and check out

See Appendix 2.

Chapter 14

Special Occasions

Think back to how we celebrated birthdays and Christmas as children. Were we given parties, presents and lots of excitement: things we wanted to repeat when we became parents, yet which seem not to 'work' with our traumatised children? Understanding why it is often difficult for our children to celebrate the special occasions that form part of ordinary family life begins, as always, with considering their early histories and how these experiences colour their perceptions. For example, birthdays for adopted and fostered children represent families lost as well as families gained. They are potent, wordless reminders that ours were not the wombs in which they grew or the faces and smiles they saw on entering the world. Similarly, the sensations, sounds and smells that formed their earliest experiences were very different from those they experience now, unconsciously reinforcing children's 'not-belonging' and that change means loss.

Birthday celebrations in birth families may have been 'over-done', with lavish gifts to 'make up for' abuse or neglect, 'under-done', with parents too preoccupied to mark these special occasions, or, often, an unpredictable mix of experiences. Moreover, in some families, siblings or half-siblings may have been treated quite differently by close or extended family members: some children receiving piles of expensive presents and others little or nothing. Common, hurtful, underlying messages are 'You're not worth it', 'It's all your fault' or 'You're different'. Since birthdays may have been handled quite differently by subsequent foster carers, they can also carry hidden reminders of further hurts and losses 🏠. Hence loss becomes an almost inevitable part of birthday associations, often not just of children's own but of everyone else's too.

However, the build-up to birthdays can become a forum for exploring what loss means to our children, if we choose times when both we and they are feeling calm and comfortable. Engaging in 'loss-based' conversations when our children are most able to engage their top-storey 'talking and thinking brains', through soothing, accepting body language and voice tones, we can instigate 'quick chats': using short, clear phrases that invite conversation without insisting on it or persisting for too long. We might say:

> *'It's your birthday next month. I bet you're excited and hoping for lots of presents. I wonder if it also reminds you about your birth mum and what life was like then. I know lots of adopted children struggle with that.'*

Perhaps give a small example of what happened back then, followed by:

> *'I know it's difficult for you to sort out these mixed-up feelings and I'm here to help. It's my job to help sort your muddles out, so let's give it a go.'*

> *'You know, I don't feel any different now I'm a year older. More grey hair maybe, but still the same inside.'*

Such brief exchanges carry very important messages to our children that:

- we understand they have complex and contradictory feelings about birthdays
- many other fostered and adopted children feel the same way
- it takes time to feel they belong here
- it's not their fault

- it's OK to have these feelings and share them with us

- change can be scary

- together we can make sense of what is going on and make things more manageable.

We might also encourage our children to draw or write about their feelings; letters written to birth parent(s) can be very powerful messages they may eventually choose to rip up, or burn, 'ceremonially', rather than send. Remember that our children are likely to have confused and confusing feelings towards their birth families, especially anger and sadness, due to their distressing and unpredictable experiences. They may continue to miss abusive or neglectful birth parents, yet feel unable to share this with us due to divided loyalties. They may also not remember, or 'choose to forget', much that was painful from their past and cling to an idealised image of early family life. Moreover we may become distressed by our feelings of rejection and may need to work on this before we can support our children. Bearing in mind that we often take things out on those closest to us, we can then interpret our children's reactions more positively .

Our children need to be able to share all their feelings with us and feel that we can handle and accept them as they are. Simultaneously we must ensure their memories are reality-based. It may be painful for us and our children to think about their past hurts, but this in no way equals the pain of bearing them in isolation, or handling them alone as they were happening. We need to remind ourselves that our children were *there* when the neglect or abuse occurred and were unlikely to have had anybody to turn to for comfort or support. They were in the intolerable position of having to deny what happened or accept responsibility for it. Being therapeutic parents means 'walking with', and talking to, our children about the reality of their past in ways that allow them to 'think the unthinkable' and 'speak the unspeakable'. By enabling them 'to go there' they can release themselves from the shame that poisons their lives . With our help they can begin the 'share, care and repair' process: but only if they feel we accept them for all of who they are and were, including those events about which they feel most shame. The maxim 'a trouble shared is a trouble halved' is invaluable here.

If we have shared several birthdays together we can remind our children, in matter-of-fact, '*I just happened to notice*', non-shaming ways, of previous difficulties and 'wonder' how we can work together to make this birthday more manageable. Taking some responsibility for past difficulties by letting our children know we made a mistake in forgetting their experiences of birthdays are not the same as ours, we might say:

> *I noticed you really struggled with your party last year. I'm sorry about that. When I was a child, I really liked parties and I forgot it's not the same for you. Let's see how YOU would like to celebrate your birthday this year.'*

We might then go on to suggest alternative ways of marking their birthday, such as a trip to the swimming pool or cinema together, having a sleep-over with just one friend, or a family weekend camping in the garden. These ideas will be very personal and, as their parents, we are best placed to offer choices that work best for each individual child each year. We should also remind ourselves that each of our children is unique, has acquired differing coping mechanisms and needs 'custom-built' birthday celebrations.

Sometimes it may be preferable not to celebrate children's birthdays at all, choosing a pre-birthday occasion to acknowledge they are a year older, or suggesting we have extra hugs every day to celebrate 'being us and being together'. This reassures our children that we have not forgotten their birthday yet eliminates potentially distressing messages, feelings and 'meltdowns'. We might wish to inject an extra note of fun by suggesting, for example, that we have a 'Mad Hatter's Tea-party' where the guests celebrate non-birthdays. Downloading the 'un-birthday song' from the internet could help here.

If our children have difficulties with peer relationships, or struggle with sharing or unstructured time, we need to think carefully about whether to arrange a party – birthday or otherwise. Activities involving peers may at best be fraught: add in over-excitement, unfulfilled expectations, 'showing off' and negative feedback to and from other parents, they can become a recipe for disaster. Our children may struggle to know who to invite, especially if they have difficulty sustaining relationships. Their best friend may be their worst enemy between invitations being sent out and the party. It is not uncommon for children to struggle so much with the anticipation of who will and will not come and the fear of rejection that they engage in unwitting 'sabotage', such as falling out with their friends pre-party: giving them some perverse 'control' over an intolerable situation.

If parties go ahead, the levels of supervision and structure required may make it impossible for us to ensure our children and their guests are kept safe and happily entertained. Even if we are prepared to 'give it a go' ourselves, parents of other children may take the easy way out and find 'reasons' for refusing our invitation and avoid inviting our children to their children's parties, compounding our children's feelings of exclusion and alienation. Remember that, even if our children manage playing with peers on an average day, raised stress neurochemicals such as cortisol resulting from heightened anticipation and excitement are likely to reduce their capacity to cope and spoil their special day, or their friends'. Discretion can be the better part of valour here. In the latter case suggesting an alternative activity to coincide with a party invitation (and a diplomatic word with the parents of would-be inviters) can be invaluable.

Christmas and New Year, while lacking such obvious connotations or reminders of earlier losses than birthdays, may also be very fraught times for our children. If birth family members had drug or alcohol problems these may have intensified during the festive season, traditionally a time of excess. Birth parents may have made promises of wonderful times only for things to go awry in the lead-up to Christmas, or on the day itself. Broken promises may have been compounded when expected presents did not materialise and natural disappointment led to acrimony and perhaps abuse. Now feelings of anticipation in our homes can trigger the same neurobiological and biochemical responses as in the past, leading to feelings of fear over-riding their excitement. MN circuits will fire in response to situations reflecting earlier experiences, so, for example, first sight of a Christmas tree, talk of compiling letters to Santa or writing Christmas cards or the smell of alcohol, though likely to have positive associations for us, can herald disaster to our children and comfortable family life.

The general build-up to Christmas and New Year also brings changes to structure and routine in school and in out-of-home activities. Since historically change has become associated with fear and loss, any change in the present can dysregulate our children and disorganise their behaviour patterns. Ends and beginnings of years and terms are often fraught, as such transitions represent greater losses than gains; tensions are likely to be noticeably heightened in the flurry of special classroom activities associated with the festive season. It may be difficult for us to have much impact on school activities directly; however, we can work with staff to help them understand these issues and mitigate the distress for our children. We might arrange that our children attend only part time in the run-up to the end of term and limit optional activities to those we feel they can manage well. We may need to weather comments from relatives, friends and other parents who view our actions as punitive (or pandering) to our children, rather than as helping them cope. We must hold faith that by adopting developmental reparenting principles we are doing our best for our children: finding like-minded foster and adoptive parents, family and friends can provide the strength we need to take the long view.

At home we should keep celebrations as low-key as possible, our own 'partying' too, and keep routines as 'normal' as possible. This is a time to anticipate potential difficulties, talk through our plans in advance with our family and empathise with our children's difficulties during the festive period. Who knows, this may create a more relaxed end of year for everyone than we are used to! We might say:

'My guess is that Christmas time is exciting and also scary for you. I know it's hard when things change and you're not sure what's happening. I know I'd struggle if I'd had as many changes as you. Let's draw up an events diary and stick it on the fridge so we know what's going on.'

'Tomorrow's the day we're going to put the Christmas tree up. I wonder how you feel about helping me fetch it and dig out the decorations?'

'I hate all this chaos and hype. Let's have a "business as usual day" and relax.'

'Things don't always have to change when the year changes. We could make a New Year's resolution to stay the same until we feel like changing!'

'We'll still be the same old family in the same old house even if we put up decorations, wear silly hats and eat special foods.'

Encouraging our children to check the family events diary daily helps them see there is structure within the changes to routine we have planned. Reframing old traditions, such as Father Christmas bringing a single special present and leaving it in our bedroom, can reduce hyped expectations and also fears associated with abusive night-time visitors. Creating new family traditions, like the New Year's 'no change' resolution or making our own Christmas crackers, Advent calendars or personal presents, can build positive seasonal associations, strengthen OC (C) and help rewire MN systems.

We can talk about joint activities, reducing the surprise element and giving our children expectations for future years:

'Do you remember we did…last year? How much fun was that? I'm really looking forward to doing…this year.'

This reminds our children that last year was different from Christmases before they came home to us, that we have kept them safe and that they have already been with us for 'a long time'.

Providing a plethora of presents to 'keep up with the Jones', or as outward expressions of love, is not in our children's best interests, leading to distress and family disharmony. Many traumatised children have so little sense of self-esteem or self-worth they feel they should not have gifts or that 'lots' is still not enough. This can lead to leaving presents untouched, trying to give them away, or finding fault with them. They may 'lose', break or take others' presents; the costly toys we spent loving hours buying and wrapping may be in pieces by Boxing Day. This is likely to create angry and hurt feelings all round, leading to major arguments, sulking or violence. So it can be better to limit expenditure and gifts and spread what we have bought over the festive period or even the rest of the year. Beginning this process in advance of birthdays and Christmas reduces the challenges and 'surprises' with which our children may struggle.

Surprises are particularly difficult for those for whom 'surprises' led to, or followed, incidents of abuse and neglect. The surprises we offer our children may be well intentioned but may have unexpected consequences, including fear, sadness, shame or even self-harm. Establishing a tradition of having small daily or weekly 'surprises' at fixed times over a longer period can reduce levels of anticipation and distress, give children opportunities to practise accepting presents and build a realistic sense of entitlement. We, too, are likely to feel less anger and disappointment if an inexpensive present is 'lost' or damaged. Another, perhaps more unconventional, way of minimising adverse responses to surprises can be to let children know which presents they will receive or to choose them together from within a price range or limited list we draw up. Pictures from catalogues can provide invaluable visual reminders of choices, further reducing anxiety levels.

We may also need to consider other important anniversaries in our children's lives, such as the anniversary of their move to our home or from their birth family into care. Even if they were 'too young to remember' events or dates, their bodies will be sensitised to, for example, day length or seasonal changes, and will send out 'red alert' signals. Our children's behaviour may deteriorate as unconscious memories trigger feelings and behaviours they struggle to comprehend. It is important to be aware of these significant anniversaries, using both historical records and current behaviour patterns as clues. Helping children make sense of the 'dips and troughs' of their feelings and actions enables them to make sense of their internal world and move towards gaining control of their external world.

In general, devising our own anniversaries can help our children feel settled with us: that they belong. 'Anniversaries' might include daily, weekly or monthly small treats or special activities, creating opportunities to celebrate our shared lives and reminding them of their time with us. This can be particularly important for children who had frequent changes in caregiver or circumstance. Reminding our children of the weeks, months and years they have lived with us and reflecting on what we did last week, last month and last year can help our children 'remember' in their bodies, brains and minds that we have a growing shared history: one that is very different from before. It will take time and ingenuity to develop their trust in us, strengthen self-regulation, encourage OP and OC (○ and alter their MN systems – but then who said developmental reparenting was easy?! As long as our spirit is willing, our flesh will not let us down.

In Appendix 1 we offer an inspirational poster for the festive season.

Chapter 15

Handling Holidays

Whilst holidays (vacations) clearly fall within the remit of 'special occasions', we should give equal importance to the principles involved in managing changes.

As prospective parents we probably had visions of family holidays as times of fun and laughter, when we could relax and spend quality time with our children. Once we have families we may start looking forward to escaping the pressures of daily family life, with well-earned breaks from the structure and routine normally needed to ensure, for example, that our children arrive at school on time with all the appropriate kit. Letting our hair down is also a vital survival tool. However, holidays with our children are often characterised by additional stresses, laced with periods of mayhem. In order to understand why our dream family holiday differs so much from the lived reality, we need to consider what holiday times mean for our children. As ever, this involves thinking about the experiential journey our children took to reach our families. We might ask ourselves the following questions:

- How many previous changes of carer did our children have, bearing in mind that they are likely to have experienced additional changes not identified in case files?

- What was the nature of these changes?

- Were they planned or unplanned?

- What preparation, or involvement in planning, did our children have?

- Were they given help to make sense of each move or to express anxieties about what was happening to them?

- Did they pack their own things or were they handed a bag of 'stuff' as they left or arrived at their new 'home'?

- What transport was used and who went with them?

- How were our children perceived as coping with the moves?

We then need to work out what these experiences meant, and continue to mean, to our children in terms of their expectations and behaviour. Often separations from birth families were abrupt and traumatic; a caregiver may have suddenly disappeared out of our children's lives as parents split up or perhaps 'went on little holidays' to prison. There may have been numerous 'going back homes' with periods of formal or informal care elsewhere before children were removed permanently. Some rehabilitation attempts may have been in accommodation away from their family base. As they were officially removed, our children may have been told by birth family members that they were 'just going away for a little while' and, if they remain in contact, may continue to hear that 'one day soon' they will be reunited as a family. Sometimes 'going away' becomes associated with new toys or clothes, as birth families struggle to let go and try to make themselves, and their relinquished children, feel better. Initially, becoming 'looked after' may also have connotations of material gain or the 'feel good' of a 'honeymoon period'.

Subsequently, temporary foster carers may have held parties when children moved on again, intending to mark this as a time for celebration and implying that they would be missed. Instead our children may have inferred that foster carers were celebrating their leaving and would not miss them. Moreover, foster families' holiday arrangements may have meant yet another move for our children, this time into temporary respite care. They will have witnessed the pleasure and excitement foster family members displayed as they prepared, yet felt excluded or even punished for 'not being good enough'. Indeed their behaviour may have played a significant part here, confirming that they are unlovable and deserve to be left out or abandoned.

Consider, too, our children's response to meeting us. Did they appear to settle reasonably well, with little upset at leaving previous carers? At the time we may have felt reassured that this boded well for the placement; the reverse is likely to be true. A more realistic interpretation would be that our children experienced this move as just one more to be survived. Their intense fear of separation and loss may have caused them to 'shut down' such overwhelming feelings: the line of least resistance is often the last battle-line of all and the only one available to them.

Now, when we look at our children's response to holidays, we may see many of the same dynamics at play. Rather than thinking: 'Oh goody! How exciting, we're going away', our children may feel distressing tension in their bodies and emotions, such as fear of the unknown, they do not understand. They are more likely to think 'Not again! What have I done this time?' or 'Why can't I stay here, I was just beginning to get used to this house and this family?' than to relish the idea of another change. We should remember, too, that our children tend to have poor emotional literacy, so the excitement they pick up may be experienced as equally distressing and inexplicable as fear, anger or grief. Add to this the inevitable family stresses as packing gets under way, items are lost, pets need to be temporarily 'rehomed' and other last-minute preparations made, and we have a potential recipe for disaster.

To consider the impact on our children of these separation experiences, visualise being visited by a colleague we do not know well who says she has heard we are having some relationship difficulties with our partner and that she has great news for us: she has found us a new partner. What feelings emerge as we picture this? Would we happily pack our bags, anticipating that this might be just the opportunity we need, or would we be filled with trepidation about the implications? Would we feel able to ask who this person was and why they wanted us to live with them? Would we go, or would we dare refuse? Had we seen the move coming or was it a bolt out of the blue? Would we view it objectively, feel it was 'all our fault' or blame our colleague or new partner? Moreover, how would we feel if our colleague grabbed a few of our things at random and led us out to their car there and then? And what if our ex-partner decided to host a 'goodbye' party: would we feel they are saying how much we would be missed or 'good riddance'?

Alternatively, consider how previously divorced persons might feel if someone they met only a month previously proposed out of the blue? Would they be likely to trust that this time the marriage would be successful, or have doubts about whether this relationship would be better than the previous one? Probably most people would have grave reservations and feelings of trepidation: such natural emotions are likely to be highly intensified in children who have had ambiguous relationships with several carers, often feeling powerless to control their own destiny. Moreover, unlike adult divorcees, our children's experiences occurred when their neurobiological 'wiring' was still 'under construction' and the MN 🔍 systems that help them make sense of the world were still immature. They are less likely to have experienced lasting, positive attachment relationships with which to balance the negative ones.

Repeated changes in carer will also have affected our children's ability to develop a secure base and sound OP. Consider how many houses they have lived in and how many 'mother-figures' our children have known before coming home to us. Often these previous 'knowns' seemed to 'disappear' arbitrarily, with any returns 'home', or contact, tenuous or intermittent. Subsequently our children may come to associate 'security' with the concrete building of our dwelling and see us merely as 'part of the ever-changing scenery'. No wonder many of them struggle with the concept of holidays – leaving the one thing they are beginning to see as permanent – and let us know through their behavioural language just how distressed they feel.

These visualisations can help us make some sense of our children's difficulties around holidays. So whilst we frequently use the term 'going away' to mean taking short recreational breaks and gaining some 'me' time, for our children 'going away' is overshadowed by 'forever' and loss: of home, family, sense of belonging, sense of self. Furthermore, the difficulties they face in relation to changes in routine and structure are highly relevant when thinking about holidays, which by their very nature involve changes in daily rhythms. We can help our children feel more comfortable with these by acknowledging their difficulties openly, empathising, and validating their feelings during the holiday planning and preparation stages. We might say:

> 'I know it's hard for you when things change. My guess is this is because you've had so many scary changes in your life.'

> 'We're all going on holiday soon, so we'll change where we'll be sleeping for two weeks. We'll be doing lots of different things when we're there too. I can see this might be scary to you. Remember I'll always be here to help you with your feelings.'

> 'We're all going together – you don't get rid of us that easily!'

> 'Here's the brochure with pictures and information about where we're going. Let's make a drink and have a look.'

> 'We can make a "countdown calendar" later today so we know when we're going and when we're coming back.'

> 'Let's think. What things would you like to take with you?'

These exchanges are not intended to reassure children that the changes involved in going on holiday with us are different or less important than those of the past. Instead we begin from the bottom up, acknowledging the continuing fear-based nature of our children's responses: giving them clear messages that we understand their world and their feelings and are there to help them. We should then create ample opportunities to talk to them about the early experiences that caused them to feel this way: providing as many concrete examples as possible. We might say:

> 'You and Terri went to live in a hostel in Cadlington when you were just a baby because Max was hurting her. There were lots of strange people and it was so noisy. Babies don't like changes or lots of noisy people.'

> 'When you were three and lived with your birth mum she was rushed into hospital and you went to stay at Mary's. You didn't know why, or when you'd be going home. You must have felt so scared and lonely. That would put me off going away too.'

Gently exploring these painful circumstances helps them gain sufficient insights to recognise that how they feel 'now' reflects how they felt 'then', yet this time they are not alone. This is a challenge that requires much forethought, yet it is essential if our children are to develop coherent narratives with us, alongside the feeling of gaining greater control over their lives. Having validated, and empathised with, our children, our next step is to explore with them how they can manage their feelings. Recognising that they may not know what will help, we need to be prepared to come up with suggestions. We might begin by thinking about the type of holiday that might work best for them. This is where the element of reassurance can enter into the equation.

> 'Holidays are important for this family, so let's see if we can figure out how to make it easier for you to feel OK.'

'Lots of adopted children hate going away on holiday. It feels like a huge upheaval. Remember, I'll be with you every step of the way.'

'Some families find it works better to go caravanning or camping – that's a bit like taking your house with you. That could be good and we could practise in the garden.'

'You love swimming, so maybe staying near a lake or the sea would work?'

'We won't go too far. Then if it gets too much for us we can always come home.'

Children may be able to manage days out or overnight trips close to home, rather than two weeks abroad, at least for their initial holidays with us (despite the lure of better weather). Talking to our children about this, letting them know where we are going and why, shows that we recognise their difficulties, shows them that we are considering their needs alongside our own and gives them some control over events. We should not assume that our children will recognise our intentions as positive without being clear about this, often to the point of exaggeration. Nor should we expect that they will feel more relaxed about the holiday simply because we have made our choice with them in mind. We will need to continue listening to and validating their unspoken feelings, making it clear that we understand they may struggle to cope with even brief absences from home.

Clearly it is vital to take into account our children's early histories when planning holidays. For example, taking children on holidays to farms or countryside, providing freedom to explore without the restrictions of our more regulated home environment, can be positive. However, if this is likely to trigger sensory responses associated with, for example, odours within an abusive or neglectful birth family, this would be a poor choice. Similarly the child-centred amusements of 'Disneyworld' may appeal to everyone superficially, yet the noise, sights, smells and movement are likely to set off cascades of bodily and emotional sensations (bottom and middle-storey responses) that threaten to overwhelm children. Being strapped into a vehicle packed with belongings can evoke the terror of previous moves and painful separations. Fear of the unknown 'out there' can threaten to destabilise even the most seemingly 'together' children. We must use our 'forensic knowledge' to inform our holiday choices, to help us work out 'which brain storey they are in' 🏠 and to let our children 'know what we know' and help them make sense of their distress.

On previous moves our children may have moved alone, or with siblings, to strange new environments: leaving the adults in the familiar home and surroundings. It is up to us to help our children experience 'going away' as different this time, emphasising that we are all going on holiday together and returning together, remembering that actions speak louder than words. Rather than giving our children their own suitcase, we might choose to have a family suitcase to hold everybody's clothes. Encouraging our children to help pack allows them to feel part of the decision-making and more in control. This is crucial because children learn through feeling and doing; simultaneously our words can act as 'connectors' linking the 'thinking' (top), and 'feeling' and 'doing' (bottom and middle-storey) areas of their semi-detached brains.

Obtaining photographs and information about what to expect from the holiday, to share with our children, can reduce their fear levels and help them gain a sense of self-agency. While the internet is a useful initial tool, downloads, brochures and pictorial reminders of the holiday that we can touch and look at repeatedly with our children are more useful. Demonstrating the route from home to holiday destination using a route planner or Google Maps (printed off) could also help. Stories and songs from the area we intend to visit can set the scene too – alongside local foodstuffs and traditions. Try a practice themed picnic in the garden or kitchen with, say, Welsh cakes, Chelsea buns, scottish shortbread, Irish soda bread or Cornish pasties as centrepieces, depending on your destination. A few local words or sayings could be introduced and practised, just as if travelling abroad;

such 'off-the-wall happenings' take the edge off the strangeness of new places and are great fun!

If we have been on previous holidays together, photographs of leaving and returning home can provide concrete reminders to our children that we are coming back. Talking about previous holiday journeys also helps to reinforce this and to stimulate changes to their MN systems. If this is our first holiday together, talking about previous short trips or days out will reinforce the 'coming home' OP message. Children can draw maps of the footpaths or route with 'our house' clearly depicted at both ends, completing their holiday 'narrative'. Similarly planning the return journey from holiday destinations is very reassuring, perhaps noting the main towns and villages along the way and conspicuously flagging up 'our town'. Taking photographs of home (inside and out) on holiday with us and deliberately and openly leaving something we treasure behind for the return can reduce children's fears. We might also discuss a number of post-holiday activities with them to further emphasise that we are all returning home together.

It is important to talk about home, and when we are going home, during the holiday and to remain conscious of our children's potential distress. They will let us know, through their behaviour, when they are struggling: if we are able to remain open to 'hearing' and 'interpreting' their behavioural language we will be able to offer the therapeutic reparenting experiences our children need. We could reflect their unspoken feelings by wondering whether the digi-box will record our favourite TV programmes whilst we are away or whether the cat left with next-door neighbours misses us as much as we miss her. We might send postcards to the house, letting it know we are looking forward to sleeping in our own beds when we return, as another fun way of reinforcing this message and strengthening OP.

Having considered some of the difficulties with holidays, it is equally important to consider the opportunities. Going on holiday with our children, if managed well, creates opportunities to spend quality time together we can use to our children's advantage.

Unless we are going on holiday with friends, the people we meet on holiday are unlikely to form part of our normal social network. This may make it possible for us to let our hair down and act in less routine or restrained ways than in our home environment. Not only does this give us a chance to be 'all of ourselves', it allows our children to see other parts of us too: consolidating OSC.

We might declare a 'food amnesty' or suggest eating dessert before the main course: the stickier and messier the better. This can help our children develop a different relationship to food: particularly relevant with children who have food-related, or cleanliness, issues. Sharing an ice-cream with our children rather than having one each may feel easier on holiday; agreeing to taking licks in turn provides valuable opportunities for closeness, eye contact and sharing. We might issue a challenge that the one who licks the most ice-cream wins a cuddle. We can then be the one mock-crying 'not fair', subsequently collapsing into giggles, as of course we get the cuddle too! Changing the usual parent–child dynamics is unlikely to undermine the boundaries and roles we have attempted to establish at home, since these experiences will be 'state-dependent': responses and memories relating specifically to the holiday will not be generalised to home routines if we are clear that these are *things we usually only do when away together*. Again this encourages the development of OC and OSC.

We might also like to engage in activities that are outside our own normal experiences, bearing in mind that our children's emotional age may make chronologically age-appropriate activities less valuable for them. At the seaside burying parts of our children in the sand and finding them is a fun alternative to hide-and-seek and helps with OP, especially if we vocalise that '*we know they're there somewhere*' when searching for hidden bits. We may feel more relaxed going on swings, see-saws or roundabouts with our children than we would in our local park. This can 're-do', in safe, nurturing ways, the pre-birth and early post-natal experiences that may not have gone well for our children, if for example their birth mother concealed the pregnancy, was bed-bound, or left them lying unattended. Subsequently we may feel able to take these new activities back home: providing a better and more memorable legacy than photographs or videos alone.

There may also be occasions when our children have the opportunity to go away individually, perhaps on school trips. Whilst we might relish the peace this could offer us temporarily, there can be many stresses building up to such events. Fear of separation and of the unknown can come into play, making it well-nigh impossible for children to contemplate leaving home. Rather than offering 'reassurance' and encouragement to our children, often generating increased resistance, offering them opportunities to choose not to go allows them to feel in control – and often results in the decision to take part. If they are planning to go, we may need to negotiate special conditions, such as being allowed to receive or make phone calls home or to limit the period away. Teaching staff and group leaders are often sympathetic once our children's special circumstances are explained and will 'bend the rules'. We should also make sure our children take with them TOs, such as photos of us or a scarf that smells of home, and write little cards reminding them we are thinking of them to be received each day either by post or through an understanding accompanying adult.

The element of choice is also important when it comes to us, as parents, contemplating breaks away from home without our children. Even if these are work related we should first consider the likely impact on our children's security and stress levels and, if they are non-negotiable, ensure we do everything we can to help them survive. Whilst we might easily argue that taking time away for 'R and R' is essential to our survival, both in the short and longer term we must balance this against the distress it may cause our children. Remember that their sense of security and belonging is weak and try to think what we would do if our children were still babies or toddlers (bottom and middle-storey mode). Keeping the separation period short, empathising with their difficulties and keeping children's routines as normal as usual can help them to practise managing separations, as will providing TOs and staying in contact by telephone, Skype, text or email. Here the choice must ultimately be ours not our children's: only we can decide. However, if we are tuned into their feelings, we can make that choice balancing their needs with ours. Similarly only we can judge how much notice we should give our children if we choose to go; some need time to get used to the idea of any change, whilst stress levels can 'crank up' with too much warning for others.

Summary

The central message of this chapter is that while holidays (vacations) may be challenging for our children, recognising and validating their feelings, being realistic about what they can manage and working towards reducing their fears and muddles can allow us to seize the opportunities that change brings. Breaks in routine and sharing an unfamiliar environment provide opportunities for us to bond and have fun with our children. In doing so we help them perceive and relate to us and to the ever-changing world in less fear-based (bottom-storey) ways: providing opportunities for healthier neurobiological development (connecting to middle and top storeys), changes in MN systems, strengthening OP and OC and increasing wellbeing and resilience. It can also help them learn that going away is not forever. Changes that involve separations from us are clearly fraught with more difficulty. Taking the developmental reparenting perspective allows us to recognise that, just like small infants, the more we keep our children close and in familiar surroundings now, the more they will flourish independently in the future, *as and when they are ready*. 'Checking in and checking out' (see Appendix 2) allows us to put our therapeutic parenting skills into practice in developmentally appropriate ways.

Chapter 16

Juggling Siblings

Few children placed for adoption today avoid significant physical or emotional trauma in their birth families; many suffer additional trauma whilst being looked after. Even babies removed at birth are likely to suffer pre-birth trauma, perhaps through poor nutrition or exposure to drugs, alcohol or nicotine. At the very least they experience the trauma of separation from the mother whose bio-rhythms they have grown to know in the womb. In all cases, their worlds will have been ones of confusion, dysregulation and fractured attachments. We now explore this in terms of the particular complexities brought to our families by siblings.

Siblings come in many shapes, sizes and ways: born into our families (as neonates, usually one at a time and relatively healthy), or placed with us, usually beyond babyhood, singly or as 'a set'; we can further sub-divide this group into siblings raised together and those with differing family or care histories. When hurt children are placed in new families with existing born-to children it can create tensions based on a sense of difference, of 'not-really-belonging' and of lack of entitlement, over and above their trauma-related issues. If coming into families where there are already hurt children, their developmental attachment difficulties can be further magnified, since these children's behaviour may also still reflect their early chaotic and inconsistent care. Competition for what they perceive to be limited attention increases each child's anxieties and consequently their difficult behaviour, as they struggle to 'tell' us how they feel and be 'heard' above the daily hubbub.

Where siblings come 'as a set', they bring with them existing, distorted sibling interactions, to which they are likely to cling and which further threaten attachment relationships within our families. Different dynamics again can come into play where siblings placed as a group have differing family or care histories. Moreover, all children develop unique responses to their traumatic experiences that significantly impact their understanding of relationships, including those with siblings. While our children may have spent their first months or years in the same family, issues like their age, stage of development and position in the family influence the effect these experiences have had on them and the expectations they bring with them. Thus, far more than born-to siblings, children coming home to us can vary in their feelings about, relationships with and behaviour towards their siblings. We need to devise individual 'reparenting programmes' taking into account each child's history and current behaviour, derived from developmental attachment principles.

One aspect to be considered that can significantly influence children's developmental attachments is the length of time they spent within their dysfunctional family of origin. We might presume that it would be the eldest children in sibling groups who suffered the greatest trauma, having lived in that environment longest. However, as their families expand, struggling parents may have been able to offer more positive caregiving to their first-born than to subsequent children. This is significant since children's earliest, pre-verbal experiences (in terms of good enough parenting) are the most influential in determining their neurobiological make-up. There may also have been gender differences in the way parents related to their offspring, or one child may have become the favourite. These differences influence the way children view both themselves and each other, affecting inter-sibling relationships and their expectations of subsequent caregivers.

In deciding how to parent siblings, whether already in our families or placed with us, we must begin by observing their behaviour in conjunction with their trauma histories to provide us with the essential clues to understanding their world. The effects of children's early traumatic experiences begin at the physical level, and are strongly linked to emotional feelings and memories beneath their conscious awareness. These in turn inform their current perceptions and behaviour and form the basis for their unconscious, perhaps contradictory, beliefs that:

- they are not good enough to be kept safe
- they are not special or important
- no-one listens to, or cares, about them
- there is not enough love to go round
- they must fight for adult attention
- their needs, and those of their siblings, will not be met
- if one sibling behaves badly, they may all be sent away
- all parents will eventually abandon or mistreat them
- it is not safe to be dependent
- siblings must look to each other for help.

For both favoured and non-favoured children, moving into families where parents provide nurture and structure and treat their children equally is likely to be distressing since it threatens their perception of themselves, their siblings and their inter-relationships. Helping our children learn the 'language of equality' will be a protracted process, as it threatens to undermine the rocky foundations upon which they have constructed their perceptions of themselves and their world. Consequently they tend to continue to misread our actions and misconstrue our feelings and intentions. This may be more obvious in the case of favoured children, who need help to accept that, whilst they are indeed important, their siblings deserve our attention just as much. The dynamics are different yet equally significant for less favoured or 'scapegoated' children, who find the idea that they are special and worthy of our attention alien. They, too, may have no language through which to interpret our intentions towards them: responding to positive attention with fear and becoming subdued, or conversely 'acting out' to 'stay safe' and 'let us know they know' they do not deserve it.

Another relevant issue is that of 'parentified' children. Older children have often felt responsible and protective towards younger siblings and continue to try to compensate for what they now perceive as inadequate parental responses by attempting to provide the care themselves. They may fear that if their siblings misbehave, they will all be 'sent away'. They may resist being parented themselves and are likely to feel 'displaced' when we assume the parental role for their siblings. The caring role they assumed may have been the only way they obtained a sense of self-worth: lacking the belief that parents could love them for themselves as children, rather than as quasi-parents. While their actions might superficially be seen as laudable, they can have serious consequences for siblings placed together in new families.

Even children who had 'good enough' parenting experiences lack the emotional maturity to meet the needs of other children; traumatised children have far fewer resources to deal with the pressures of daily life. Their compromised neurobiological and socio-emotional development means our children are unlikely to be able to offer their siblings sufficient positive 'parenting' experiences. Furthermore, children struggling to survive hostile family environments can feel understandable resentment, or contradictory feelings, towards their younger siblings: feelings they may act out in their current relationships.

In new families, many 'parentified' children continue to act as 'caregivers' for their siblings, perhaps encouraging their siblings to turn to them, rather than their new parents. They fear that their siblings are at risk from adults in general, and feel an overwhelming sense of shame when they perceive (however unjustified) that their new parents have not fully understood their siblings' needs. Moreover, younger siblings unfamiliar with having their needs met by adult caregivers often turn to elder siblings for support: rejecting the role of their new parents and perpetuating early, unhealthy attachment relationships. Altering these enmeshed relationships can be a difficult process: we need to work hard to prevent 'parentified' children from feeling 'displaced', 'devalued' or 'shamed', or increasing our 'parented' children's fear-based reactions to adult caregivers. These dynamics can pose particularly difficult challenges for substitute caregivers since they have been through intensive assessment and training processes focused on their ability to be 'good' parents. These unexpected challenges can undermine their confidence and intensify feelings of inadequacy if the parenting they offer is rejected.

Since our children have not experienced a consistent secure base and may have lived in families where attention to one child meant loss or abandonment, encouraging close and supportive sibling relationships can engender fear and inter-sibling competition. With these beliefs and behaviours embedded in their MN systems, hurt children view our interactions with them and their siblings through a distorting prism. The 'normal' sibling rivalry of securely attached sibling relationships is exacerbated for children who had to 'fight for survival' in environments where their needs were not met consistently.

Again it is its frequency, intensity, duration and meaning that sets our children's behaviour apart. In parenting siblings we must therefore identify and meet each child's needs individually whilst simultaneously recognising the distressed relationships between them. This can mean acting in counter-intuitive ways, for example allowing one child to attend swimming lessons whilst keeping the others at home for some one-to-one attention, since they are not yet able to handle group situations or may 'sabotage' their siblings' enjoyment. Similarly we may need to ensure that children are not left together unsupervised, when bullying or teasing may occur.

Allowing children to play together can lead to re-enactment of early, traumatic sibling relationships, in turn limiting opportunities for practising new ways of interacting, and reducing the development of healthier MN circuits. Conversely, encouraging children to play separately may increase their levels of anxiety that neither they, nor their siblings, are safe. A sibling may represent the only OP 🐾 and secure base they have experienced; playing separately they may lose sight of this, both visually and emotionally; they may only see themselves in relation to their siblings. Moreover, they may worry that siblings are being singled out either for further abuse or more love and attention. We need to work hard to recognise these feelings in our children and find ways of helping them. We might, for example, encourage them to play separately within the same room as us, joining in with them alternately: perhaps encouraging them to build with Lego separately, with a view to combining their constructions into a 'family creation'. This parallel play can simultaneously alter MN circuits and strengthen OP and OC.

Moreover, starting with short periods of time when children play separately, alongside short periods of supervised play, we should choose toys, games and activities that encourage their sense of safety and security. Competitive games may not be appropriate; often our children's fragile self-esteem means they cannot manage being 'winners' or 'losers', leading to increased conflict; non-competitive games are frequently more appropriate. Baking, making sand-barriers against the sea, digging 'group holes', planting flowers, washing the car, tickling Mummy, painting, gluing or sticking family pictures, putting up tents, singing songs or listening to stories together can all provide acceptable shared fun. Shared chores, such as fluffing up pillows or picking up socks, can work and can be great fun if engaged in light-heartedly and with limited expectations of standards!

Family picnics also offer opportunities of 'doing it together', although we may need to pack each child's food in separate containers to minimise cries of 'It's not fair, they've got more than me!' Often trips to the cinema work well, as children tend to focus more on the screen (and popcorn) than on each other, as long as there are enough adults to sit between them. Eventually, inventing games like 'the-messiest-spaghetti-eater-wins' can introduce limited elements of competition that challenge expectations, make taking part fun in itself, and even out chances of 'losing'. The 'prize' for everyone could then be a 'group hug'.

Parenting our children equally does not always mean treating them the same, since they all have distinct personalities, interests and needs. We should resist knee-jerk responses of 'it's not fair' from our children, recognising that we may never succeed, in their view, in being fair to them! Instead we can offer messages of empathy for their feelings while remaining equally attentive to everyone's needs and difficulties. We may also need to reassure one sibling that another's behaviour does not mean they will be seen in the same light and give them repeated messages that they are separate individuals with distinct needs. All this can feel like sawing ourselves in half! Where there are two, or more, caregivers we need not spread ourselves so thinly: separate play and talking spaces with separate adults, allowing us more readily to help each child feel unique, valued and understood. However, we need to use agreed 'family rules' to ensure our children experience a consistent parenting approach.

Managing outside-the-home activities can also feel like an impossible juggling act if we operate a '*we'll all do this together*' policy. Whilst the logistics of taking children to separate activities, such as swimming lessons, takes some organisation, the benefits can be remarkable. Again, 'being fair' is clearly easier with more than one caregiver available. Maybe one partner could take a child to gym club whilst the other offers '*aren't-we-lucky-it's-just-us*' time, at home or elsewhere. Relatives and trusted friends can also provide 'equal but different' opportunities: each child experiencing 'being spoiled' in their own space. Since grandparents often relish these 'one-on-one' times, and our children may behave better singly and with non-parent-figures, this is definitely a 'win-win' situation! Again, for consistency, and to reinforce OC ©, regular 'family' rules should apply, unless otherwise agreed.

We must also help our children recognise the feelings inherent in their sibling relationships. By monitoring when situations are approaching the point of disruption and stepping in early, we can reduce negative sibling interactions. We can guard against our children feeling 'losers' or 'failures' by ending play sessions when they are still fun, so they still feel good about themselves and each other. If our children can manage 15 minutes of safe play together, we might allow them just five or ten minutes before intervening and congratulating them on playing well. Allowing play to go on too long until fights and arguments have started is distressing to everyone and prevents children learning new ways of interacting. Top-storey interventions can be introduced both before and after sibling play sessions:

- Talking honestly and uncritically about our children's difficulties demonstrates empathy whilst helping them cope better. These interactions work best when we (and our children) are feeling relaxed and at ease, use the PARCEL approach and hold in mind their histories.

- We might say: *'I've noticed it's hard for you to share with your brother. I can understand that: when you lived in your birth family you didn't always get enough to eat. Perhaps we can practise some sharing games, to help you begin to learn that there's always enough to go round.'*

- If children struggle to share our attention we could reflect that: *'I've noticed it's hard for you when I pay attention to your sister. I wonder if you think I love her more? That makes sense: I'd believe I wasn't good enough if I'd been in five foster homes when I was little. Let's have some cuddles now and see whether this helps you feel you're very special to me, even when I'm helping your sister with her homework.'*

- Children need to be congratulated on how well they were able to survive an unsafe environment: *'You did so well looking after yourself and your sister when your birth parents were fighting. Now you're here, let's practise me looking after you and your sister.'*

- *We need to help our children 'practise' new messages: 'Maybe now you need help to learn that it's safe for me to take care of you. I wonder how I can help you know you're just as special as your sister?'*

All these issues can be intensified where related children are placed together yet had a different birth parent, differing experiences, or perhaps entered our home at separate times. Moreover, introducing traumatised children into our home is likely to unsettle any existing children in the family: the traumatised children reawakening memories of past distress in our more settled ones. Without careful planning we are likely to have less time for our established children, understandably feeling we need to prioritise our new arrival. Suddenly the world becomes less predictable as our established children seek to find ways to relate both to us and their new sibling. These issues, faced by all birth parents of second or subsequent babies to some degree, are magnified when they involve children in 'socially created' families and further intensified with neglected and abused youngsters.

Established children are likely to feel a sense of displacement, while 'new' children must adjust to their new setting and share, compete for or feel they must 'earn' attention. This reduces their opportunities to feel special: an essential antidote to early traumatic hurts, rejection and abandonment. If, additionally, our existing children were placed separately from their birth siblings, comparisons and feelings of divided loyalty can emerge, perhaps alongside 'the grass is greener syndrome', where newly acquired siblings are viewed less favourably than separated birth siblings. Where some children have continued contact with birth family members it can generate further ill feeling about adoptive siblings or about themselves as 'unlovable' and anticipating rejection. Holding this in mind, we can let our children know that we see they struggle with these issues, validate their feelings and help them make sense of them in terms of their differing past histories.

Introducing traumatised children into families with birth children may superficially appear less complex. Our birth children will be operating from a secure base, with healthy neurobiological connections, including MN systems that reflect the love and commitment they received from us; in most cases they did not have significant breaks in their attachments. However, difficulties can still emerge. Our born-to children are likely to have been involved in the decision-making and assessment processes and committed themselves to supporting us and their adoptive siblings. Nevertheless, the reality of living with troubled siblings is often very different from their expectations: perhaps internalised from popular literature or peers. Having never experienced children who express their underlying fears through challenging behaviours, birth children can be ill-equipped to deal with rudeness, aggression, lying, attention-seeking or withdrawal. They may struggle to cope with their 'bad' feelings when siblings break their favourite toys or 'borrow' precious items and then 'lose' them.

Born-to children may find it difficult to share their hurt and angry feelings with us because they feel guilty about having them: after all they agreed with the plan for adoption and recognise their siblings have had a 'rough deal'. They are likely to have a strong sense of family loyalty and, not wishing to increase our burden when they see us struggling with a traumatised child, feel unable to talk about their anxieties and doubts. We must work hard to demonstrate empathy for each of our children, giving them 'permission' to speak and ensuring that we meet their individual needs with equanimity. This can itself pose problems for us when we are already over-stressed and over-stretched: taking care of ourselves may slip even further down our 'to do' list – to our own, and the family's, cost.

We must also consider our own sibling relationships and how these may influence our expectations of siblings now. If we were raised in healthily functioning families we will have experienced sibling relationships very different from our hurt children's. We must be aware of, and reflect on, our own relationships and the ways they differ from, or mirror, our children's, to avoid interpreting their relationship interactions through the lens of our own experiences. If we had relatively positive sibling relationships it can be difficult to see beyond 'all children do that'. Should we overlook, choose to ignore or minimise our 'created' siblings' difficulties, we will be unable to provide appropriate opportunities for repair and healing. If our sibling relationships were stressed, or gender-biased, we must guard against inadvertently interpreting our children's relationships in this light. For example, if we were teased or bullied by an older sibling, it may be harder for us to empathise realistically with, and recognise the fear-based nature of, children who act aggressively with their siblings, and hence over- or under-react.

A further, unfortunately common, dimension can be that we live in communities where there are different expectations and a lack of understanding for families like ours. At school or within our wider family and social networks our children will often be encouraged to 'look out for each other' and be expected to share. This may run counter to their best interests, since it replicates the 'parentified' roles or 'lack-of-enough-to-go-round beliefs' we are trying to alter. Furthermore, unwitting comparisons between siblings made by 'outsiders' will negatively impact their sense of self and self-worth: both of which are already likely to be compromised. We may need to seek support to inform teachers, friends and extended family about these issues, so they can recognise our children's special needs and help them devise ways of dealing with them effectively.

Check in and check out

See Appendix 2.

Chapter 17

Taking Care of Ourselves

It goes with the territory that parents are expected to put their children first, that our children's needs should be prioritised and ours sacrificed to theirs. On becoming parents we may have given up activities we previously enjoyed and reduced our friendship circle, in part due to these expectations and in part as a result of lack of time or energy, or feelings that the pressures we face differ from our friends'. This pattern is exaggerated when we take on traumatised children whose needs far exceed those of born-to children. It may therefore come as both a surprise and a relief to learn that the central theme of this chapter is the importance of prioritising our own and our partners' needs. This is a natural feature of evolution. In life-threatening circumstances, species survival requires the prioritising of mothers over the unborn; vulnerable youngsters are unlikely to make it if their source of safety and nutrition is lost; poorly nourished or distressed parents are less likely to raise healthy children.

Earlier we looked in depth at the neurobiological impact of early trauma and considered how the development of babies' brains is mediated by their experiences pre-birth and in their first years. We argued that the brain is plastic: body–brain–mind connections can be changed as a result of later experiences; this principle underpins therapeutic, or developmental, reparenting of hurt children. We now consider the potential impact on our own bodies, brains and minds of living with traumatised children, how our neurobiological patterns can be adversely affected due to the secondary trauma of sharing our lives with them, and the changes we can make to protect or improve our 'wiring'. We can begin by considering the expectations we had when we began the adoption process. What sort of parents did we imagine we would be? What experiences did we anticipate sharing with our children? What were our expectations of how our children would manage at home and school? How close are these expectations to the reality of life with our children now?

If our expectations and reality are 'out-of-synch' we may have feelings of failure, especially if our children's behavioural difficulties seem to have increased rather than diminished post placement, or if we feel angrier or more helpless than we could ever have imagined. If we feel out of control and on edge as we await the next battle with our children, feel misunderstood and blamed by friends, family and professionals and stressed in our couple relationships, these emotions will be intensified and reflected in increased stress neurochemicals such as cortisol. This, in turn, affects our physical health and immune systems and effects changes in our neurobiological systems. We can become 'trauma-sensitised': 'hot-wired' to respond at primarily bottom and mid-storey levels rather than through (top-storey) mature thinking and reasoning 🏠. While we may feel uncomfortable accepting this, it is important to emphasise that these are normal reactions to living with both acute and chronic stress.

For example, having money regularly taken out of our purse may lead to our monitoring how much money we have and remembering the location of the purse at every moment, ensuring it has been hidden away from temptation. Increased distress (including shame) follows when, despite our best efforts, money still goes missing and we repeatedly go over whether money has in fact disappeared or we spent it when shopping. Stress levels increase further as we consider how and when to deal with this issue. If we have several children we may have to determine who took the money and work out how to be fair and reasonable. We are likely to feel guilt and anger, blaming ourselves for failing to keep our purse safe, to become anxious about our children's visits to friends' homes and to worry where this pattern of stealing might lead.

Dealing with such events on a regular, yet often inconsistent, basis can lead to us feeling we are over-reacting or misjudging our children. We are likely to feel we are constantly 'walking on eggshells' and speaking to other adults about this might mean they see our children as 'bad' or invite them less often. Moreover, knowing that confronting the issue may lead to our children's denial, anger or withdrawal adds a further dimension of distress when we may already be facing a myriad of other issues: school-based difficulties, food and control issues, sleep problems. This is a far cry from the 'normal' family life we visualised; yet is one shared daily by many parents of traumatised children.

Living with this level of distress can lead to us becoming permanently stressed: a concept often referred to as 'secondary trauma'. Conrad (2004, p.1) defines secondary trauma as 'the stress resulting from helping or wanting to help a traumatised or suffering person'. He is clear that 'empathic engagement can lead to secondary trauma' and that its development is prevalent in those caring for traumatised children because 'empathy is often the most important tool foster parents bring to helping the children in their care. Unfortunately, the more empathic they are, the greater their risk for internalising the trauma of the children they care for.' In essence Conrad suggests that the better we are at empathising with traumatised children the better we are able to help them *and* the more likely we are to suffer secondary trauma. Thus, rather than being a sign of poor parenting, or personal weakness, secondary trauma is often indicative of good parenting and that we need to be good to ourselves!

Having said that, it is important to identify any signs of secondary trauma we may display and take action to address our trauma issues sooner rather than later, for the sake of our own health and wellbeing and that of the whole family. Children can only make progress if parents model the change process; we must have the courage to show we can face that challenge. By changing first, not because we are necessarily 'getting it wrong' but because it is always possible to change for the better, we improve our children's life-chances. We cannot do this if our stress levels and sense of failure affect our self-view and our ability to parent our children positively. For this reason, and because we deserve it, we should instigate our process of change right away through taking good care of ourselves.

We could begin by congratulating ourselves on the excellent job we are doing as parents of traumatised children; repeating at frequent intervals mantras such as 'I'm a great parent and deserve treats'. Since this may initially be difficult, try imagining a friend in similar circumstances and considering the stresses she is facing. Would we feel she has failed if at times she gets angry at having every reasonable request challenged or would we empathise and try to help? Would we blame her if she left her purse out, money went missing and she felt crazy with worry? Would we think she was a bad parent? Most of us are more understanding and forgiving of our friends than we are of ourselves and would recognise that they were doing their best in challenging situations. We should practise empathising with and praising ourselves in the way we would our friends, perhaps saying out loud 'Well done me!' after remaining calm in dealing with challenges from our children. If we do become angry or act in ways we later regret, try saying out loud: 'This is not the end of the world. I've been angry today, but even my best friend would have been angry. I'm a good mum/dad and will practise being less angry again tomorrow.' To reinforce this we could ask our partner or friends to remind us of what a good job we are doing.

Putting notices that proudly state 'I'm a great parent, doing a tough job' in places only we will see, such as on the inside door of our wardrobe, or as wallpaper on our computer or mobile phone, can help us feel better about ourselves. Repeating the message five times daily will begin to alter our neurobiological patterns for the better. This will help us feel better about ourselves and more effective as parents, messages that will also convey to our children that we feel empowered and in control. Looking in the mirror, smiling and repeating positive messages about ourselves will alter our neurobiological settings and MN firing whilst simultaneously reminding us that we are good enough parents.

Alongside these simple practices we must find space and time for ourselves, perhaps taking time when our children are at school to do something for ourselves or to have a break from chores. Thirty minutes' light reading will be more beneficial for family life than half an hour spent vacuuming or dusting! We could phone friends and arrange to meet them for coffee or walks in the park, endeavouring, of course, to talk about anything other than children. We might just lie on the sofa and snooze! The final poster in Appendix 1 offers several more ideas for taking care of ourselves. Taking time to nurture our adult relationships is equally important. If it is impossible to arrange a night out, we could have a 'night in'. Dressing up as we would for a night out, ordering a meal to ensure we need not cook and agreeing to discuss any interests other than parenthood will make us feel better about ourselves and our partners or friends and promote feelings that life has not been totally swamped by the stresses of parenting. We should find lots of reasons to praise our partners and 'hear' and practise thanking them when they praise us.

Alongside providing some rest and relaxation in our life, it is important to consider our psychological and emotional health: not only in the 'here and now' but also from a historical perspective. We are all products of our past, and taking time to reflect on situations with which we now struggle and exploring how these reflect past experiences will be salutary. We could work with our partner or trusted friend on this, although we may also choose to engage in formal therapeutic work to help us address any past issues that increase stress in ourselves and our family now. Simultaneously we must hold on to the knowledge that we are good enough and doing the best we can.

Try listing the behaviours in our children that cause us particular angst alongside the messages these behaviours convey to us. Then imagine the messages we might have received from our parents had we acted the way our children are acting now. Comparing and contrasting these messages and recognising the differences and similarities between our experiences and theirs allows us to see that the criteria by which we judge ourselves as parents reflects how we were parented and may not be the optimal way to parent our children, since our parenting patterns may not match our children's developmental attachment needs.

Summary

We need to take care of, and nurture, ourselves if we are to take care of and nurture our families. Practise right now by saying out loud 'I am a great parent doing a brilliant job' before putting this book down and celebrating how amazing we are. Making sure we have fun as we do so and reminding ourselves that we deserve this because we are wonderful and creative human beings will stand us in good stead to provide the understanding and care our children need, survive the threat of secondary trauma and thrive as therapeutic parents.

Check in and check out

See Appendix 2.

Chapter 18

Getting Help

The mantra 'It takes a village to raise a child' acknowledges that parenting is a difficult task, one that cannot be successfully achieved alone. It becomes more challenging if family and friends do not support our parenting approach and their actions are critical of, or counter-productive to, our therapeutic philosophy. Therefore getting help often involves accepting that developmental reparenting principles fly in the face of many social expectations and 'normal' parenting principles. Whilst 'cognitive-behavioural' approaches (CBT) involving 'reward and punishment', 'ignoring "bad" behaviour' or using the 'naughty stair' are frequently recommended to parents, they are seldom effective with children whose development has been impacted by early traumatic experiences (see Archer 2003) and can reinforce their tendency to 'become stuck' (in their behaviour). By reminding ourselves that family and friends are doing their best and that they really do wish to understand how to help us, we can begin the essential process of educating them about our children's special needs. This will allow us to explore with them how our families can best be supported over the long term.

It is unlikely that members of our family, friends and professional support networks will have the time or drive to read this book thoroughly; we therefore need to offer them shorthand ways of 'getting it'. We could offer them comparisons between the needs of traumatised and non-traumatised children using the hand-out below (pp.255–258), and begin a dialogue about what this means for our children. We can then assess which of our family and friends are best placed to join our essential support network. These will be the people from whom we might seek child-minding, a shoulder to cry on, or an extra pair of hands when the going gets tough. Even the friends who do not 'get it' can offer support. They may be able to meet us for coffee, or go for walks, to help take our minds off our difficulties (avoiding child-related issues). This can boost our self-esteem by reminding us we have skills and talents outside our role as caregivers: especially helpful when our children's behaviour threatens our confidence as parents.

We should use the same assessment criteria when seeking professional support, although we may have to show great courage and patience to hold out for what we need. Educating professionals requires tact as well as commitment and time to provide just the right level of information without appearing to 'know it all'. We may also need to practise our 'asking for help' skills, since we may have always been the ones to whom others turned for help in the past or are striving to prove we are 'up to the job'. Remember that asking for help is a sign of strength not weakness; getting what we need is even more empowering.

Types of support
Support from people who understand because they've 'been there, done that'
Alongside support from family and friends we need to consider ways of eliciting support from other parents of hurt children. Adoption UK is an important source of support we could consider contacting to discuss our individual support needs and to identify local support groups in our area.

Specific support groups for difficulties, such as dyslexia, dyspraxia, ADHD, autistic spectrum disorders and speech and language disorders, may also feel appropriate.

Professional support

Since our children have special developmental attachment needs, we should consider whether we, and they, might benefit from more formal support from their placing agency, local Post Adoption Support or Child and Family teams. Be aware that social work practitioners within independent (and Local Authority) post-adoption services are more likely to be aware of developmental attachment issues than generic child and family workers. However, access to the specialist support services our families need may still be limited.

Additional support in school can prove invaluable, but it may first be necessary to help school staff recognise our children's special needs by providing material specifically relating to schools (see 'Useful Webiste Contacts' and 'Particularly Relevant Book Titles' on p.281).

Therapeutic support

This can prove extremely helpful for our children *if* it is the right sort of therapy. We might first discuss their needs with our doctor or social worker. However, before agreeing to any therapeutic intervention for our children, we need to assess its appropriateness.

Therapeutic interventions that exclude parents from the therapeutic process and non-directive interventions that work only with 'what children bring into the room' are unlikely to be helpful (e.g. Vaughan 2003). Similarly, Cognitive Behavioural Therapy (CBT) may only be of use in some cases (Siegel ithou. org/node2730) since it addresses the top storey of the brain to utilise top-down controls yet when they are most in need of such controls hurt children are likely to be stuck in lower storey sensori-emotional functioning. Moreover, children need to feel that we are an integral part of the healing process and can 'hear' and accept the worst parts of them. They also need help to recognise what is going on for them and, with help from us, explore their histories gradually if they are to heal from the trauma that is interfering with their ability to form secure and trusting relationships with us. To do this they will need a level of security, support and encouragement only we can provide.

We need therapeutic supports that can 'reach the parts others cannot': trauma- and attachment-focused therapy that preferably includes an understanding of developmental neurobiology (van der Kolk 2005; Siegel 2010b). Parent mentors and post-adoption 'buddies' e.g. through Adoption UK (see Resources) can add an added dimension to our support system, the former providing us with expert guidance using a developmentally based attachment approach, the latter offering an in-the-know sounding board and informal guide to managing our families and identifying further supports.

HANDOUT

Telling It Like It Is

Starting from the statement 'All children do that', friends and family must recognise that while it's true many children:

- steal

- tell lies

- 'lose it' sometimes

- fall out with friends

- have sibling rivalry issues

- argue about what shoes/clothes to wear to school

- suddenly decide they don't like vegetables

- fight with their siblings

- feel 'it's not fair'.

It is the intensity, duration, frequency and intent that are different in traumatised children. We can use 'apples and onions' to highlight these differences: apples representing 'neuro-typical' children and onions 'trauma-normal' children.

APPLE CHILDREN:

- trust parents love them

- know parents are 'there for them'

- feel safe and secure

- feel comfortable in themselves and can return to their 'comfort zone'

- know they are remembered

- know where 'home' is

- know they will be fed and cared for

- bounce back from temporary set-backs.

ONION CHILDREN:

- don't trust parents and caregivers
- believe no-one is 'there for them'
- feel the world is unsafe
- have fear and anxiety as their 'default setting'
- do not feel 'held in mind'
- are unsure where or what home is
- are not certain they will be fed and cared for
- struggle to get over everyday 'ups and downs'.

APPLE CHILDREN:

- tend to be sweet
- easily show and heal from their bruises
- have core belief systems consistent with the world around them
- develop self-assurance and self-worth
- become increasingly able to regulate their emotions and behaviours over time
- have feelings and thoughts consistent with their bodily sensations, emotions and current experiences
- experience appropriate guilt for what they do
- internalise social expectations and learn to modify their behaviour accordingly.

ONION CHILDREN:

- can be sharp, bitter or bitter-sweet
- tend to hide their hurts or wear them 'on their skin'
- perceive the world from fear-based belief systems
- have little self-belief or self-worth

- struggle to regulate their bodies, feelings and behaviours
- often react from the past not the present
- respond with shame rather than guilt
- tend not to learn from experience and persist with inappropriate 'survival' responses.

IMPLICATIONS:

All children need to feel safe, secure and loved. Without that secure base they often resist closeness and seem at odds with the world.

APPLE CHILDREN had parents who provided:

- consistent nurture that met their needs
- firm structure that helped them feel safe
- regulation of their body responses to promote regulation of their feelings
- help to develop a coherent sense of themselves and their world.

ONION CHILDREN had parents who failed to do this, or did so inconsistently. They therefore struggle with:

- close relationships and accepting help
- taking care of themselves and staying safe
- physical and emotional self-regulation
- self-awareness, self-control and self-esteem.

THERAPEUTIC PARENTS OF ONION CHILDREN NEED:

- friends, family and professionals who understand the impact of trauma on children and adults

- support and encouragement both informally and from professionals and experienced mentors or 'buddies' who have 'been there'

- recognition that they are doing their best in very difficult situations

- practical support: childcare; understanding; a shoulder to cry on; someone to share problems with and laugh with

- space to relax and take care of themselves and their relationships

- access to effective therapeutic supports, individually and as a family.

SOMEONE WHO SAYS:

- 'I know how hard it is for you.'

- 'You're doing your best.'

- 'What can I do to help?'

NOT:

- 'You're worrying too much.'

- 'All children do that.'

- 'It's just a phase.'

Appendix 1
Posters to Print

Anger Poster

When you're angry you get lots of a chemical called adrenalin in your body. This makes it hard to think well and make good decisions. Here are some ways you can get rid of angry feelings and adrenalin.

- Squeeze a bean bag
- Run around outside
- Try to accept there are things you can't do
- Jump up and down 20 times
- Do 20 sit-ups
- Punch a pillow
- Write down your feelings
- Tear up paper and think (or shout) about what makes you angry
- Blow up a balloon with an angry thought with every puff. Then punch it until you get rid of your anger or burst it to explode your anger (or both)
- Jump on a trampoline. Start jumping really high and fast and then slow down and jump lower until your anger is gone
- Run around the garden until you feel calmer
- Deep breathing can really help
- Look at your family poster
- Try to remember that anger is really about being scared
- Try to figure out whether the anger is about now or about feelings from the past
- Try to remember that Mum and Dad love you even when they say no
- Try to remember that you are special and deserve to be happy
- Ask Mum or Dad for a hug. I bet they can help you feel calm when you're not able to do this for yourself.

Mum and Dad have lots of other good ideas to get rid of adrenalin. They can help you if you ask. If you have too much adrenalin in your body to remember to ask Mum or Dad to help you, they will help to remind you.

Muir Family Plan

If Pete gets  this is our plan.

Mum will take Flo upstairs to keep her safe ♡ and we will have a 🛁 then we'll put cream 🧴 on and Mum will put nail polish ✋ on Flo. Then we can watch telly 📺 from Mum's bed 🛏.

Dad will ask Pete to try his jumps 🏃 and then cuddle 👪 Pete. Dad will keep cuddling Pete until he feels safe ♡ and not angry. Then Pete and Dad and maybe Mum can talk 😮😮, wonder why Pete was angry and try and find ways to help Pete feel happy 😊.

We can all then go to sleep 😴 because we all love ♡ each other sooooooooooooooooooo much.

Create the Spirit of Christmas

Create a calm family atmosphere by following these rules.

Have a hype-free Christmas by reducing visitors and activities to a minimum: our children don't cope well with surprises, change and excitement, experiencing these as threats to their wellbeing.

Remind family and friends of our children's special emotional needs and ask them to help co-create a stress-free Christmas.

Inappropriate presents: how many of the toys received last year were still in one piece by Boxing Day? Give inexpensive presents and reduce the number of gifts to those children can easily manage. Spread them out over several days if the child will manage this better.

Simple: Keep it simple. Remember: Boring is best.

Tradition: Create a family tradition to keep year on year. This gives children a sense of stability, continuity and belonging, especially if they are involved in the choice of the 'tradition'. Tell friends and family about this when they visit and encourage children to talk about it too.

Make time for ourselves. We need to pace ourselves and make sure we have time for ourselves and our partners. Children and guests will survive frozen vegetables!

Accept and acknowledge children's difficulties with understanding and empathy. Their behaviour might feel like a deliberate attempt to reject our love; in fact it's based on fear of abandonment and lack of self-worth. They are doing the best they can.

Success (or at least less dis-Stress) is likely if we follow these rules. Have a peaceful and happy **Christmas**!

Suggestions for Taking Care of Ourselves

- Buy ourselves a bunch of flowers.
- Take time to sit down with a book and a cup of tea.
- Play our favourite piece of music. Use it to alter our mood: rousing music if we need to let off steam; quiet, calm music to relieve stress.
- Go for a walk. Find a special place to let go of our feelings safely. A windy wood or sea in a storm can resonate with feelings of anger and allow us to shout and scream out frustrations unnoticed.
- Start swimming: it's an excellent way of relaxing.
- Take a long bath, adding soothing essential oils.
- Arrange to have an aromatherapy massage.
- Get in touch with friends and fix a night out with them – ban talking about children.
- Plan a meal out with our partner – or dine 'in' if childcare is difficult.
- Write positive messages on 'Post-its', such as 'I am a good enough parent', and place these around the house to remind us of our special qualities.
- Find ways of having fun and laughing. We live in a stressful environment and need to release some of the stress. Laughter is an excellent way of discharging adrenalin and cortisol, releasing serotonin, and improving our all-round health.

These are just a few suggestions for nurturing ourselves: we should adopt ways that suit us and our lifestyles best. It's really important to set aside time at least weekly to do something for ourselves; better still, do something daily. Even taking 15 minutes for ourselves can have very positive effects. Try hard not to think about the children, or indeed any problems, during this self-nurturing time. This may require practice!

Protect the time we lay aside for ourselves. Don't let anything short of an emergency intrude on this precious space.

Appendix 2

Check In and Check Out Outline

Stage 1: checking ourselves out

- Check out how we feel physically, emotionally, cognitively.

- Identify whether we are functioning primarily from our bottom, middle or top-storey brain, sensing whether we are breathing too quickly, feeling too hot or cold, hungry, thirsty or wobbly. Explore our feelings, observing whether we are upset, angry, powerless or scared.

- Using our awareness of 'top down' controls, make conscious efforts to re-regulate ourselves from the bottom up. Adjusting our breathing, nurturing ourselves, dealing with our feelings sensibly, we can 'switch on' our thinking brain circuits.

Stage 2: practising by ourselves

- Experiment with the facial expressions, gestures, tone of voice and words that feel most comfortable to us.

- Practise making these with partners or friends, checking out the feelings this generates in them and in us.

- Try out these exercises both when we feel relaxed and when we feel stressed, to get a feel for how our reactions vary depending on our circumstances.

- Take into consideration our unique family circumstances, such as whether we are on our own or whether we have other children who may also need our help during times of stress.

- Establish ways of getting some additional help if we, or our other children, need it. Test these out in non-stressful situations.

Stage 3: checking out our children

- Observe how our children 'make' us feel, physically and emotionally, think and react, when we 'tune in' to them.

- Check ourselves out again, in case we need to re-regulate and reconnect ourselves once more.

- Use the information we gain from 'tuning into' our children to work out whether they are mostly functioning out of their bottom, middle or top-storey brains 🏠 and where their 'loose connections' lie.

- Use what we know about bottom-up development to identify where our children most need our help. If in doubt, start at the bottom and work up.

- Remind ourselves of our children's early histories to gain insights into their disconnections and resultant perceptions, expectations and behaviours.

- Integrate this awareness to identify where they most need our help.

- Find healthy ways of connecting with our children and 'retuning' them to our better-regulated neurobiological systems (co-regulating), to help them become more able to regulate, organise and make connections internally.

- Remind ourselves that we are the experts on our children and are best placed to create the best 'knitting patterns' for them.

- Be aware of potentially difficult situations and be prepared to deal with them. Having a well-rehearsed plan can sometimes be enough to reduce the likelihood of difficulties arising.

Stage 4: practising with our children

- 'Notice' our children and let them know we have noticed them – smiling, winking, waving, laughing *with* them, hugging, 'high-fiving', giving the 'thumbs up', chatting, singing, rocking, bouncing (the list is endless!).

- Comment on what you see or feel they are feeling and doing: 'I can see...' – being careful to avoid sounding critical or that we are laughing *at* them.

- If we cannot see them, 'check in' verbally from time to time – a 'quick' call is enough to reconnect. With older children, a short text, 'smiley' icon or photo could be good.

- Show interest in our children and in what interests them. This is a vital tool in helping them to feel connected and to gain a sense of self-competence and self-worth.

- Shared attention is essential to the development of inter-communication: encouraging this need not be obvious.

- Suggest shared activities – and have fun!

- Devise games that 'accidentally' create opportunities to interact. Play is the ideal environment for connecting, learning, reducing fear and increasing feelings of security and comfort.

- Once we are comfortable with these 'tweaks' to our parenting interactions in 'normal circumstances', identify

one or two 'tricky' situations where we might try them out
with our children.

Stage 5: dealing with difficult situations

- Take time to assess the situation and how best to approach
it.

- 'Think toddler' – working out our children's functional age
at that moment and treating them as we would a child of that
age. If in doubt, go lower.

- 'Think hurt animal' – checking out their current emotional
state ⊡ and adjusting our 'approach' accordingly.

- Attempt to make *some* eye contact whilst staying aware of
our children's difficulties in this area; on the other hand,
do not *force* eye, or physical, contact, as either may trigger
fight, flight, freeze or shame reactions.

- Provide simple, loving, accepting, verbal messages to
accompany simple, loving, accepting, non-verbal messages
through our eyes, facial expressions and body language.

- Speak calmly and gently, showing acceptance of our
children for who and what they are *at that moment*, staying
aware that they are so sensitised to perceived threat and
shame that we may inadvertently trigger powerful, negative
responses by 'looking too hard'.

- Meet our children's basic nurturing needs, for example
through cuddles, shared stories or TV programmes, snacks.
'Sharing, caring time' simultaneously encourages calming,
'feel good' neurochemical messengers such as oxytocin,
endorphins, serotonin and dopamine to circulate.

- Suggest physical activities we have previously identified
that work for our children to help them burn off over-
arousing biochemical messengers, such as cortisol and
adrenalin, circulating through their bodies. Nervous energy

has to go somewhere, and introducing regular 'burn-off' sessions' can begin to 'rewire' trigger-happy systems. Join in or be 'the coach'.

- 'Read' what we 'see' and empathise, gradually use our own bodies and *expressions* to co-regulate our children and alter the emotional climate for the better.

- Initially, match our communications to what we 'read' before moving children 'up' or 'down' the arousal scale and, once in their 'comfort zone', into their top-storey thinking brain.

- Extend what we have seen to other difficult situations.

Healing early trauma and developmental
attachments using therapeutic parenting

RELATE

REGULATE

REFLECT

REHEARSE

REPAIR

REWIRE

RESILIENCE

Glossary

Adrenalin – neurochemical messenger (neurotransmitter) produced by adrenal glands in response to stress which prepares individual for fight or flight.

Amygdala (plural: amygdalae) – area of mid-storey brain (limbic system) important for processing emotion, including pre and non-verbal memories. Right hemisphere develops more dynamically than left.

Attachment – enduring shared relationship created between individuals. Since human infants are unable to care for themselves, attachment facilitates physical survival. It is also the matrix for emotional, social and intellectual development, leading to health, resilience and wellbeing.

Attachment-trauma – impact of early adversity, such as distressed or disrupted intrafamilial relationships, affecting attachment and neurobiological development.

Attunement – process of getting in touch (in synch) with another's sensations and feelings and resonating, or empathising, with them.

Autistic spectrum disorder (ASD) – neurobiologically-based disorder characterised by poor integration, social awareness and 'mindreading' capacities.

Autonomic nervous system (ANS) – part of nervous system; consisting of network of glands producing neuro-hormones, which is responsible for involuntary responses such as fight, flight and freeze. Characterised in trauma-normal children by high arousal (sympathetic NS) and/or low arousal (parasympathetic NS).

Biofeedback loops – inter-connectivity of neuronal and neurochemical messengers, where each can influence the functions of the other.

Brainstem – developmentally one of the 'oldest' parts of the brain, regulating basic bodily functions such as heart rate, respiration, body temperature, sleep and elimination.

Broca's area – the area of the brain primarily responsible for expressive language.

Central nervous system (CNS) – system of neuron and neural networks linking the brain to every part of the body.

Coherent narrative – explicit memories (stored in hippocampi) that can be accessed, recalled and interpreted in a consistent, sequential, organised manner, creating a 'self-story'.

Corpus callosum – the 'white matter' connecting the right and left hemispheres of the brain.

Cortisol – neuro-hormone that allows individual to respond to stress, including immune functions. In moderation, cortisol releases energy within the body and promotes healing. Excess cortisol due to chronic stress can lead to the destruction of nerve cells and connections and adversely affects long-term health.

Dance of attachment – active, synchronous inter-relationship between parent and child creating reciprocity and mutual feedback.

Developmental trauma disorder (DTD) – diagnosis proposed by van der Kolk *et al.* to define more accurately the altered neurobiology and constellation of symptoms resulting from early attachment-trauma.

Disorganised attachment patterns – dysfunctional attachment patterns, normally resulting from early childhood maltreatment, that adversely affect developmental neurobiology and interfere with the capacity to form healthy relationships. Typified by states of high arousal, dissociative responses, poor ability to self-regulate or to use caregivers to provide co-regulation. There is a high correlation between disorganised attachment patterns in childhood and serious adult mental health problems.

Dissociation – lack of connection between senses, emotions, awareness, behaviour and memories; occurs on a continuum and can be partial or total.

Dopamine – 'feel good' neurotransmitter that enhances glucose uptake which stimulates neural growth in the prefrontal cortex and so promotes top-down controls, positive expectations and wellbeing.

Dysregulation – disturbance in ability to monitor and modulate neurobiological arousal.

Emotional literacy – capacity to identify, 'read' and make sense of one's own feelings that enables individual to identify, 'read' and make sense of others' emotions.

Empathy – the ability to get in tune with, or share, another's sensations, emotions, thoughts or needs.

Endorphins – internally produced opioid compounds released into the blood stream to create sense of wellbeing or as natural analgesic.

Hippocampus (plural: hippocampi) – area of mid-storey limbic brain involved with verbal memory formation, storage and retrieval. Greater development occurs in left hemisphere of brain; comes 'on line' at three years plus.

Internal working models (IWMs) – internalised 'road maps' of self, others and 'how they work': affecting perceptions, expectations and responses.

Limbic system – 'mid-storey' areas of brain associated with attachment, emotional connections and memory (both non-verbal and verbal).

Mirroring – act of attuning to, and reflecting back, another's sensations, emotions or thoughts. In doing so parents provide awareness and insights for their children that enable them to make sense of themselves and others.

Neo-cortex – most recently evolved area of the brain that enables reflection, social communication, language development, 'top down' controls, decision-making and inter-personal negotiation.

Neural networks – complex connections between neurons in the brain and central nervous system.

Neuro-biochemicals – chemical 'messengers' that carry information around the brain and nervous system (both CNS and ANS).

Neurobiological – relating to the structure and function of the brain and nervous system.

Neurodevelopment – sequential formation and inter-connection of nervous systems and brain according to experience: with developmental 'windows' providing opportunities for optimal maturing and healthy development.

Neuro-hormones – neuro-biochemicals carrying information within the brain and nervous system.

Neurophysiological – relating to the functioning of the nervous systems, rather than to their structure.

Neuroplasticity – ability of neural networks to create new connections and hence 'fill in the gaps' in terms of physical, emotional, social and intellectual functioning.

Neurotypical – Cartwright and Morgan (2008) use this term rather than 'normal' to remind readers that ASD children have underlying neurobiological difficulties. It is used here for similar reasons: to distinguish betweeen 'normal' children and those whose neuro-development has been affected by attachment trauma.

Orbito-prefrontal cortex (OFC) – provides vital neurobiological connections between the brainstem and limbic area and the neo-cortex, or top-storey 'thinking brain'. Right hemisphere is dominant in the earliest years of life.

Oxytocin – the 'altruistic' neuro-hormone. Promotes caregiving in mothers, bonding between individuals and pleasurable feelings.

Regulation – ability to monitor, sustain or return to 'normal' comfortable levels of physical, emotional and cognitive arousal. Infants and young children are unable to self-regulate and depend on primary caregivers to help them develop self-regulation through repeated, consistent co-regulation.

Sensori-motor – sensations, perceptions and responses relating to the body and/or movement.

Serotonin – 'feel good' neuro-messenger (neurotransmitter). Excess cortisol (due to stress) reduces serotonin levels, which in turn are associated with aggressive behaviour.

Stress – the demands and pressures of daily living are essential to healthy life. Healthy individuals have the capacity to 'bounce back', to get back in balance, once the immediate stress recedes or is dealt with. However, excessive or chronic stress overwhelms the system and makes recovery problematic: stress responses become normalised (trauma-normal).

Transitional object (TO) – tangible item (such as a teddy) that represents the caregiver and can provide security and comfort to child during periods of anxiety and separation.

Toxic stressors – can be chemical (e.g. tobacco, alcohol, toxic metals), adverse events (e.g. hospitalisation) or inter-personal (e.g. loss of, or breaks in, significant relationships).

Trauma – an 'injury' to body, brain or mind due to excessive stress. The lasting distress of abandonment, loss, maltreatment and lack of 'containment' of affect in the early years adversely affects neurobiological development and therefore ongoing perceptions, responses and relationships.

Trauma-normal – describes individuals whose neurobiology is geared to anticipate and react to perceived threat (see 'Stress' above).

References

Adoption, Attachment Issues and Your School. Available at: www.postadoptioncentral support.org, accessed 27 November 2012.

Archer, C. (1999a) *First Steps in Parenting the Child Who Hurts: Tiddlers and Toddlers.* London: Jessica Kingsley Publishers.

Archer, C. (1999b) *Next Steps in Parenting the Child Who Hurts: Tykes and Teens.* London: Jessica Kingsley Publishers.

Archer, C. (2003) 'Weft and warp: Developmental impact of trauma and implications for healing.' In C. Archer and A. Burnell (eds) *Trauma, Attachment and Family Permanence.* London: Jessica Kingsley Publishers.

Archer, C. and Gordon, C. (2004) 'Parent mentoring: An innovative approach to adoption support.' *Journal of Adoption and Fostering 28,* 4, 27-38.

Archer, C. and Gordon, C. (2006) *New Families, Old Scripts.* London: Jessica Kingsley Publishers.

Archer, C. and Gordon, C., (2006) *New Families, Old Scripts: A Guide to the Language of Trauma and Attachment in Adoptive Families.* London: Jessica Kingsley Publishers.

Attachment, Developmental Trauma and Executive Functioning Difficulties in the School Setting. Available at www.familyfutures.co.uk, accessed 27 November 2012.

Baron-Cohen, S. (1999) *Mindblindness: An Essay in Autism and Theory of Mind.* London: A Bradford Book (MIT Press).

Bomber, L.M. (2007) *Inside I'm Hurting.* London: Worth Publishing.

Bomber, L.M. (2011) *Inclusive Strategies to Support Pupils with Attachment Difficulties Make it Through the School Day.* London: Worth Publishing.

Bowlby, J. (1969) *Attachment and Loss. Volume 1: Attachment.* London: Penguin.

Bowlby, J. (1973) *Attachment and Loss. Volume 2: Separation.* London: Hogarth Press.

Bowlby, J. (1988) *A Secure Base.* London: Routledge.

Brain Gym. Available at www.braingym.org.uk, accessed on 27 November 2012.

Carr, L., Iacoboni, M., Dubeau, M-C., Maziotta, J. and Lenzi, G.L. (2003) 'Neural mechanisms of empathy in humans: A relay from neural systems for imitation to limbic areas.' *Proceedings of the National Academy of Sciences 100,* 9, 5497–5502.

Cartwright, A. and Morgan, J. (2008) *The Teaching Assistant's Guide to Autistic Spectrum Disorders.* London: Continuum.

Caspari Foundation for Educational Therapy and Therapeutic Teaching. Available at www.caspari. org.uk, accessed on 27 November 2012.

Cicchetti, D. (2010) 'Resililence under conditions of extreme stress: A miltilevel perspective.' *World Psychiatry 9,* 3 145–154.

Conrad, D. (2004), 'The cost of caring: Secondary traumatic stress.' *Fostering Communications,* 2004.

Cozolino, L. (2002) *The Neuroscience of Psychotherapy.* London: Norton.

Criscuolo, F., Monaghan, P., Nasir, L. and Metcalfe, N.B. (2008) 'Early nutrition and phenotypic development: "Catch up" growth leads to elevated metabolic rate in adulthood.' *Proceedings of the Royal Society of London series B: Biological Sciences*, 275, 1565-1570.

Damasio, A. (2006) *Descartes' Error*. London: Vintage Books.

D'Andrea, W., Ford, J., Stolbach, B., Spinazzola, J. and van der Kolk, B.A. (2012) 'Understanding interpersonal trauma in children: Why we need a developmentally appropriate trauma diagnosis.' *American Journal of Orthopsychiatry, 82*, 2, 187-200.

Davidson, R.J. (2000) 'Affective style, psychopathology and resilience: Brain mechanisms and plasticity.' *American Psychologist, 20*, 2 1196–1214.

Dawson, P. and Guare, R. (2004) *Executive Skills in Children and Adolescents*. New York: Guilford Press.

DeCasper, A. and Fifer, W. (1980) 'Of human bonding: Newborns prefer their mothers' voices.' *Science 208*, 1174–1176.

De Waal, F. (1992) *Peacemaking Among Primates*. London: Penguin.

Eliot, L. (2000) *What's Going On in There?* New York: Bantam Books.

Encyclopedia of Mental Disorders (2012) Online. Available at www.minddisorders.com.

Felitti, V.J. and Anda, R.F. (2009) 'The relationship of adverse childhood experiences to adult medical disease, psychiatric disorders, and sexual behaviour: Implications for healthcare.' In Lanius, R. and Vermetten, E. (eds) The Hidden Epidemic: *The Impact of Early Life Trauma on Health and Disease*. Cambridge: Cambridge University Press.

Fisk, N. (2000) 'Does a foetus feel pain?' E. Burns, *The Times*, 28 March.

Fonagy, P. and Target, M. (1997) 'Attachment and reflective function: Their role in self-organization.' *Development and Psychopathology 9*, 679–700.

Frank, M.C., Vul, E. and Johnson, S.P. (2009) 'Development of infants' attention to faces during the first year.' *Cognition 110(2009)* 160–170.

Gerhardt, S. (2004) *Why Love Matters*. Hove, UK: Brunner-Routledge.

Gitau, R., Menson, E., Pickles, V., Fisk, N.M., Glover, V. and MacLachlan, N. (1998) 'Umbilical cortisol levels as an indicator of the fetal stress response to assisted vaginal delivery.' *European Journal of Obstetric and Reproductive Biology, 98*, 1, 14-17.

Gluckman, P. and Hanson, M. (2005) *The Fetal Matrix: Evolution, Development and Disease*. Cambridge: Cambridge University Press.

Goddard, S. (1996) *A Teacher's Window into the Child's Mind*. Eugene, OR: Fern Ridge Press.

Goldman-Rakic, P.S. (1987) 'Development of cortical circuitry and cognitive function.' *Child Development 58*, 601–622.

Goldman-Rakic, P.S., Isseroff, S., Schwartz, M.L. and Bugbee, N.M. (1983) 'The Neurobiology of Cognitive Development.' In P.H. Mussen (ed.) *Handbook of Child Psychology*. New York: Wiley.

Gratier, M. and Trevarthen, C. (2008) 'Musical narrative and motives for culture in mother-infant vocal interaction.' *Journal of Consciousness Studies 15*, 122-158.

Hughes, D. (2003) 'Psychological interventions for the spectrum of attachment disorders and intrafamilial trauma.' *Attachment and Human Development 5*, 3, 271–279.

Hughes, D. (2006) *Building the Bonds of Attachment: Awakening Love in Deeply Troubled Children*. Lanham, MD: Jason Aronson.

Hughes, D. (2009) *Attachment-Focused Parenting*. New York: W.W. Norton & Co.

Iacoboni, M., Molnar-Szakacs, I., Gallese, V., Buccino, G., Mazziotta, J.C. and Rizzolatti, G. (2005) 'Grasping the intentions of others with one's own mirror neuron system.' Available at http.//www.plosbiology.org/article.info

Jennings, S. (2011) *Healthy Attachments and Neuro-Dramatic-Play*. London: Jessica Kingsley Publishers.

Keck, G. and Kupecky, R. (2002) *Parenting the Hurt Child*. Colorado Springs CO: Pinon Press.

Kohler, E., Keysers, C., Umilta, M.A., Fogassi, L., Gallese, V. and Rizzolatti, G. (2002) Hearing sounds, understanding actions: Action representation in mirror neurons. *Science 297*, 5582, 846–848.

Koomar, J., Kranowitz, C.S., Szklut, S. (2004) *Answers to Questions Teachers Ask About Sensory Integration.* Las Vegas (NV): Sensory Resources LLC.

Lyons-Ruth, K., Bronfman, E. and Atwood, G. (1999) 'A Relationship Diathesis Model of Hostile-helpless States of Mind: Expressions in Mother–Infant Interaction.' In J. Solomon and C. George (eds) *Attachment Disorganization.* New York: Guilford Press.

MacFarlane, J. (1975) 'Olfaction in the Development of Social Preference in the Human Newborn.' In M. Hofer (ed.) *Foundation Symposium: Parent–Child Interaction.* Amsterdam: Elsevier.

Mandela, N. (2006) *Words of Wisdom.* Dublin: Mentor Books.

Maurer, D. (1993) Neonatal synaesthesia: Implications for the Processing of Speech and Faces.' In B de Boysson-Bardies *et al.* (eds) *Developmental Neurocognition: Speech and Face Processing in the First Year of Life.* Kluwer.

Meltzoff, A.N. and Moore, M.K. (1989) 'Imitation in newborn infants: Exploring the range of gestures imitated and the underlying mechanisms.' *Developmental Psychology, 25,* 6, 954-962.

Metcalfe (2008) Proceedings of the Royal Society Journal, quoted in *The Guardian.* 09.04.08, Medical Matters, *Radio 4* (2011)

Nishitani, N. and Hari, E. (2000) 'Temporal dynamics of cortical representation for action.' *Proceedings of the National Academy of Sciences USA 97,* 2, 913–918.

Offers an Attachment Support Service for schools including assessments, consultations, therapy and training. Available at www.theyellowkite.co.uk, accessed on 27 November 2012.

Panksepp, J. (1998) *Affective Neuroscience.* Oxford and New York: Oxford University Press.

Papousek, H. and Papousek, M. (1979) 'Early Ontogeny of Human Social Interactions: Its Biological Roots and Social Dimensions'. In M von Cranach *et al.* (eds.) *Human Ethology: Claims and Limits of a New Discipline.* Cambridge: Cambridge University Press.

Perry, A. (2009) *Teenagers and Attachment: Helping Adolescents Engage with Life and Learning.* London: Worth Publishing. (Including chapters by Bomber, L.M., Hughes, D.A. and Batmanghelidjh, C.)

Porges, S.W. (1997) 'Emotion: An Evolutionary Bi-product of the Neural Regulation of the Autonomic Nervous System.' In C. Carter, B. Kirkpatrick and I. Lederhendler (eds) *The Integrative Neurobiology of Affiliation. Annals of the New York Academy of Sciences 807,* 62–77.

Porges, S.W. (2011) *The Polyvagal Theory: Neurophysiological Foundations of Emotions, Attachment, Communication, and Self-regulation.* New York: W.W. Norton & Co.

Reebye, P. and Stalker, A. (2008) *Understanding Regulation Disorders of Sensory Processing in Children.* London: Jessica Kingsley Publishers.

Rizzolatti, G., Fogassi, L. and Gallese, V. (1997) 'Parietal cortex: From sight to action.' *Current Opinion in Neurobiology 7,* 562-567.

Rizzolatti, G. and Sinigaglia, C. (2007) *Mirrors in the Brain: How Our Minds Share Actions and Emotions.* Oxford: Oxford University Press.

Roth, I. (2010) *The Autism Spectrum in the 21st Century: Exploring Psychology, Biology and Practice.* London: Jessica Kingsley Publishers.

Row, S. (2005) *Surviving the Special Needs System.* London: Jessica Kingsley Publishers.

Sanefuji, W., Wada, K., Yamamoto, T., Shizawa, M., *et al.* (2011) 'One-month-old infants show visual preference for human-like features.' *Letters on Evolutionary Behavioral Science 1,* 5–8.

Schore, A. (1994) *Affect Regulation and the Origin of the Self.* Hillsdale, NJ: Laurence Erlbaum Associates.

Schore, A. (2001a) 'Effects of a secure attachment on right brain development, affect regulation, and infant mental health.' *Infant Mental Health Journal 22*, 7–61.

Schore, A. (2001b) 'The effects of early relational trauma on right brain development affect regulation, and infant mental health.' *Infant Mental Health Journal 22*, 201–269.

Shemmings, D. and Shemmings, Y. (2011) *Understanding Disorganized Attachment.* London: Jessica Kingsley Publishers.

Siegel, D., (1999) *The Developing Mind: Towards a Neurobiology of Interpersonal Experience.* New York and London: Guilford Press.

Siegel, D. and Hartzell, M. (2004) *Parenting from the Inside Out.* New York, NY: Tarcher.

Siegel, D. (2007) *The Mindful Brain.* New York and London: W.W. Norton & Co.

Siegel, D. (2010a) *Mindsight.* Oxford: Oneworld Publications.

Siegel, D. (2010b) *The Mindful Therapist.* New York and London: W.W. Norton & Company.

Siegel, D. *Mindfulness, Psychotherapy and the Brain.* Available at www.ithou.org, accessed on 13 November 2012.

Social Exclusion Unit. Available at www.socialexclusion.gov.uk, accessed on 27 November 2012.

Solomon, J. and George, C. (1999) 'The place of disorganization in attachment theory: Linking classical observations with contemporary findings.' In J. Solomon and C. George (eds) *Attachment Disorganization.* New York and London: The Guilford Press.

Spangler, G. and Grossman, K. (1999) 'Individual and Physiological Correlates of Attachment Disorganization in Infancy.' In J. Solomon and C. George (eds) *Attachment Disorganization.* New York: Guilford Press.

Trevarthen, C. (1979) 'Communication and cooperation in early infancy: A description of primary intersubjectivity'. In M Bullowa (ed) *Before Speech.* London and Cambridge: Cambridge University Press.

Trevarthen, C. (2001) 'Intrinsic motives for companionship in understanding: Their origin, development, and significance for infant mental health.' *Infant Mental Health Journal 22*, 95–131.

Tronick, E., Adamson, L.B., Als, H. and Brazelton, T.B. (1975) 'Infant emotions in normal and perturbated interactions.' Presented at The Biennial Meeting of the Society for Research in Child Development: Denver CO.

Troxel W. *Marriage and Sleep Study,* In the Daily Mail. Available at http//:www.sleep.patt.edu/, accessed on 12 June 2012).

Van Gulden, H. (2005) *In Search of Self: Helping Children Heal.* After Adoption Training Programme: Newport, UK.

Van Gulden, H. (2010) *Adoption fostering* BAAF: YouTube:

Van Gulden, H. *Introduction to: Object Permanence and Constancy.* Available at http://youtube.com/watch?v=bd1-APMTiFY, accessed on 13 November 2012.

Van Gulden, H. *So What is Permanence?* Available at http://youtube.com/watch?v=r270CJEOo0&, accessed on 13 November 2012.

Van Gulden, H. *Building Object Permanence.* Available at http://youtube.com/watch?v=gxEsGFQuM78, accessed on 13 November 2012.

Van Gulden, H. *Permanence 5 What Are the Symptoms of a Lack of Permanence?* Available at http://youtube.com/watch?v=IVtjoJsO&fe, accessed on 13 November 2012.

Van Gulden, H. *Parts Talk - Language to Build Object Constancy.* Available at http://youtube.com/watch?v=_r270XCJEOoO, accessed on 13 November 2012.

Van Gulden, H. *Common Symptoms of Lack of Object Constancy.* Available at http://youtube.com/watch?v=jgSK2abOBrU, accessed on 13 November 2012.

Van der Kolk, B. A. 'Developmental trauma disorder' (2005) *Psychiatric Annals* (2005 pp 401-408.

Vaughan, J. (2003) 'Rationale for the intensive programme'. In C. Archer and A. Burnell (eds) *Trauma, Attachment and Family Permanence*. London: Jessica Kingsley Publishers.

Winnicott, D.W. (1958) 'Primary Maternal Preoccupation.' In *Collected Papers, Through Paediatrics to Psychoanalysis*, 300–305.

Winnicott, D.W. (1965) *The Maturational Processes and the Facilitating Environments: Studies in the Theory of Emotional Development*. London: Hogarth Press.

Young Minds. Available at www.youngminds.org.uk/training_services/young_minds_in_schools/welbeing/attachment, accessed on 27 November 2012.

YouTube (2012) Permanency and Constancy: Introduction. Described by Holly van Gulden. Available at http://youtube.com/watch?v=bd1-APMTiFY.

Selection of Useful Books for Children

(Relating to Object Permanence and Constancy, Faces, Bodies and Feelings)

Carle, E. (1997) *From Head to Toe*. London: Picture Puffin.

Carle, E. (1998) *The Mixed-up Chameleon*. London: Picture Puffin.

Carle, E. (2002) *The Very Hungry Caterpillar*. London: Puffin.

Carle, E. (2006) *Mister Seahorse*. London: Picture Puffin.

Carle, E. (2009) *The Foolish Tortoise*. London: Simon & Schuster Children's.

Carle, E. (2010) *The Bad-tempered Ladybird*. London: Puffin.

Fordham, J. (2001) *Faces*. London: Macmillan Children's Books.

Hill, E. (1983) *Where's Spot?* Harmondsworth: Puffin Books.

Hill, E. (2009) *Spot Bakes a Cake*. London: Warne.

Hill, E. (2010) *Spot Goes to the Farm*. Harmondsworth: Puffin Books.

Hill, E. (2011) *Spot Goes to the Park*. Harmondsworth: Puffin Books.

Handford, M. (2011) *Where's Wally? The Totally Essential Travel Collection*. London: Walker Books.

Handford, M. (2012) *Where's Wally? The Search for the Lost Things*. London: Walker Books.

Large, J. (2001) *Pets*. London: Macmillan Children's Books.

Large, J. (2001) *Farm*. London: Macmillan Children's Books.

McKee, D. (2005) *Mr Benn: The Complete Series*. (DVD)

Mckee, D. (2009) *The Extraordinary Adventures of Mr Benn*. London: Hodder Children's Books.

Milne, A.A. and Shepard, E.H. (2009) *The House at Pooh Corner*. London: Egmont Books Ltd.

Moran, P. (2011) *Where's the Meerkat?* London: Michael O'Mara Books.

Moran, P. (2012) *Meerkat on Holiday*. London: Michael O'Mara Books.

Parr, T. London: Little Brown Young Readers.

Things That Make You Feel Good (2001)

My Book About Me (2003)

The Okay Book (2004)

We Belong Together: A Book for Adoptive Families (2008)

It's OK to Be Different (2009)

The Feelings Book (2009)

Feelings Flashcards (2010)

The Underwear Book (2012)

Ross, T. London: Harper Collins Books.

I Want My Mummy (2006)

I Want My Dummy (2007)

I Want My Light On (2008
I Want My Tooth) (2009)
I Want a Sister (2010)

Rowe, J. Selection from *'Lift the Flap'* series:
Guess Who? (2010) London: Five Mile Press.
Guess What? (2010) London: Five Mile Press.
Whose Feet? (2000) London: Southwood Books.
Whose House (2001) London: Southwood Books.
Whose Tail? (2001) London: Southwood Books.
Whose Nose? (2005*)* London: Happy Cat Books.
Whose Poo? (2005) London: Happy Cat Books.
Whose Teeth? (2005) London: Southwood Books.

Sendak, M. (2000) *Where the Wild Things Are.* UK: Red Fox.

Essential Resources

Useful Website Contacts

Adoption, Attachment Issues and Your School. Available at: www.postadoptioncentralsupport.org.

Attachment, Developmental Trauma and Executive Functioning Difficulties in the School Setting. Available at www.familyfutures.co.uk.

Brain Gym. Available at www.braingym.org.uk.

Caspari Foundation for Educational Therapy and Therapeutic Teaching. Helps children, young people and families cope with barriers to learning and therapeutic input into schools. Available at www.caspari.org.uk.

Offers an Attachment Support Service for schools including assessments, consultations, therapy and training. Available at www.theyellowkite.co.uk.

Social Exclusion Unit. Available at www.socialexclusion.gov.uk.

Young Minds. Offers strategies to be implemented in schools to support attachment. Available at www.youngminds.org.uk/training_services/young_minds_in_schools/welbeing/attachment.

Particularly Relevant Book Titles

Bomber, L.M. (2007) *Inside I'm Hurting.* London: Worth Publishing.

Bomber, L.M. (2011) *Inclusive Strategies to Support Pupils with Attachment Difficulties Make it Through the School Day.* London: Worth Publishing.

Cartwright, A. and Morgan, J. (2008) *The Teaching Assistant's Guide to Autistic Spectrum Disorders.* London: Continuum.

Koomar, J, Kranowitz, C,S., Szklut, S. (2004) *Answers to Questions Teachers Ask About Sensory Integration.* Las Vegas (NV): Sensory Resources LLC

Perry, A. (2009) *Teenagers and Attachment: Helping Adolescents Engage with Life and Learning.* London: Worth Publishing. (Including chapters by Bomber, L.M., Hughes, D.A. and Batmanghelidjh, C.).

Row, S. (2005) *Surviving the Special Needs System.* London: Jessica Kingsley Publishers.

UK organisations

Adoption UK

Provides information and support in the areas of
adoption attachment and developmental trauma.
Linden House
55 The Green
South Bar Street
Banbury OX16 9AB
Office open Monday to Friday, 9am–5pm
Tel: 01295 752240; Fax: 01295 752241
Email: enquiries@adoptionuk.org.uk

Adoption UK Wales/Cymru

Penhavad Studios
Penhavad Street
Grangetown
Cardiff CF11 7LU
Helpline open Monday to Friday, 11am–1pm: 02920 232221
General telephone enquiries/callers – Monday to
Friday, 10am–4pm: 02920 230319
Email: ann@adoptionuk.org.uk; helen@adoptionuk.org.uk

Adoption UK (Scotland)

172 Leith Walk
Edinburgh EH6 5EA
Helpline: 0844 848 7900
Tel: 0131 555 5350
Email: scotland@adoptionuk.org.uk

Adoption UK (NI)

545 Antrim Road
Belfast BT15 3BU
Tel: 02890 775211
Email: stephenmcvey@adoptionuk.org.uk

Fostering Network

Provides information about attachment and fostering.
Advice lines:
Wales – 0800 316 7664
Scotland – 0141 204 1400
Northern Ireland – 028 9070 5056
England – 0800 040 7675

British Agencies for Adoption and Fostering
Saffron House
6-10 Kirby Street
LONDON EC1N 8TS
Tel: 0207 421 2600
www.BAAF.org

Attachment Network Wales
(Rhwydwaith Ymlyniad Cymru)
Facilitates multi-disciplinary collaboration within the field of
attachment, provides information and education on attachment-
related issues and lobbies for positive changes to social,
mental health and educational policies within Wales.
www.attachmentwales.org
Tel: 02920 230319
Email: helen@adoptionuk.org.uk

Scottish Attachment in Action
A multi-professional group committed to promoting better
experiences of attachment in the Scottish population and effecting
positive changes in social policy, education and mental health.
www.saia.org.uk

National Autistic Society
Monday to Friday: 0845 070 4004; parent-to-parent line: 0800 9520

National Autistic Society Wales
Membership: 01792 815915

British Dyslexia Association
Unit 8 Bracknell Beeches
Old Bracknell Lane
Bracknell RG12 7BW
Helpline: 0845 251 9002

Sensory Integration Network
27a High Street
Theale
Berkshire RG7 5AH
Tel: 0118 324 1588

International links (general)
Australia
www.adopting.org. Follow links to adoption/issues in adoption
www.adoption.org. Follow links to adoptions/attachment
www.adopting.org. Follow links to early intervention
www.adopting.org. Follow links to adoption/issues in adoption
www.adoption.org. Follow links to adoptions/attachment
www.attachmentparentingaustralia.com/support.htm
www.bensoc.au/post adoption
www.community.nsw.gov.au

Canada
www.adoption.ca
www.canadaadopts.com. Follow links to canada/resources
www.canadianadoption.com. Follow links to canada

New Zealand
www.cyf.govt.nz. Follow links to adoption/post adoption support
www.adopting.org. Follow links to adoption/issues in adoption
www.adoption.org. Follow links to adoptions/attachment
www.adopting.org. Follow links to early intervention
www.dyslexia-parent.com

USA
www.asa-usa.org
(Provides support services for military families.)
www.attach.org
(Professionally led international organisation promoting awareness of attachment issues and treatment choices for children and families. Email: questions@attach.org)

Index